OXFORD WORLD'S CLASSICS

THE RUSSIAN MASTER

AND OTHER STORIES

ANTON CHEKHOV was born in 1860 in south Russia, the son of a poor grocer. At the age of 19 he followed his family to Moscow, where he studied medicine and helped to support the household by writing comic sketches for popular magazines. By the end of the 1880s he was established as a writer of serious fiction, and had some experience as a playwright, while continuing to practise medicine on the small estate he had bought near Moscow. It was there that he wrote his innovatory drama *The Seagull*. Its disastrous opening performance was the cruellest blow of Chekhov's professional life, but its later successful production by the Moscow Art Theatre led to his permanent association with that company, his marriage to its leading actress, Olga Knipper, and his increasing preoccupation with the theatre. Forced by ill-health to move to Yalta in 1898 he wrote there, despite increasing debility, his two greatest plays, *Three Sisters* and *The Cherry Orchard*. The première of the latter took place on his forty-fourth birthday. Chekhov died six months later, on 2 July 1904.

RONALD HINGLEY edited and translated the nine-volume Oxford Chekhov and was Emeritus Fellow of St Antony's College, Oxford. His translations of Chekhov's short stories are available in a number of volumes in Oxford World's Classics, together with an edition of Chekhov's drama, *Five Plays*.

T0058354

OXFORD WORLD'S CLASSICS

*For over 100 years Oxford World's Classics have brought
readers closer to the world's great literature. Now with over 700
titles—from the 4,000-year-old myths of Mesopotamia to the
twentieth century's greatest novels—the series makes available
lesser-known as well as celebrated writing.*

*The pocket-sized hardbacks of the early years contained
introductions by Virginia Woolf, T. S. Eliot, Graham Greene,
and other literary figures which enriched the experience of reading.
Today the series is recognized for its fine scholarship and
reliability in texts that span world literature, drama and poetry,
religion, philosophy and politics. Each edition includes perceptive
commentary and essential background information to meet the
changing needs of readers.*

OXFORD WORLD'S CLASSICS

ANTON CHEKHOV

The Russian Master
and Other Stories

Translated with an Introduction and Notes by
RONALD HINGLEY

OXFORD
UNIVERSITY PRESS

OXFORD

UNIVERSITY PRESS

Great Clarendon Street, Oxford OX2 6DP

Oxford University Press is a department of the University of Oxford.
It furthers the University's objective of excellence in research, scholarship,
and education by publishing worldwide in

Oxford New York

Athens Auckland Bangkok Bogotá Buenos Aires Calcutta
Cape Town Chennai Dar es Salaam Delhi Florence Hong Kong Istanbul
Karachi Kuala Lumpur Madrid Melbourne Mexico City Mumbai
Nairobi Paris São Paulo Singapore Taipei Tokyo Toronto Warsaw

with associated companies in Berlin Ibadan

Oxford is a registered trade mark of Oxford University Press
in the UK and in certain other countries

Published in the United States
by Oxford University Press Inc., New York

Translations and editorial material © Ronald Hingley 1965, 1970, 1971, 1975
Chronology © Oxford University Press 1984
Select Bibliography © Patrick Miles 1998

Reissued as an Oxford World's Classics paperback 1999
Reissued 2008

British Library Cataloguing in Publication Data

Data available

Library of Congress Cataloging in Publication Data

Chekhov, Anton Pavlovich, 1860–1904.
The Russian master and other stories.
(Oxford world's classics)
Bibliography: p.
1. Chekhov, Anton Pavlovich, 1860–1904—Translations,
English. I. Hingley, Ronald. II. Title.
PG3456.A15H56 1984 891.73'3 83–23719

ISBN 978-0-19-955487-4

12

Printed in Great Britain by
Clays Ltd, Elcograf S.p.A.

CONTENTS

CONTENTS

INTRODUCTION

THE eleven items in this book have been chosen from the short stories of the author's maturity (1888–1904). One of these, *The Russian Master*, will be familiar to some readers under the arguably inaccurate title given to it by other translators: *The Teacher of Literature*. So Chekhovian a work is it that it might almost be called, without disparagement, a parody of the master by himself. Here we have the usual romantic illusions about love and marriage shipwrecked on the usual submerged reefs of domestic triviality and provincial vulgarity: all forming a most original sermon on the theme 'man does not live by bread alone'.

The Russian Master has a fascinating history. In 1889 Chekhov published what is now the first of its two chapters as a self-contained story under a different title, *Mediocrities*. It then had the happy ending which the text of Chapter I still retains, except, of course, that Chapter II now follows it, gradually but remorselessly reversing any such impression. As it happens, we know why Chekhov originally published his story in this incomplete and misleadingly optimistic form. He had read out a draft of what is now Chapter I to members of his family, confiding in them his intention of providing a continuation in which he would blow his young couple's happiness 'to smithereens'. Only when these kind-hearted listeners had appealed to him not to spoil the ending did he agree to publish the story in truncated form. But the happily-ending *Mediocrities* of 1889 turned out too 'sloppy' in its author's view, and by 1894 he was ready with the very different version, expanded and transformed by the addition of the astringent Chapter II, which we have here.

Since frustration so often accompanies love and marriage in Chekhov we need not be surprised at this course of events. But we may also note that the unfortunate Russian master and bridegroom Nikitin would have been equally doomed had he chosen to remain single. That option was one that Chekhov fully explored in *Doctor Startsev* (1898). Startsev (the 'Nikitin' of the later story) rejects his 'Masha' (Catherine Turkin), but only to sink into the bog of provincial complacency, card-playing and wine-bibbing against which Nikitin proclaims his revolt—with what prospects of success we do not learn—in the last paragraph of *The Russian Master*.

Frustration in love, that typical Chekhov theme, is lavishly represented elsewhere in this volume.

In the short but powerful *His Wife* the sick doctor is the victim of his hateful, predatory Olga. In *Terror* the woman is more the victim of the man, while *The Order of St. Anne* has a male predator, the ludicrous Modeste Alekseyevich, seeking to victimize his beautiful young wife, only to have the tables turned on him in the end in one of the mature Chekhov's rare snap conclusions. Yet other amorous postures are found in *A Lady with a Dog*, perhaps the best-known of all Chekhov's stories. But though *chagrin d'amour* does indeed suffuse this saga of an experienced philanderer unexpectedly caught up in a profound passion, the dénouement by no means excludes some kind of happy solution. We are reminded that *A Lady with a Dog* was written during the early stages of the author's love affair with Olga Knipper, the actress who eventually became his wife. It reflects Chekhov's own hopes, but also his irritation with his invalid condition which forced him to winter in the south away from her—and from the city of Moscow for which he once said that he had come to yearn as much as any of his own Three Sisters.

Far more anomalous is the love pattern in another of Chekhov's most renowned stories, which also happens to have been Tolstoy's favourite: *Angel*, known to other translators as *The Darling*. The heroine, another of Chekhov's many Olgas, is remarkable for her habit of contracting happy marriages or marital unions—three in all, whereas we may search almost in vain elsewhere for any other Chekhov character who enjoys even one such satisfactory relationship. The story is exceptional too in that Chekhov for once describes provincial life without the contempt, unmistakable though restrained, which we detect in *Doctor Startsev*, *The Russian Master* and even *A Lady with a Dog*. And yet we shall err if we read *Angel* solely as the charming study of a kindly, simple woman whose heart overflows with love for her various spouses and the little boy whom she eventually looks after. We must also be alive, as always with this author, to contrary undercurrents; not sentiment unalloyed but the tension between sentiment and irony is the clue to *Angel*.

Yet another marital or cohabitational episode dominates *The Duel*, included here as an especially fine specimen of Chekhov's longer work. It also contains the most sustained portrayal of a quarrel to come from a writer who was himself a notably peaceable man, but could yet delineate the squabbles of others with admirable skill. This he does in pitting *The Duel*'s slovenly, slipper-shufflling Layevsky (paramour of the no less slovenly Nadezhda) against the forthright, puritanical zoologist von Koren: that prophet of the survival of the fittest. But though von Koren eventually finds himself in a position to exterminate Layevsky—demonstrably unfit to live and therefore liquidation-ripe—in a pistols-at-dawn contest, that contest fizzles out in the predictable Chekhovian fiasco; and the text explicitly makes the point that the heroic age of duels *à la* Lermontov and Turgenev has now given way to a humdrum era when issues are less majestically clear-cut. How disappointing, though, that Chekhov should have fallen, in the last few pages of his *Duel*, from his usual high standards by suddenly pretending that the problems so successfully ventilated in his first ninety-odd pages were in fact no problems at all. *The Duel*'s feeble last chapter—in which a reformed Layevsky is seen married to a reformed Nadezhda, and in which both are forgiven by a reformed von Koren—gives the answer to those who complain of Chekhov's many unhappy endings. Here, after all, is a 'happy' ending: but one so unconvincing and banal that, though it cannot spoil so superb a story, it yet remains a considerable minor blemish.

Peasants reflects very different preoccupations. Of all Chekhov's works this created the greatest stir among his contemporaries in his own country. It may seem disappointingly slight on first reading, being hardly a story at all—rather a sequence of sketches set in an unprepossessing Russian village peopled by the usual drunkards, wife-beaters and wiseacres. Chekhov had drawn on his own experiences as resident from 1892 onwards of the village of Melikhovo near Moscow to illustrate all the most typical elements in late nineteenth-century Russian rural life. And since such down-trodden, backward rustics constituted four-fifths of the total population of the Russian Empire, numbering about a hundred million in all, his *Peasants* is a document of outstanding social importance. It also happens to furnish the quickest short cut available to understanding a crucial area of Russian society in his day. But if we choose, as well we may, to call *Peasants* a documentary, we must add that it is a documentary of genius. Only supreme literary skill could purvey, in a mere thirty pages,

more about this complex social situation than many another author
has contrived in an entire volume, besides which Chekhov's
restrained and subtle humour gives *Peasants* a dimension beyond
the reach of other Russian rural studies. As for the abuse which
greeted *Peasants* in Russia on first publication, that too forms a
significant comment on the age. Chekhov had sinned, in the
opinion of many contemporary intellectuals, by flouting an unspoken taboo whereby no author might mention such unedifying
features of village life as dirt, squalor, dunkenness, brutality and
deceitfulness without simultaneously proclaiming or implying the
Russian muzhik to be a paragon of certain mysterious virtues
visible only to the eye of faith. But Chekhov's eye was always that
of a critical observer who, frankly, could not discern these mysterious rustic virtues. Whether he was discussing peasants or anything
else, he always believed in reporting accurately what he saw. And
in any case his unconventional and apparently unfavourable picture
of the muzhik is fundamentally sympathetic, as must surely be
evident to any sensitive reader of *Peasants*. Nor was Chekhov the
squire of Melikhovo in the least hostile to the local rustics, for his
outstanding record as devoted village doctor, assiduous school-
builder and good neighbour demonstrates the very opposite.

Finally there are the three remarkable stories *A Hard Case*,
Gooseberries and *Concerning Love*. They are sometimes called a
'trilogy', being unique in Chekhov's fiction in possessing a single
unifying theme illustrated by characters who spill over from one
story to another. Each item in the trilogy contains as its principal
element a story-within-the-story told by one of three narrators to
one or both of the others. And all three stories denounce the
tendency whereby, in Chekhov's view, human beings tend arbit-
rarily to fetter themselves with superfluous encumbrances—
ideology, ambition, love—thus renouncing man's most precious
birth-right, freedom. The hidebound schoolmaster Belikov who
tyrannizes the townsfolk in *A Hard Case*; the ludicrous Nicholas
Chimsha-Gimalaysky who sacrifices his whole life for a single plate
of sour gooseberries; the unenterprising Alyokhin who cravenly
renounces the one true love of his life—all three key characters
admirably exemplify Chekhov's central theme. They have all made
the wrong choice, as he shows, while also reminding us by
implication of something which he does not show: that in Chekhov,
alas, virtually all choices are wrong. What if Alyokhin had in fact

gone off with the seductive Mrs. Luganovich? What if the unfortunate Nicholas had never saved up to buy his estate complete with
its gooseberry patch, and what if Belikov had never taught Greek
or bullied his colleagues? They would only have embraced some
other activity equally futile, equally self-limiting. Of this we may
be certain, for anti-climax and the frustration of illusions remain
basic to Chekhov's art at its best. And, as we are again reminded,
the last pages of *The Duel* are there to show how right he was to
stick to his true métier, how disastrous any attempt to break out of
it might prove. We are also reminded that Chekhov, at his best,
usually focuses on what does not—seldom on what does—happen.

By no means all Chekhov's readers will agree in finding failure
and disillusionment to be such inseparable features of life as he
seems to suggest in his works. And that Chekhov himself, as a
man, had an outlook far less melancholy than that seemingly
implied by Chekhov the artist we know from the rich source
material of his biography: his personal letters, totalling over 4,000,
and the many memoirs about him. Nor, in order to enjoy
Chekhov's work, need readers feel any more obliged than did he
himself (in his non-literary capacity) to adopt the philosophy of all-
embracing frustration apparently deducible from his writings.

Rather may we marvel at the skill with which this arguably
distorted philosophy has been used as a prism to display the human
predicament in so original, so exhilarating, and above all so
ultimately undistorting a projection.

RONALD HINGLEY

SELECT BIBLIOGRAPHY

Biography and Autobiography

Heim, Michael Henry (trans.), and Karlinsky, Simon (ed.), *Letters of Anton Chekhov* (New York, 1973).

Hingley, Ronald, *A Life of Chekhov* (Oxford, 1989).

Rayfield, Donald, *Anton Chekhov: A Life* (London, 1997).

Bibliography

Lantz, Kenneth, *Anton Chekhov, A Reference Guide to Literature* (Boston, 1985).

Background

Bruford, W. H., *Chekhov and His Russia* (London, 1948).

Tulloch, John, *Chekhov: A Structuralist Study* (London, 1980).

Criticism

Bitsilli, Peter M., *Chekhov's Art: A Stylistic Analysis* (Ann Arbor, 1983).

Clyman, Toby W. (ed.), *A Chekhov Companion* (Westport, Conn., 1985).

Gerhardi, William, *Anton Chekhov: A Critical Study* (London, 1923).

Hahn, Beverly, *Chekhov: A Study of the Major Stories and Plays* (Cambridge, 1977).

Jackson, Robert Louis (ed.), *Reading Chekhov's Text* (Evanston, 1993).

Kramer, Karl D., *The Chameleon and the Dream: The Image of Reality in Čexov's Stories* (The Hague, 1970).

Llewellyn Smith, Virginia, *Anton Chekhov and the Lady with the Dog* (Oxford, 1973).

Turner, C. J. G., *Time and Temporal Structure in Chekhov* (Birmingham, 1994).

Winner, Thomas, *Chekhov and His Prose* (New York, 1966).

Further Reading in Oxford World's Classics

Twelve Plays, translated and edited by Ronald Hingley (*On the High Road; Swan Song; The Bear; The Proposal; Tatyana Repin; A Tragic Role; The Wedding; The Anniversary; Smoking is Bad for You; The Night Before the Trial; The Wood-Demon; Platonov*).

Early Stories, translated and edited by Patrick Miles and Harvey Pitcher.

The Steppe and Other Stories, translated and edited by Ronald Hingley.

Ward Number Six and Other Stories, translated and edited by Ronald Hingley.

A CHRONOLOGY OF ANTON CHEKHOV

All dates are given old style.

1860   16 or 17 January. Born in Taganrog, a port on the Sea of Azov in south Russia.

1876   His father goes bankrupt. The family moves to Moscow, leaving Anton to finish his schooling.

1879   Joins family and enrols in the Medical Faculty of Moscow University.

1880   Begins to contribute to *Strekoza* ('Dragonfly'), a St. Petersburg comic weekly.

1882   Starts to write short stories and a gossip column for *Oskolki* ('Splinters') and to depend on writing for an income.

1884   Graduates in medicine. Shows early symptoms of tuberculosis.

1885–6   Contributes to *Peterburgskaya gazeta* ('St. Petersburg Gazette') and *Novoye vremya* ('New Time').

1886   March. Letter from D. V. Grigorovich encourages him to take writing seriously.
         First collection of stories: *Motley Stories*.

1887   Literary reputation grows fast. Second collection of stories: *In the Twilight*.
         19 November. First Moscow performance of *Ivanov*: mixed reception.

1888   First publication (*The Steppe*) in a serious literary journal, *Severny vestnik* ('The Northern Herald').

1889   31 January. First St. Petersburg performance of *Ivanov*: widely and favourably reviewed.
         June. Death of brother Nicholas from tuberculosis.

1890   April–December. Crosses Siberia to visit the penal settlement on Sakhalin Island. Returns via Hong Kong, Singapore and Ceylon.

1891   First trip to western Europe: Italy and France.

1892   March. Moves with family to small country estate at Melikhovo, fifty miles south of Moscow.

1895   First meeting with Tolstoy.

1896   17 October. First—disastrous—performance of *The Seagull* in St. Petersburg.

1897   Suffers severe haemorrhage.

1897–8   Winters in France. Champions Zola's defence of Dreyfus.

1898   Beginning of collaboration with the newly founded Moscow Art Theatre. Meets Olga Knipper. Spends the winter in Yalta, where he meets Gorky.

           17 December. First Moscow Art Theatre performance of *The Seagull*: successful.

1899   Completes the building of a house in Yalta, where he settles with mother and sister.

           26 October. First performance by Moscow Art Theatre of *Uncle Vanya* (written ?1896).

1899–1901 First collected edition of his works (10 volumes).

1901   31 January. *Three Sisters* first performed.

           25 May. Marries Olga Knipper.

1904   17 January. First performance of *The Cherry Orchard*.

           2 July. Dies in Badenweiler, Germany.

HIS WIFE

'I THOUGHT I told you not to tidy my desk,' said Nicholas. 'I can't find anything when you've been round tidying. Where's that telegram got to? Where did you put it? Would you mind having a look? It's from Kazan, dated yesterday.'

The maid, a pale, very slim girl, seemed unconcerned. She did find several telegrams in the basket under the desk and handed them to the doctor without a word, but those were all local telegrams from his patients. Then they searched the drawing-room and his wife Olga's room.

It was past midnight. Nicholas knew that his wife would not be back for a long time, not till five in the morning at least. He did not trust her and felt depressed and could not sleep when she stayed out late. He despised his wife, her bed, her looking-glass, her boxes of chocolates and all these lilies-of-the-valley and hyacinths that came from someone every day and made the whole house smell as sickly-sweet as a florist's shop. On nights like this he grew irritable, moody and snappish, and he felt that he simply must have yesterday's telegram from his brother, though there was nothing in the thing beyond the compliments of the season.

On the table in his wife's room he did turn up a telegram under a box of writing-paper and glanced at it. It came from Monte Carlo and was addressed to his wife, care of his mother-in-law. The signature was *Michel*. The doctor could not make head or tail of it as it was in some foreign language, English apparently.

Who could *Michel* be? Why Monte Carlo? And why send it care of his mother-in-law?

Suspicions, conjectures, deductions—seven years of married life had made such things second nature to him and he often thought that he had had enough practice at home to turn him into a first-class detective.

He went back to his study and began thinking things over, where-upon it all came back to him. About eighteen months ago he had been in St. Petersburg with his wife. They had lunched at Cubat's Restaurant with an old school friend of his, a transport engineer who had introduced a young man of twenty-two or twenty-three called Michael with a short, rather odd surname—Rees. Two months later the doctor had seen the young man's photograph in his wife's album with some

writing in French: 'In memory of the present and in hope for the future.'
Then he had run across the man a couple of times at his mother-in-
law's. That was when his wife had taken to going out a lot and coming
home at all hours of the morning. She kept asking him to let her have
a passport so that she could go abroad. He had refused and for days on
end all hell had been let loose at home and he could hardly face the
servants.

Six months ago Nicholas's medical colleagues had decided that he
was developing T.B. and advised him to drop everything and go to the
Crimea, hearing which Olga put on an air of great alarm and started
making up to her husband. She told him how cold and boring the
Crimea was and how much better Nice would be. She would go with
him and nurse him and see that he had some peace and quiet.

Now he knew why his wife was so set on Nice This *Michel* lived
at Monte Carlo.

He picked up an English–Russian dictionary and gradually put together the following by translating the words and guessing the meaning:

> **DRINK TO MY DEARLY BELOVED KISS TINY FOOT**
> **THOUSAND TIMES EAGERLY AWAIT ARRIVAL**

Now he saw what a laughing-stock he would have made of himself if
he had agreed to take his wife to Nice. He was so upset that he was
ready to cry, and began stalking from room to room in great distress.
A sensitive man of humble origins, he felt wounded in his pride. He
clenched his fists and scowled disgustedly, wondering how he—the
son of a village priest, brought up at a church school, a plain, blunt
man and a surgeon by profession—could ever have let himself be
enslaved. Why this shameful surrender to a creature so feeble, mean-
spirited, dishonest and generally beneath contempt?

'Tiny foot!' he muttered, screwing up the telegram. 'Tiny foot my
foot!'

Falling in love, proposing, seven years of marriage—nothing remained of all that but the memory of long, fragrant hair, clouds of
soft lace and a tiny foot. Yes, it actually was very small and pretty.
Those early embraces now seemed to have left him with the feel of silk
and lace on his hands and face, and nothing else.

Nothing else, that is, unless you count hysteria, screams, reproaches,
threats and lies—barefaced, treacherous lies.

At his father's house in the village, he remembered, a bird sometimes
chanced to fly in from outside and would crash furiously against the

windows and knock things over. And that is what this woman was like, flying into his life from a completely different world and creating sheer havoc. The best years of his life were over and they had been hell, his hopes of happiness had been dashed and mocked, his health was gone, and his house was full of the paraphernalia of a vulgar coquette. Out of the ten thousand roubles that he earned each year he could not raise even ten to send to his old mother and he was in debt to the tune of fifteen thousand. A gang of thugs could have camped out in his home without making such a total wreck of his life as this woman had done, or so it seemed.

He began coughing and gasping for breath. He should have gone to bed to get warm, but he could not. He kept walking about the house or sitting down at his desk, doodling nervously with a pencil and writing automatically, 'Writing practice. . . . Tiny foot. . . .'

By five o'clock he felt quite weak and was blaming himself for everything. He felt that Olga should have married someone else who could have had a good influence on her. That might have turned her into a good, decent woman—who knows?—whereas he was a poor psychologist who knew nothing of the female heart, quite apart from being so dull and insensitive. . . .

'I'm not long for this world,' he thought. 'A walking corpse like me shouldn't get in living people's way. To stand out for one's supposed rights now—that really would be silly and eccentric. I'll have it out with her. Let her go off with her lover—I'll give her a divorce and take the blame. . . .'

Olga arrived in the end. She came straight into the study without taking off her white coat, hat and galoshes, and flopped down in an armchair.

'Horrid, horrid fat boy!' she panted with a sob. 'Thoroughly dishonest, I call it! Beastly!' She stamped. 'I can't, I won't, I shan't put up with it!'

'Why, what is it?' asked Nicholas, going towards her.

'A student—Azarbekov—has been seeing me home and he's lost my purse with fifteen roubles that Mother gave me.'

She was crying in real earnest, like a little girl, and not only her handkerchief, but even her gloves were wet with tears.

'It can't be helped,' sighed the doctor. 'If it's lost it's lost and that's that. Do calm down, I want a word with you.'

'I'm not made of money and I can't afford to be so slapdash. He says he'll pay it back, but I don't believe him, he's too poor. . . .'

Her husband asked her to calm down and listen, but she kept on about the student and this missing fifteen roubles.

'Look,' he said irritably, 'I'll let you have twenty-five roubles in the morning. Only please do shut up.'

'I must go and change,' she sobbed. 'Well, I can't talk seriously with my coat on, can I? Whatever next!'

Helping her off with her coat and galoshes, he caught a whiff of the white wine that she liked with oysters—she could certainly put away the food and drink, for all her dainty looks.

She went to her room and came back after a while, having changed her clothe. and powdered her face, but with eyes swollen from crying. She sat down and vanished inside her lace négligé, and all her husband could make out in this sea of pink billows was her hair all over the place and that tiny foot in a slipper.

'Well, what is it?' she asked, rocking herself in the chair.

'I happened to see this,' said the doctor and handed her the telegram.

She read it and shrugged.

'What of it?' she asked, rocking harder. 'It's an ordinary New Year's greeting, that's all. There's no mystery about it.'

'You're banking on me not knowing English. I know I don't, but I do have a dictionary. That telegram's from Rees. He drinks to his beloved and sends you a thousand kisses. But never mind that, never mind that,' the doctor hurried on. 'I haven't the faintest wish to reproach you or make a scene. We've had scenes and reproaches enough and it's about time we stopped. What I say is this—you're free to live as you like.'

There was a short silence. She began crying softly.

'I'm giving you your freedom so that you won't need to pretend and lie any more,' went on Nicholas. 'If you love that young man, well then, love him. And if you want to join him abroad, go ahead. You're young and healthy and I'm an invalid, I'm not long for this world. In other words—well, you see what I mean.'

He felt too upset to go on. Weeping, Olga admitted in a self-pitying voice that she did love Rees, had been with him on jaunts out of town, visited him in his hotel room—and really was very keen on this trip abroad.

'You see, I'm not hiding anything,' she sighed. 'I'm putting my cards on the table and I implore you once again to do the decent thing and give me my passport.'

'That's just what I'm telling you—you're free.'

She moved to a chair nearer him so that she could look at his face. She distrusted him and wanted to read his innermost thoughts. She never trusted people and always suspected them, however well-meaning, of being up to some dirty little trick and having an eye to the main chance. As she scrutinized his face her eyes seemed to flash green like a cat's.

'Then when do I get my passport?' she asked quietly.

'Never,' he suddenly wanted to answer, but took a grip on himself and said, 'Whenever you like.'

'I'm only going for a month.'

'You can stay with Rees for good. I'm giving you a divorce and taking the blame, so Rees can marry you.'

Olga looked astonished. 'But I don't *want* a divorce!' she said forcefully. 'I'm not asking for one. Just give me the passport, that's all.'

'But why no divorce?' The doctor was beginning to lose his temper. 'You're a strange woman, I must say. If you're really fond of him and he loves you, you two can't do better than marry, placed as you are. Don't tell me that given the choice you actually prefer adultery to marriage!'

'Oh, I *see*,' she said, moving away. An evil, vindictive expression came into her face. 'I see your little game. You're fed up with me and you just want to get rid of me by landing me with this divorce. But I'm not quite such a fool as you think, thank you very much. I'm not having a divorce and I'm not leaving you, oh dear me no. Firstly, I want to keep my social position,' she went on quickly as though afraid that he might stop her. 'Secondly, I'm twenty-seven and Rees is only twenty-three. In a year's time he'll tire of me and throw me over. And what's more, I'm not sure I shall be so keen on him much longer, if you want to know. . . . So there! I'm sitting tight!'

'Then out of this house you go!' shouted Nicholas, stamping. 'I'll throw you out! You're a vile, disgusting creature.'

'We'll see about that,' she said and left the room.

It was broad daylight outside, but the doctor still sat at his desk doodling and automatically writing, 'My dear Sir. . . . A tiny foot. . . .'

Or else he walked about, stopping in the drawing-room in front of a photograph taken soon after his wedding seven years ago. He looked at it for some time.

It was a family group. There were his father-in-law, his mother-in-law and his wife Olga, then aged twenty. And there was he in his role of happy young husband. Father-in-law was clean-shaven, plump, dropsical, a senior civil servant, cunning and avaricious. Mother-in-law, a stout woman with the small, predatory features of a ferret, loved her daughter to distraction and helped her as much as she could. If her daughter had strangled someone she would not have said a word to the girl, but would just have shielded her behind her apron.

Olga had small, predatory features too, but they were bolder and more expressive than her mother's—no ferret she, but a nastier piece of work altogether!

Nicholas himself looked such a decent, straightforward fellow in the photograph—such a terribly nice chap! A hearty, good-natured, boyish grin lit up his whole face. He looked as if he believed in his simple way that this brood of vampires, into which fate had thrust him, was going to bring him adventure, happiness and all that he had dreamt of when he was a student and sang, "Tis better to have loved and lost than never to have loved at all.'

Once again he asked himself in utter bafflement how he—son of a village priest and brought up at a church school, a plain, straight-forward, blunt man—could have surrendered so abjectly to this contemptible, lying, vulgar, mean-spirited, wholly alien creature.

At eleven o'clock that morning he was putting on his coat before going to the hospital when the maid came into his study.

'What is it?'

'Madam has just got up. She wants the twenty-five roubles you promised her yesterday.'

A LADY WITH A DOG

I

THERE was said to be a new arrival on the Esplanade: a lady with a dog.

After spending a fortnight at Yalta, Dmitry Gurov had quite settled in and was now beginning to take an interest in new faces. As he sat outside Vernet's café he saw a fair-haired young woman, not tall, walking on the promenade—wearing a beret, with a white Pomeranian dog trotting after her.

Then he encountered her several times a day in the municipal park and square. She walked alone, always with that beret, always with the white Pomeranian. Who she was no one knew, everyone just called her 'the dog lady'.

'If she has no husband or friends here she might be worth picking up,' calculated Gurov.

He was still in his thirties, but had a twelve-year-old daughter and two schoolboy sons. His marriage had been arranged early—during his second college year—and now his wife seemed half as old again as he. She was a tall, dark-browed woman: outspoken, earnest, stolid and—she maintained—an 'intellectual'. She was a great reader, she favoured spelling reform, she called her husband 'Demetrius' instead of plain 'Dmitry', while he privately thought her narrow-minded, inelegant and slow on the uptake. He was afraid of her, and disliked being at home. He had begun deceiving her long ago, and his infidelities were frequent—which is probably why he nearly always spoke so disparagingly of women, calling them an 'inferior species' when the subject cropped up.

He was, he felt, sufficiently schooled by bitter experience to call them any name he liked, yet he still couldn't live two days on end without his 'inferior species'. Men's company bored him, making him ill at ease, tongue-tied and apathetic, whereas with women he felt free. He knew what to talk about, how to behave—he even found it easy to be with them without talking at all. In his appearance and character, in his whole nature, there was an alluring, elusive element which charmed and fascinated women. He knew it, and he was himself strongly attracted in return.

As experience multiple and—in the full sense of the word—bitter had long since taught him, every intimacy which so pleasantly diversifies one's life, which seems so easy, so delightfully adventurous at the outset ... such an intimacy does, when reasonable people are involved (not least Muscovites—so hesitant and slow off the mark), develop willy-nilly into some vast, extraordinarily complex problem until the whole business finally becomes quite an ordeal. Somehow, though, on every new encounter with an attractive woman all this experience went for nothing—he wanted a bit of excitement and it all seemed so easy and amusing.

Well, he was eating in an open-air restaurant late one afternoon when the lady in the beret sauntered along and took the next table. Her expression, walk, clothes, hair-style ... all told him that she was socially presentable, married, in Yalta for the first time, alone—and bored.

Much nonsense is talked about the looseness of morals in these parts, and he despised such stories, knowing that they were largely fabricated by people who would have been glad to misbehave themselves, given the aptitude! But when the young woman sat down at the next table, three paces away, he recalled those tales of trips into the mountains and easy conquests. The seductive thought of a swift, fleeting *affaire*—the romance with the stranger whose very name you don't know—suddenly possessed him. He made a friendly gesture to the dog. It came up. He wagged his finger. The dog growled and Gurov shook his finger again.

The lady glanced at him, lowered her eyes at once.

'He doesn't bite.' She blushed.

'May I give him a bone?'

She nodded.

'Have you been in Yalta long, madam?' he asked courteously.

'Five days.'

'Oh, I've nearly survived my first fortnight.'

There was a short pause.

'Time goes quickly, but it *is* so boring,' she said, not looking at him.

'That's what they all say, what a bore this place is. Your average tripper from Belyov, Zhizdra or somewhere ... he doesn't know what boredom means till he comes here. Then it's "Oh, what a bore! Oh, what dust!" You might think he'd just blown in from sunny Spain!'

She laughed. Then both continued their meal in silence, as strangers.

After dinner, though, they left together and embarked on the bantering chat of people who feel free and easy, who don't mind where they go or what they talk about. As they strolled they discussed the strange light on the sea: the water was of a soft, warm, mauve hue, crossed by a stripe of golden moonlight. How sultry it was after the day's heat, they said. Gurov described himself as a Muscovite who had studied literature but worked in a bank. He had once trained as an opera singer but had given that up and owned two houses in Moscow.

From her he learnt that she had grown up in St. Petersburg, but had married in the provincial town where she had now been living for two years, that she was staying in Yalta for another month, that her husband (who also wanted a holiday) might come and fetch her. She was quite unable to explain her husband's job—was it with the County Council or the Rural District?—and even she saw the funny side of this. Gurov also learnt that she was called Anne.

In his hotel room afterwards he thought about her. He was very likely to meet her tomorrow, bound to. As he went to bed he remembered that she had not long left boarding-school, that she had been a schoolgirl like his own daughter—remembered, too, how much shyness and stiffness she still showed when laughing and talking to a stranger. This must be her first time ever alone in such a place, with men following her around, watching her, talking to her: all with a certain privy aim which she could not fail to divine. He remembered her slender, frail neck, her lovely grey eyes.

'You can't help feeling sorry for her, though,' he thought. And dozed off.

II

A week had passed since their first meeting. It was a Sunday or some other holiday. Indoors was stifling, and outside flurries of dust swept the streets, whipping off hats. It was a thirsty day, and Gurov kept calling in at the café to fetch Anne a soft drink or an ice-cream. There was no escaping the heat.

In the evening things were a little easier, and they went on the pier to watch a steamer come in. There were a lot of people hanging around on the landing-stage: they were here to meet someone, and held bunches of flowers. Two features of the Yalta smart set were now thrown into sharp relief. The older women dressed like young ones. There were lots of generals.

As the sea was rough the steamer arrived late, after sunset, and manœuvred for some time before putting in at the jetty. Anne watched boat and passengers through her lorgnette as if seeking someone she knew. Whenever she turned to Gurov her eyes shone. She spoke a lot, asking quick-fire questions and immediately forgetting what they were. Then she lost her lorgnette: dropped it in the crowd.

The gaily-dressed gathering dispersed, no more faces could be seen, and the wind dropped completely while Gurov and Anne stood as if waiting for someone else to disembark. Anne had stopped talking, and sniffed her flowers without looking at Gurov.

'The weather's better now that it's evening,' said he. 'So where shall we go? How about driving somewhere?'

She did not answer.

Then he stared at her hard, embraced her suddenly and kissed her lips. The scent of her flowers, their dampness, enveloped him, and he immediately glanced around fearfully: had they been observed?

'Let's go to your room,' he said softly.

They set off quickly together.

Her room was stuffy and smelt of the scent which she had bought in the Japanese shop.

'What encounters one does have in life,' thought Gurov as he looked at her now.

He still retained memories of the easy-going, light-hearted women in his past: women happy in their love and grateful to him for that happiness, however brief. He also recalled those who, like his wife, made love insincerely, with idle chatter, affectations and hysteria, their expressions conveying that this was neither love nor passion but something more significant. He thought of two or three very beautiful frigid women whose faces would suddenly flash a rapacious, stubborn look of lust to seize, to snatch more from life than it can give . . . women no longer young, these: fractious, unreasonable, overbearing and obtuse. When Gurov had cooled towards them their beauty had aroused his hatred, and the lace on their underclothes had looked like a lizard's scales.

In this case, though, all was hesitancy, the awkwardness of inexperienced youth. There was the impression of her being taken aback, too, as by a sudden knock on the door. Anne, this 'lady with a dog', had her own special view—a very serious one—of what had happened. She thought of it as her 'downfall', it seemed, which was all very strange and inappropriate. Her features had sunk and faded, her long hair drooped sadly down each side of her face. She had struck a pensive, despondent pose, like the Woman Taken in Adultery in an old-fashioned picture.

'This is all wrong,' she said. 'Now you'll completely despise me.'

There was a water-melon on the table. Gurov cut a slice and slowly ate. Half an hour, at least, passed in silence.

He found Anne touching. She had that air of naïve innocence of a thoroughly nice unworldly woman. A solitary candle, burning on the table, barely lit her face, but it was obvious that she was ill at ease.

'Why should I lose respect for you?' asked Gurov. 'You don't know what you're saying.'

'God forgive me,' she said, her eyes brimming with tears. 'This is terrible.'

'You seem very much on the defensive, Anne.'

'How *can* I defend what I've done? I'm a bad, wicked woman, I despise myself and I'm not trying to make excuses. It's not my husband, it is *myself* I've deceived. I don't just mean what happened here, I've been deceiving myself for a long time. My husband may be a good, honourable man, but he *is* such a worm. What he does at that job of his I don't know—all I know is, he's a worm. I was twenty when I married him—I longed to know more of life. Then I wanted something better. There must *be* a different life, mustn't there? Or so I told myself. I wanted a little—well, rather *more* than a little—excitement. I was avid for experience. You won't understand me, I'm sure, but I could control myself no longer, I swear, something had happened to me, there was no holding me. So I told my husband I was ill and I came here. And I've been going round here in a daze as if I was off my head. But now I'm just another vulgar, worthless woman whom everyone is free to despise.'

Gurov was bored with all this. He was irritated by the naïve air, the unexpected, uncalled-for remorse. But for the tears in her eyes he might have thought her to be joking or play-acting.

'I don't understand,' said he softly. 'What is it you want?'

She hid her face on his breast and clung to him.

'Please, please believe me,' she implored. 'I long for a decent, moral life. Sin disgusts me, I don't know what I'm doing myself. The common people say the "Evil One" tempted them, and now I can say the same: I was tempted by the Evil One.'

'There there, that's enough,' he muttered.

He looked into her staring, frightened eyes, kissed her, spoke softly and gently. She gradually relaxed and cheered up again. Both laughed.

Then they went out. The promenade was deserted, the town with its cypresses looked quite dead, but the sea still roared, breaking on the beach. A single launch with a sleepily glinting lamp tossed on the waves.

They found a cab and drove to Oreanda.

'I've only just discovered your surname, downstairs in your hotel,' Gurov told her. '"Von Diederitz", it says on the board. Is your husband German?'

'No, his grandfather was, I think, but he's Russian.'

They sat on a bench near the church at Oreanda, gazing silently down at the sea. Yalta was barely visible through the dawn mist, white clouds hung motionless on the mountain peaks. Not a leaf stirred on the trees, cicadas chirped. Borne up from below, the sea's monotonous, muffled boom spoke of peace, of the everlasting sleep awaiting us. Before Yalta or Oreanda yet existed that surf had been thundering down there, it was roaring away now, and it will continue its dull booming with the same unconcern when we are no more. This persistence, this utter aloofness from all our lives and deaths . . . do they perhaps hold the secret pledge of our eternal salvation, of life's perpetual motion on earth, of its uninterrupted progress? As he sat there, lulled and entranced by the magic panorama—sea, mountains, clouds, broad sky—beside a young woman who looked so beautiful in the dawn, Gurov reflected that everything on earth is beautiful, really, when you consider it—everything except what we think and do ourselves when we forget the lofty goals of being and our human dignity.

Someone—a watchman, no doubt—came up, looked at them, went away. Even this incident seemed mysterious—beautiful, too. In the dawn they saw a steamer arrive from Feodosiya, its lights already extinguished.

'There's dew on the grass,' Anne said, after a pause.

'Yes, time to go home.'

They went back to town.

After this they met on the promenade each noon, lunched, dined, strolled, enthused about the sea together. She complained of sleeping badly, of palpitations. Disturbed by jealousy, and by the fear that he did not respect her enough, she kept repeating the same old questions. And often in the Square or Gardens, when there was nobody near them, he would suddenly draw her to him and kiss her ardently. This utter idleness, these kisses in broad daylight, these glances over the shoulder, this fear of being seen, the heat, the sea's smell, the repeated glimpses of idle, elegant, sleek persons . . . it all seemed to revitalize him. He told Anne how pretty she was, how provocative. He was impetuous, he was passionate, he never left her side, while she was for ever brooding and begging him to admit that he did not respect her, that he loved her not at all, that he could see in her no more than a very ordinary woman. Late almost every evening they would drive out of town: to Oreanda or the waterfall. These trips were invariably a great success, leaving an impression of majesty and beauty.

They had been expecting the husband to arrive, but he sent a letter to say that he had eye trouble, and begged his wife to come home soon. Anne bestirred herself.

'It's just as well I *am* leaving,' she told Gurov. 'This is fate.'

She left by carriage and he drove with her. This part of her journey took all day. When she took her seat in the express train, which was due to leave in five minutes, she asked to look at him once more.

'One last look—that's right.'

She did not cry, but was so sad that she seemed ill. Her face quivered.

'I'll think of you, I'll remember you,' she said. 'God bless and keep you. Don't think ill of me. We're parting for ever. We must, because we should never have met at all. God bless you.'

The train departed swiftly, its lights soon vanishing and its noise dying away within a minute, as though everything had conspired to make a quick end of that sweet trance, that madness. Alone on the platform, gazing into the dark distance, Gurov heard the chirp of grasshoppers and the hum of telegraph wires, feeling as if he had just awoken. Well, there went another adventure or episode in his life, he reflected. It too had ended, now only the memory was left.

He was troubled, sad, somewhat penitent. This young woman whom he would never see again . . . she hadn't been happy with him, now, had she? He had treated her kindly and affectionately. And yet his attitude to her, his tone, his caresses had betrayed a faint irony: the rather crude condescension of your conquering male—of a man nearly twice her age into the bargain. She had kept calling him kind, exceptional, noble—so she hadn't seen him as he really was, obviously, and he must have been deceiving her without meaning to.

Here at the station there was already a whiff of autumn in the air, and the evening was cool.

'It's time I went north too,' thought Gurov, leaving the platform. 'High time.'

III

Back home in Moscow it was already like winter. The stoves were alight. It was dark when his children breakfasted and got ready for school in the mornings, so their nanny lit the light for a short time. The frosts had begun. It is always such a joy to see the white ground and white roofs when the snow first falls, on that first day of sleighriding. The air is so fresh and good to breathe, and you remember the years of your youth. White with frost, the old limes and birches have a kindly look, they are dearer to your heart than any cypresses or palm-trees, and near them you no longer hanker after mountains and sea.

A Moscow man himself, Gurov had come home on a fine frosty day. He put on his fur coat and warm gloves and strolled down the Petrovka, he heard church bells pealing on Saturday evening . . . and his recent trip, all the places he had visited, lost all charm for him. He plunged deeper and deeper into Moscow life. He was zealously reading his three newspapers on principle! He felt the lure of restaurants, clubs, dinner parties, anniversary celebrations; he was flattered to be visited by famous lawyers and actors, flattered to play cards with a professor at the Doctors' Club. He could tackle a large helping of 'Moscow hotpot' straight from the pan.

In a month or two's time the memory of Anne would become blurred, thought he—he would just dream of her, of her adorable smile, occasionally as he used to dream of those other ones. But more than a month passed, real winter set in, and yet everything was still as clear in his mind as if they had parted only yesterday. His memories flared up ever more brightly. When, in the quiet of evening, his children's voices reached his study as they did their homework, when he heard a sentimental song or a barrel organ in a restaurant, when a blizzard howled in his chimney . . . it would all suddenly come back to him: that business on the pier, the early morning with the mist on the mountains, the Feodosiya steamer, the kisses. He would pace the room for hours, remembering and smiling until these recollections merged into fantasies: until, in his imagination, past fused with future. Though he did not dream of Anne, she pursued him everywhere like his shadow, watching him. If he closed his eyes he could see her vividly—younger, gentler, more beautiful than she really was. He even saw himself as a better man than he had been back in Yalta.

She gazed at him from the book-case in the evenings, from the hearth, from a corner of the room. He heard her breathing, heard the delightful rustle of her dress. In the street he followed women with his eyes, seeking one like her.

He was plagued, now, by the urge to share his memories. But he could not talk about his love at home, and outside his home there was no one to tell—he couldn't very well discuss it with his tenants or at the bank! What was there to say, anyway? Had he really been in love? Had there really been anything beautiful or idyllic, anything edifying—anything merely interesting, even—in his relations with Anne? He was reduced to vague remarks about love and women, and no one guessed what he had in mind. His wife just twitched those dark eyebrows and told him that 'the role of lady-killer doesn't suit you at all, Demetrius'.

As he was leaving the Doctors' Club one night with his partner, a civil servant, he could not help saying that he had 'met such an enchanting woman in Yalta—did you but know!'

The civil servant climbed into his sledge and drove off, but suddenly turned round and shouted Gurov's name.

'What is it?'

'You were quite right just now, the sturgeon *was* a bit off.'

For some reason these words, humdrum though they were, suddenly infuriated Gurov, striking him as indelicate and gross. What barbarous manners, what faces, what meaningless nights, what dull, featureless days! Frantic card-playing, guzzling, drunkenness, endless chatter always on one and the same topic. Futile activities, repetitious talk, talk, talk . . . they engross most of your time, your best efforts, and you end up with a sort of botched, pedestrian life: a form of imbecility from which there's no way out, no escape. You might as well be in jail or in a madhouse!

Gurov lay awake all night, fuming—then had a headache all next day. He slept badly on the following nights, too, sitting up in bed thinking, or pacing the room. He was fed up with his children, fed up with his bank, there was nowhere he wanted to go, nothing he wanted to talk about.

Towards Christmas he prepared for a journey. He told his wife that he was going to St. Petersburg on a certain young man's business—but he actually went to the town where Anne lived. Why? He didn't really know himself. He wanted to see her, speak to her—make an assignation if he could.

He reached the town one morning and put up at a hotel, in the 'best' room with wall-to-wall carpeting in coarse field-grey material. On the table stood an inkstand, grey with dust and shaped as a horseman holding his hat up in one hand and minus a head. The porter told him what he needed to know: von Diederitz lived in Old Pottery Street in his own house near the hotel. He did things in style, kept his own horses, was known to everyone in town. The porter pronounced the name as 'Drearydits'. Gurov sauntered off to Old Pottery Street, found the house. Immediately facing it was a long, grey fence crowned with nails: 'a fence to run away from', thought Gurov, looking from windows to fence and back.

Local government offices were closed today, so the husband was probably at home, Gurov reckoned. In any case it would be tactless to go into the house and create a disturbance. If he sent a note, though, it might fall into the husband's hands and ruin everything. Better trust to chance. He paced the street near the fence, awaiting this chance. He saw a beggar go through the gate, saw him set upon by dogs. An hour later he heard the faint, muffled sound of a piano—that must be Anne playing. Suddenly the front door opened, and out came an old woman with the familiar white Pomeranian running after her. Gurov wanted to call the dog, but his heart suddenly raced and he was too excited to remember its name.

He paced about, loathing that grey fence more and more. In his irritation, he fancied that Anne had forgotten him and might be amusing herself with another man—what else could be expected of a young woman compelled to contemplate this confounded fence morning, noon and night? He went back to his room, sat on the sofa for hours not knowing what to do, then lunched and dozed for hours.

'It's all so stupid and distressing,' he thought, waking up and seeing the dark windows—it was already evening. 'Now I've had a good sleep for some reason, but what shall I do tonight?'

He sat on the bed—it was covered with a cheap, grey hospital blanket.

'So much for your ladies with dogs!' said he in petulant self-mockery. 'So much for your holiday romances—now you're stuck in this dump.'

In the station that morning his eye had been caught by a poster in bold lettering advertising the opening of *The Geisha*. Recalling this, he drove to the theatre, reflecting that she very probably attended first nights.

The theatre was full. As usual in provincial theatres a mist hung above the chandelier, while the gallery was restive and rowdy. In the first row before the performance began stood the local gallants, hands clasped behind their backs. In the Governor's box, in front, sat that worthy's daughter complete with feather boa, while the Governor himself lurked modestly behind a *portière*, only his hands showing. The curtain shook, the orchestra tuned up protractedly. As the audience came in and took its seats, Gurov peered frantically around.

In came Anne. She sat down in the third row, and when Gurov glimpsed her his heart seemed to miss a beat. He saw clearly, now, that she was nearer, dearer, more important to him than anyone in the whole world. Lost in the provincial crowd, this very ordinary little woman carrying her vulgar lorgnette now absorbed his whole being. She was his grief, his joy—the only happiness he wanted, now. To the strains of that abominable orchestra with its atrocious, tasteless fiddling he thought how lovely she was . . . thought and brooded.

A young man with short dundrearies, very tall, round-shouldered, had come in with Anne and sat down beside her. He kept bobbing his head as if making obeisance with every step he took. It must be the husband whom, in that bitter outburst back in Yalta, she had dubbed a 'worm'. His lanky figure, his side-whiskers, his small bald patch . . . there actually *was* something menial and flunkey-like about them. He gave an ingratiating smile, the emblem of some learned society glinting in his buttonhole like a hotel servant's number.

The husband went for a smoke in the first interval, while she remained seated. Gurov—his seat was also in the stalls—approached her. His voice trembling, forcing a smile, he wished her good evening.

She glanced at him, she blenched. Then she looked again—aghast, not believing her eyes, crushing fan and lorgnette together in her hands in an obvious effort to prevent herself from fainting. Neither spoke. She sat, he remained standing—alarmed by her discomfiture, not venturing to sit down beside her. Fiddles and flute started tuning up, and he suddenly panicked: from all the boxes eyes seemed to be staring at them. Then she stood up and quickly made for the exit, while he followed, both walking at random along corridors, up and down stairways, glimpsing men in the uniforms of the courts, the schools and the administration of crown lands, all wearing their decorations. There were glimpses of ladies and fur coats on pegs. A draught enveloped them with the smell of cigarette ends.

'Oh God—why all these people, this orchestra?' wondered Gurov, his heart pounding.

Suddenly he recalled the evening when he had seen Anne off at the station, when he had told himself that it was all over and that they would never meet again. How far they were now, though, from any ending!

On a narrow, gloomy staircase labelled ENTRANCE TO CIRCLE she stopped.

'How you did scare me,' she panted, still pale and dazed. 'I nearly died, you scared me so. Why, why, why are you here?'

'Try and understand, Anne,' he said in a rapid undertone. 'Understand, I implore you——'

She looked at him—fearfully, pleadingly, lovingly. She stared, trying to fix his features in her memory.

'I'm so miserable,' she went on, not hearing him. 'I've thought only of you all this time, my thoughts of you have kept me alive. Oh, I did so want to forget you—why, why, why are you here?'

On a landing higher up two schoolboys were smoking and looking down, but Gurov did not care. He pulled Anne to him, kissed her face, cheek, hands.

'Whatever are you doing?' she asked—horrified, pushing him from her. 'We must be out of our minds. You must go away today—leave this very instant, I implore you, I beg you in the name of all that is holy. Someone's coming.'

Someone indeed was coming upstairs.

'You *must* leave,' Anne went on in a whisper. 'Do you hear me, Gurov? I'll visit you in Moscow. I've never been happy, I'm unhappy now, and I shall never, never, never be happy. So don't add to my sufferings. I'll come to Moscow, I swear it, but we must part now. We must say good-bye, my good, kind darling.'

She pressed his hand and went quickly downstairs, looking back at him, and he could see from her eyes that she really was unhappy. Gurov waited a little, cocked an ear and, when all was quiet, found the peg with his coat and left the theatre.

IV

Anne took to visiting him in Moscow. Once every two or three months she would leave her home town, telling her husband that she was going to consult a professor about a female complaint. The husband neither believed nor disbelieved her. In Moscow she would put up at the Slav Fair Hotel, and at once send a red-capped messenger to Gurov. Gurov would visit her hotel, and no one in Moscow knew anything about it.

It thus chanced that he was on his way to see her one winter morning —her messenger had called on the previous evening, but had not found him at home. He was walking with his daughter, wanting to take her to her school, which was on his way. There was a heavy downpour of sleet.

'It's three degrees above zero, yet look at the sleet,' said Gurov to his daughter. 'But it's only the ground which is warm, you see—the temperature in the upper strata of the atmosphere is quite different.'

'Why doesn't it thunder in winter, Daddy?'

He explained this too, reflecting as he spoke that he was on his way to an assignation. Not a soul knew about it—or ever would know, probably. He was living two lives. One of them was open to view by— and known to—the people concerned. It was full of stereotyped truths and stereotyped untruths, it was identical with the life of his friends and acquaintances. The other life proceeded in secret. Through some strange and possibly arbitrary chain of coincidences everything vital, interesting and crucial to him, everything which called his sincerity and integrity into play, everything which made up the core of his life . . . all that took place in complete secrecy, whereas everything false about him, the façade behind which he hid to conceal the truth— his work at the bank, say, his arguments at the club, that 'inferior species' stuff, attending anniversary celebrations with his wife—all that was in the open. He judged others by himself, disbelieving the evidence of his eyes, and attributing to everyone a real, fascinating life lived under the cloak of secrecy as in the darkness of the night. Each individual existence is based on mystery, which is perhaps why civilized man makes such a neurotic fuss about having his privacy respected.

After taking his daughter to school, Gurov made for the Slav Fair. He removed his coat downstairs, went up, tapped on the door. Anne was wearing his favourite grey dress, she was tired by the journey— and by the wait, after expecting him since the previous evening. She was pale, she looked at him without smiling, and no sooner was he in the room than she flung herself against his chest. Their kiss was as protracted and lingering as if they had not met for two years.

'Well, how are things with you?' he asked. 'What's the news?'

'Wait, I'll tell you in a moment—I can't now.'

Unable to speak for crying, she turned away and pressed a handkerchief to her eyes.

'Let her cry, I'll sit down for a bit,' thought he, and sat in the arm-chair.

Then he rang and ordered tea. Then he drank it while she still stood with her back to him, facing the window.

She wept as one distressed and woefully aware of the melancholy turn which their lives had taken. They met only in secret, they hid from other people like thieves. Their lives were in ruins, were they not?

'Now, do stop it,' he said.

He could see that this was no fleeting affair—there was no telling when it would end. Anne was growing more and more attached to him. She adored him, and there was no question of telling her that all this must finish one day. Besides, she would never believe him.

He went up to her, laid his hands on her shoulders, meaning to soothe her with a little banter—and then caught sight of himself in the mirror.

His hair was turning grey. He wondered why he had aged so much in the last few years and lost his looks. The shoulders on which his hands rested were warm and trembling. He pitied this life—still so warm and beautiful, but probably just about to fade and wither like his own. Why did she love him so? Women had never seen him as he really was. What they loved in him was not his real self but a figment of their own imaginations—someone whom they had dreamed of meet-ing all their lives. Then, when they realized their mistake, they had loved him all the same. Yet none of them had been happy with him. Time had passed, he had met new ones, been intimate with them, parted from them. Not once had he been in love, though. He had known everything conceivable—except love, that is.

Only now that his head was grey had he well and truly fallen in love: for the first time in his life.

Anne and he loved each other very, very dearly, like man and wife or bosom friends. They felt themselves predestined for each other. That he should have a wife, and she a husband . . . it seemed to make no sense. They were like two migratory birds, a male and a female, caught and put in separate cages. They had forgiven each other the shameful episodes of their past, they forgave each other for the present too, and they felt that their love had transformed them both.

Once, in moments of depression, he had tried to console himself with any argument which came into his head—but now he had no use for arguments. His deepest sympathies were stirred, he only wanted to be sincere and tender.

'Stop, darling,' he said. 'You've had your cry—that's enough. Now let's talk, let's think of something.'

Then they consulted at length about avoiding the need for concealment and deception, for living in different towns, for meeting only at rare intervals. How could they break these intolerable bonds? How, how, how?

He clutched his head and asked the question again and again.

Soon, it seemed, the solution would be found and a wonderful new life would begin. But both could see that they still had a long, long way to travel—and that the most complicated and difficult part was only just beginning.

THE DUEL

I

IT was eight o'clock in the morning—the hour when officers, civil servants and visitors usually took a dip in the sea after the hot, stuffy night, and then went to the Pavilion for their coffee or tea. Ivan Layevsky—a thin, fair-haired young man of about twenty-eight—arrived for his bathe wearing slippers and the peaked cap of a treasury official. On the beach he found many acquaintances, among whom was his friend Samoylenko, an army medical officer.

Samoylenko had a large head, close-cropped hair and no neck to speak of. He was ruddy and big-nosed, he had beetling black eyebrows and grey dundreary whiskers. Fat, paunchy, with the deep, raucous voice of a typical army man, he struck every new arrival unpleasantly as a blustering bully. But after two or three days one began to find his face extremely kind and agreeable—handsome, even. Clumsy and rough though he was, he was also mild, infinitely easygoing, good-humoured and obliging. He was on Christian-name terms with everyone in town, lent them money, gave them medical consultations, arranged their marriages, patched up their quarrels, and organized picnics at which he grilled kebabs and brewed a most tasty grey mullet stew. A cheery soul, he was always asking favours on someone's behalf. He was commonly regarded as a paragon, having only two weak points. Firstly, he was ashamed to be so kind, and tried to hide it with his stern look and pretence of rudeness. And, in the second place, he liked medical orderlies and soldiers to call him general, though he was only a colonel.

'Answer me this, Alexander,' Layevsky began when he and Samoylenko were both shoulder deep in water. 'You fall in love with a woman, let's say, and have an affair with her. You live with her for over two years, say, and then, as does happen, you fall out of love and start thinking of her as a stranger. What would you do?'

'No problem. "Clear out, old thing," you tell her, and that's that.'

'It's easily said. But say she has nowhere to go? She's alone in the world, she has no family, she's completely broke, she can't get a job——'

'All right then—let her have five hundred roubles down, or twenty-five a month, and no argument. Very simple.'

'Granted you have five hundred roubles and the twenty-five a month—even so, I'm talking about a proud, educated woman. Could you really bring yourself to offer her money? And how would you set about it?'

Samoylenko made to reply, but a large wave broke over both and crashed on the beach, roaring back down the shingle. The friends came out of the water and started dressing.

'If you don't love a woman, it's not easy to live with her—obviously,' said Samoylenko, shaking sand out of his boot. 'But one must be reasonably humane, Ivan. If it was me, I'd pretend I still did love her, and I'd live with her till my dying day.'

Suddenly ashamed of his words, he pulled himself up.

'If you ask me,' said he, 'we'd be a sight better off without women, blast them!'

The friends finished dressing and went into the Pavilion, where Samoylenko—one of the regulars—even had his own cups, plates and so on. Every morning he was served a tray with a cup of coffee, a tall, cut-glass tumbler of iced water and a glass of brandy. First he would sip his brandy, then his hot coffee, then his iced water. They must have tasted good, for a glint would come into his eyes when he had drunk, and he would stroke his whiskers with both hands.

'Remarkably fine view,' he would say, gazing at the sea.

After a long night frittered away on dismal, futile thoughts which had kept him awake, seeming to intensify the stifling blackness, Layevsky felt haggard and jaded. His bathe and coffee had done him no good.

'About what we were saying, Alexander,' he said. 'I shan't hide anything, I'll tell you frankly, as a friend. Things are in a bad way with me and Nadezhda, a very bad way. I'm sorry to be confiding in you, but I must get it off my chest.'

Sensing the conversation's drift, Samoylenko lowered his eyes and drummed his fingers on the table.

'I've lived with her for two years and I don't love her any more,' Layevsky went on. 'Or rather I've come to see that I never did love her. These two years have been a snare and delusion.'

While speaking, Layevsky had the trick of scrutinizing the pink palms of his hands, biting his nails or crumpling his cuff. He did so now.

'You can't help me, that I realize,' he said. 'But I'm telling you because talk's the only escape for us failures and Superfluous Men. I have to base whatever I do on general principles. I must find an explanation, an excuse for my futile life in somebody's theories, in literary types—say in the fact that we, the gentry, are going to the bad, and so on. Last night, for instance, I kept consoling myself with the thought of Tolstoy—he's so right about things, so fiendishly right—and it made me feel better. He's a really great writer, old man—say what you like.'

Never having read Tolstoy, but meaning to every day, Samoylenko was abashed.

'Yes,' he said. 'All writers draw on their imagination, but he draws direct from nature.'

'Ye Gods,' Layevsky sighed. 'How civilization does cripple us! I fall in love with a married woman, she falls in love with me. It all starts with kisses, quiet evenings, vows, Herbert Spencer, ideals and common interests. How utterly bogus! We're really running away from her husband, but we pretend we're escaping from the futility of our life as intellectuals. We see our future as follows. Firstly the Caucasus—getting to know the place and the people. I'm to dress up as a bureaucrat, and do an office job. Then we take a plot of land somewhere in the wide open spaces. We live by the sweat of our face—we dig vineyards, we till fields and all that. In my place you—or your zoologist friend Von Koren—would probably have gone on living with Nadezhda for thirty years, and you'd have left your heirs a prosperous vineyard and a couple of thousand acres of maize. But I felt a complete flop from the first day. This town's unbearably hot and boring, there's no one to talk to. Take a trip into the country, and every bush and stone seems to hide monstrous spiders, scorpions and snakes, while further out there's just a wilderness of mountains. Foreign people, foreign scenery, a pathetic level of culture—these things, my friend, are a sight harder to take than dreaming about warm countries as you saunter down the main street of St. Petersburg in a fur coat with Nadezhda on your arm. What's needed here is a man who'll fight tooth and nail. But I'm no fighter, I'm just a miserable, namby-pamby neurotic. My ideas about hard work and vineyards add up to damn all, I've known that from the first day. As for love, living with a woman who has read Herbert Spencer and followed you to the ends of the earth—that's just as boring as cohabiting with any more common or garden specimen, you take it from me. There's the same smell of ironing, face-powder and medicines, there are the same curl-papers every morning, there's the same old pretence.'

'You can't run a house without ironing,' said Samoylenko, blushing because he knew the woman of whom Layevsky had spoken so frankly. 'You're in a bad mood this morning, Ivan, I see. Nadezhda's a splendid, cultivated woman and you're a highly intellectual chap yourself. You two aren't married, of course,' Samoylenko went on with a glance at the next tables. 'But that's not your fault, is it? Besides, one mustn't be prejudiced, one must move with the times. I'm all for civil marriage myself, indeed I am. But in my view, once you do start living together you should keep it up for the rest of your life.'

'Without love?'

'I'll explain,' said Samoylenko. 'Eight years ago we had an old shipping-agent here, a highly intelligent chap. Well, he used to say that the most important thing in family life is patience. Hear that, Ivan? Patience—not love. Love can't last. You've lived and loved for a couple of years, and now your domestic life has obviously entered a phase when you must call on all your patience—to preserve the balance, as it were.'

'You believe your agent, but the old man's advice makes no sense to me. Perhaps he was only pretending. He may well have been testing his powers of endurance, and using his unloved partner as an object essential to such exercises. But I haven't yet sunk so low. Should I wish to practise endurance, I shall buy dumb-bells or a high-spirited horse—and leave human beings out of it.'

Samoylenko ordered chilled white wine.

'Tell me,' Layevsky asked him suddenly, when each had drunk a glass, 'what is softening of the brain?'

'It's—what shall I say?—a disease which makes the brain soft, as if it was dissolving.'

'Can it be cured?'

'Yes, if it hasn't gone too far. It needs cold showers, plasters—oh yes, and something taken internally.'

'Ah. Well, you see how I'm fixed. I can't live with her, it's quite beyond me. When I'm with you I can pass the time of day like this and smile, but at home I'm utterly depressed. I feel so awful that if I was told I had to spend another month with her, say, I think I'd blow my brains out. Yet I can't leave her. She has no one else, she can't get a job, and neither of us has any money. Where can she go, who can she turn to? Ideas fail one. So come on, tell me what to do, can't you?'

'Well, er,' growled Samoylenko, at a loss for a reply. 'Does she love you?'

'Yes—to the extent that a woman of her age and temperament requires a man. It would be as hard for her to part with me as to give up her face-powder or hair-curlers. I'm an essential component of her boudoir.'

Samoylenko was embarrassed.

'You're out of sorts this morning, Ivan,' he said. 'You must have had a bad night.'

'Yes, I slept badly. I'm in a pretty bad way altogether, old man—I feel so hopeless, my heart sinks, and I'm faint somehow. Must get away!'

'Where will you go?'

'Up north—back to the pines, the mushrooms, the people, the ideas. I'd give half my life to be somewhere in Moscow County or Tula now, plunge in a stream, cool off and then, you know, wander for about three hours with someone—even some dull little undergraduate would do—and talk, talk, talk. Remember the scent of hay? And evening strolls round the garden when you hear a piano in the house, a passing train——'

Layevsky gave a delighted laugh. Tears came to his eyes, and to hide them he reached over for a box of matches on the next table without rising from his seat.

'It's eighteen years since I was last up north,' said Samoylenko. 'I've forgotten what it's like. The Caucasus is the finest place in the world for my money.'

'There's a picture by Vereshchagin of some prisoners under sentence of death wasting away at the bottom of a deep well, and to me your wonderful Caucasus is a similar hell-hole. Given the choice of chimney-sweeping in St. Petersburg or lording it here, I'd take the chimneys every time.'

Layevsky fell into a reverie. Looking at the stooped body, the staring eyes, the pale, sweaty face, the sunken temples, the chewed nails and the slipper hanging at the heel to reveal a badly darned sock, Samoylenko was consumed with pity.

'Is your mother still alive?' he asked, probably because Layevsky reminded him of a helpless child.

'Yes, but we don't see each other. She couldn't forgive me this entanglement.'

Samoylenko was fond of his friend, seeing in Layevsky a good sort, a typical student, a hail-fellow-well-met kind of chap with whom you could have a drink, a laugh and a good talk. What he understood about Layevsky he intensely disliked. Layevsky drank to excess and at the wrong times. He played cards, despised his work, lived beyond his means, was always using bad language, wore his slippers in the street, quarrelled with Nadezhda in public. These were the things that Samoylenko disliked. As for Layevsky's having once belonged to a university arts faculty, subscribing now to two literary reviews, often talking so cleverly that most people couldn't understand him, and living with an educated woman—none of these things did Samoylenko understand, and them he liked. He thought Layevsky his superior, and looked up to him.

'One other point,' Layevsky said, shaking his head. 'But keep this to yourself—I'm not letting on to Nadezhda just yet, so don't blurt it out in front of her. The day before yesterday I had a letter to say that her husband's died of softening of the brain.'

'May he rest in peace,' Samoylenko sighed. 'But why keep it from her?'

'Showing her that letter would be like offering to take her straight to the altar. We must clarify our relations first. Once she's convinced we can't go on living together, I'll show her the letter. It will be safe then.'

'Know what, Ivan?' said Samoylenko, and his face suddenly assumed a sad, pleading look as if he was about to ask a great favour but feared to be turned down. 'You get married, old man.'

'What for?'

'Do the right thing by this wonderful woman. In her husband's death I see the hand of Providence showing you your way ahead.'

'But, my dear man, that's out of the question, can't you see? Marrying without love—it's like an atheist celebrating mass, it's base, it's beneath a man's dignity.'

'But it's your duty.'

'Oh! And why is it my duty?' Layevsky asked irritably.

'You took her from her husband and assumed responsibility.'

'But I tell you in plain language—I don't love her!'

'Well, in that case show her respect. Pretend a bit——'

'Respect? Pretend?' mocked Layevsky. 'Do you take her for a mother superior or something? You're a poor psychologist and physiologist if you think honour and respect will get you very far where living with a woman's concerned. A woman's chief need is bed!'

'But, my dear Ivan,' said Samoylenko in embarrassment.

'You're an old baby—it's all words with you. Whereas I'm prematurely senile and actually involved, so we'll never understand each other. Let's change the subject. Mustafa,' Layevsky shouted to the waiter. 'What do we owe you?'

'No, no, no!' panicked the doctor, clutching Layevsky's arm. 'I'll pay, it was my order. Chalk it up to me,' he shouted to Mustafa.

The friends stood up and set off in silence along the front. At the boulevard they stopped to say good-bye and shook hands.

'You're a spoilt lot, gentlemen,' sighed Samoylenko. 'Fate sends you a young, beautiful, educated woman—and you don't want her. But if God sent me even a crippled old crone, I'd be so happy, if she was only affectionate and kind. I'd live with her in my vineyard and——'

Samoylenko pulled himself up.

'And the old bitch could damn well keep my samovar going!' said he.

He took farewell of Layevsky, and set off down the boulevard. Ponderous, imposing, stern of countenance, in his snow-white tunic and highly-polished boots, he paraded the boulevard, thrusting out a chest which sported the Order of St. Vladimir and ribbon. At such times he was very pleased with himself, feeling as if the whole world enjoyed watching him. He looked from side to side without turning his head, and found the boulevard's amenities excellent. The young cypresses, eucalyptus trees and ugly, spindly palms were fine indeed, and would spread a broad shade in time. The Circassians were a decent, hospitable people.

'Odd how Layevsky dislikes the Caucasus,' he thought. 'Very odd, that.'

He met five soldiers with rifles who saluted him. On the right of the boulevard a civil servant's wife was walking on the pavement with her schoolboy son.

'Morning, Mrs. Bityugov,' Samoylenko shouted with a pleasant smile. 'Been for a dip? Ha, ha, ha! My regards to your husband.'

He walked on, still smiling pleasantly. But seeing an army medical orderly approach, he suddenly frowned and stopped the man.

'Is there anyone in the hospital?' he asked.

'No one, General.'

'Eh?'

'No one, General.'

'Fine. You run along then.'

Swaying majestically, he made for a lemonade stand kept by a full-bosomed old Jewess who tried to pass as a Georgian.

'Kindly give me some soda water!' he yelled in his best parade-ground bark.

II

Layevsky's dislike of Nadezhda was based principally on the falsity—or veneer of falsity, as it seemed to him—of everything she said and did. If he read anything attacking women and love, it always seemed to fit himself, Nadezhda and her husband to perfection.

When he arrived home, she had already dressed and done her hair, and was sitting at the window drinking coffee with an anxious air as she leafed through a literary review. It struck him that the consumption of coffee was not an occasion so earth-shaking as to justify her air of concern, and that it was a waste of her time to cultivate a fashionable hair-style when there was no one around worth pleasing and no point in pleasing anyone anyway. He also thought that intellectual review an affectation. It struck him that just as she dressed and did her hair to make herself look beautiful, so also her reading was designed to make her look intelligent.

'Is it all right if I bathe today?' she asked.

'Suit yourself. Bathe or don't bathe—I doubt if the skies will fall either way.'

'I asked in case the doctor might be cross.'

'Then ask the doctor—I don't happen to be medically qualified.'

What riled Layevsky most about Nadezhda on this occasion was her bare, white neck with the curls at the back. When Anna Karenin ceased to love her husband, he remembered, it was the man's ears that had especially displeased her.

'How true, how very true,' he thought.

Feeling faint and hopeless, he went into his study, lay on the sofa and covered his face with a handkerchief to stop the flies bothering him. Listless, dismal, repetitious thoughts plodded through his brain like a long line of wagons on a foul autumn evening, as he sank into drowsy despondency. Where Nadezhda and her husband were concerned, he felt guilty—felt himself to blame for the husband's death. He felt guilty, too, of ruining his own life, and of letting down his high ideals of scholarship and hard work. Not here on this seashore trodden by starving Turks and lazy Abkhazians did that marvellous sphere of activity seem a real possibility, but in the north with its opera, theatre, newspapers and manifold intellectual work. There, and only there, could one be decent, intelligent, high-minded and pure. Not here. He blamed himself for having no ideals, no guiding principle in life, though he did now dimly discern what that meant. Falling in love with Nadezhda two years earlier, he had felt that he only needed to become her lover and take her to the Caucasus to be saved from the shoddy hopelessness of existence. Similarly, he was now convinced that to abandon Nadezhda and leave for St. Petersburg was to satisfy his every need.

'Escape,' he muttered, sitting up and biting his nails. 'Must get away.'

He imagined himself boarding the steamer, lunching, drinking cold beer, and talking to the ladies on deck. Then he catches a train in Sevastopol and rides off. Freedom, here we come! Stations flash past in quick succession, the air grows colder and sharper. Now birches and firs appear. Here is Kursk, here Moscow.

The station buffets have cabbage stew, mutton with *kasha*, sturgeon, beer—not oriental squalor, in other words, but Russia, the real thing. The passengers on the train discuss business, new singers and the Franco-Russian *entente*. Everything seems so vital, so cultured and intellectual, so high-spirited.

Faster, faster! Here at last is St. Petersburg's Nevsky Prospekt. Here are Great Morskoy Street and Kovensky Lane, where he had once lived as a student. Here are the dear, grey sky, the dear old drizzle, the drenched cab-drivers.

'Mr. Layevsky,' called someone from the next room, 'are you in?'

'Here,' Layevsky replied. 'What is it?'

'I have some papers.'

Layevsky stood up lazily, his head spinning, and went into the next room, yawning and shuffling in his slippers. There in the street by the open window stood one of his young colleagues, laying out official documents on his window-sill.

'Very well, old man,' said Layevsky gently, going to look for his ink-well. He returned to the window and signed the papers without reading them.

'It's hot,' he said.

'Yes indeed. Are you coming in today?'

'I doubt it, I don't feel too well. Tell Sheshkovsky I'll call on him after dinner, old man.'

The official left, and Layevsky lay down on his sofa again.

'Well,' he thought, 'I must weigh all the factors and work things out. I must pay off my debts before leaving here. I owe two thousand roubles odd. I have no money—but that's not important, of course. I'll pay part of it now somehow or other, and send some of it on later from St. Petersburg. The main thing is Nadezhda. We must first clarify our relations, indeed we must.'

A little later he was reflecting whether he might not do better to go and ask Samoylenko's advice.

'I might do that,' he thought, 'but what would be the use? I'd only speak out of turn again, all about boudoirs, women and doing the decent thing—or the indecent thing. Why, hang it, how can I possibly discuss what's decent or indecent if my very existence is at stake as I suffocate and fight for my life in these blasted shackles? To go on living like this would be so sordid and cruel as to dwarf all other considerations into nothingness, and it's about time that was realized!'

'Escape!' he muttered, sitting up. 'Must get away!'

The deserted beach, the sweltering heat, the monotony of the hazy, mauve mountains—for ever unchanging and silent, for ever lonely—filled him with sadness. They seemed to be lulling him to sleep, frustrating him. Perhaps he was highly intelligent and gifted—a remarkably honest man. Had he not been hemmed in on all sides by sea and mountains, he might have made an excellent rural welfare worker, a statesman, an orator, a publicist, or a great man of action—who could tell? And if so, how stupid to argue whether one was doing the decent thing or not! Suppose some able, useful person—a musician or artist, say—broke down a wall and tricked his gaolers so that he could escape from prison? In such a situation any action is honourable.

Layevsky and Nadezhda sat down to lunch at two o'clock and the cook served rice soup with tomatoes.

'We have the same thing every day,' Layevsky said. 'Why can't she make cabbage stew?'

'There's no cabbage.'

'Odd. At Samoylenko's they make cabbage stew, Mary Bityugov makes cabbage stew. Why am I alone forced to eat these sickly slops? It won't do, old girl.'

Like nearly all married couples, Layevsky and Nadezhda had once been unable to get through lunch without tantrums and scenes. But since Layevsky had decided that he was no longer in love, he had tried to let Nadezhda have everything her own way, addressing her gently and politely, smiling and calling her 'old girl'.

'This soup tastes like liquorice,' he said with a smile, but could not keep up this parade of amiability.

'No one does any housekeeping round here,' he said. 'If you're too ill or busy reading, all right—I'll handle our meals.'

In the old days she would have told him to go ahead, or said that she could see he only wanted to make a cook out of her. But now she only looked at him timidly and blushed.

'Well, how are you today?' he asked kindly.

'Not bad—a bit feeble, though.'

'Look after yourself, old girl. I'm very worried about you.'

Nadezhda suffered from some complaint. Samoylenko called it undulant fever and fed her quinine. The other doctor, Ustimovich, was a tall, lean, unsociable person who stayed at home by day and strolled quietly along the sea-front of an evening—coughing, with his hands clasped behind him and a cane held down his back. Ustimovich decided that she had some female complaint and prescribed hot compresses. When Layevsky had loved Nadezhda her ill health had alarmed him and made him feel sorry for her, but now he thought even her illness a sham. Nadezhda's yellow, drowsy face, her lifeless look, the yawning fits which came over her after bouts of feverishness, her habit of lying under a rug during these attacks and looking more boyish than feminine—all these things, together with the unpleasantly stuffy smell of her room, wrecked any romantic illusion, he thought, and were a strong argument against love and marriage.

As his second course he was served spinach and hard-boiled eggs, while Nadezhda had jelly and milk because she was unwell. She touched the jelly with her spoon, looking preoccupied, and then began to eat it languidly between sips of milk. Hearing her gulps, Layevsky was seized by such utter loathing that it actually made his scalp tingle. His feelings would be insulting to a dog, even, he realized. But it was not himself he was annoyed with—he was annoyed with Nadezhda for provoking such emotions in him, and he could see why it is that lovers sometimes murder their mistresses. He would never do that himself, naturally—but were he serving on a jury at the moment, he would vote such a murderer not guilty.

'Thanks, old girl,' he said when the meal was over, and kissed Nadezhda on the forehead.

He went to his study, and paced up and down for five minutes, glancing sideways at his boots, then sat on the sofa.

'Get away, must get away,' he muttered. 'Clarify relations and escape.'

He lay on the sofa, and remembered once again that the death of Nadezhda's husband might be his fault.

'It's silly to blame people for falling in or out of love,' he admonished himself, lying down and kicking up his legs to put on his riding-boots. 'Love and hate are outside our control. As for the husband, I may have been an indirect cause of his death—but once again, can I help it if his wife and I fall in love?'

He stood up, found his cap and went off to Sheshkovsky's—the colleague at whose house local officials met daily to play bridge and drink cold beer.

'I'm as bad as Hamlet,' Layevsky thought on the way there. 'How neatly Shakespeare hit him off—how very true to life.'

III

As there was no hotel in town, Dr. Samoylenko kept a sort of eating-house to relieve the general boredom, and meet the urgent needs of newcomers and people living on their own who had nowhere else to eat. He had only two guests at present—the young zoologist Von Koren, who came to the Black Sea in summer to study the embryology of the jelly-fish, and Deacon Pobedov, fresh from college and assigned to the little town to stand in for the old deacon who had gone away to take a cure. They each paid twelve roubles a month for lunch and dinner, and Samoylenko made them swear to be punctual for two o'clock lunch.

Von Koren was usually first to arrive. He would sit down quietly in the drawing-room, pick up an album from the table, and scrutinize faded snap-shots of unknown men in wide trousers and top hats, and of ladies in crinolines and mob-caps. Samoylenko could name only a few of them, and of those whom he had forgotten he would sigh: 'Grand fellow, highly intelligent chap.' When he had done with the album, Von Koren would pick up a pistol from the shelves, screw up his left eye and take lengthy aim at a portrait of Prince Vorontsov. Or he would face the mirror and inspect his swarthy face, his large forehead, his black hair as curly as a Negro's, his shirt of neutral-coloured cotton printed with huge flowers like a Persian rug, and his wide leather belt worn instead of a waistcoat. This self-inspection gave him almost greater pleasure than his scrutiny of the snap-shots or of the pistol in its sumptuous case. He was well pleased with his face and handsomely trimmed beard, as with his broad shoulders—witness to good health and a strong frame. He was also delighted with his modish rig, from the tie matching his shirt down to his yellow boots.

While he examined the album and stood in front of the mirror,

Samoylenko was busy in kitchen and pantry. Wearing neither coat nor waistcoat, much excited and bathed in sweat, he was fussing about the tables—preparing salad, a sauce, meat, gherkins and onions for cold soup, while angrily glaring at the orderly who was helping, and brandishing a knife or spoon at him from time to time.

'Vinegar!' he ordered. 'No, not vinegar, I meant salad oil!' he shouted, stamping his feet. 'And where do you think you're going, you swine?'

'For butter, General,' quavered the disconcerted orderly in a high-pitched voice.

'Then hurry up! It's in the cupboard. And tell Darya to put more dill in the gherkin jar. Dill, I say! And cover up that sour cream, you cretin, or the flies will get it.'

The whole house seemed to buzz with his shouts. At ten or fifteen minutes to two, the deacon arrived—a young man of about twenty-two, thin, long-haired and clean-shaven but for a barely formed moustache. Going into the drawing-room, he crossed himself before the icon, smiled, and held out his hand to Von Koren.

'Good day,' the zoologist said coldly. 'Where have you been?'

'Fishing for gobies in the harbour.'

'I might have known it. Obviously you'll never get down to a real job of work, Deacon.'

'I don't see why not. It's never too late to put your nose to the grindstone,' said the deacon, smiling and thrusting his hands into the deep pockets of his white cassock.

'You're incorrigible,' the zoologist sighed.

Fifteen or twenty minutes passed without lunch being announced, and the orderly could still be heard scurrying back and forth from pantry to kitchen with a clattering of boots.

'Put it on the table!' Samoylenko shouted. 'What are you up to? Wash it first!'

Both famished, the deacon and Von Koren began stamping their heels on the floor to show impatience, like a gallery audience in the theatre. At last the door opened and the anguished orderly announced lunch. Crimson in the face, practically steam-cooked by the heat of his kitchen, an incensed Samoylenko greeted them, glared at them, out-rage written on his face, and raised the lid of the soup tureen to serve each a bowl. Only when he was sure that they were eating with relish and enjoying their meal did he utter a faint sigh and sit down in his deep arm-chair. His face looked relaxed and oily.

He slowly poured himself a glass of vodka.

'To the younger generation,' he said.

After his talk with Layevsky, Samoylenko had spent the whole morning in a fundamentally depressed state despite his high spirits. Sorry for Layevsky, wanting to help him, he gulped down his glass of vodka before the soup and sighed.

'I saw Ivan Layevsky today,' he said. 'Poor chap's rather up against it. Things aren't too good on the material side, but what's got him down is psychological, mainly. I'm sorry for the lad.'

'Now, there's someone I'm not sorry for,' said Von Koren. 'If that charming fellow was drowning, I'd take a stick and give him an extra shove. "Go ahead and drown, dear boy," I'd say.'

'Oh no you wouldn't.'

'Think not?' the zoologist shrugged. 'You aren't the only one who can do a good deed.'

'Drowning someone a good deed?' the deacon laughed.

'In Layevsky's case—yes.'

'I think I left something out of the soup,' said Samoylenko, wishing to change the subject.

'Layevsky's a downright pest, he's as great a threat to society as the cholera microbe,' Von Koren went on. 'Drowning him would be a public service.'

'It's no credit to you to speak of your neighbour like that. Why do you hate him then?'

'Don't talk rubbish, Doctor. To hate and despise a microbe would be idiotic, while to believe that every chance acquaintance must needs be one's neighbour, and no two ways about it—well, I'm very sorry, but that means refusing to think, refusing to take a reasonable line on people. It's washing your hands of them in fact. To my mind friend Layevsky's a bastard. I make no bones about it, and I treat him as such with a completely clear conscience. You consider him your neighbour—all right, slobber over him for all I care. But considering him your neighbour means you must have the same attitude to him as to me and the deacon—you haven't any attitude at all, in other words. You're equally indifferent to everyone.'

'To call the man a bastard!' Samoylenko muttered, frowning fastidiously. 'That's so shocking—well, words fail me!'

'One is judged by one's acts,' went on Von Koren. 'Now, judge for yourself, Deacon. I shall address myself to you, Deacon. Mr. Layevsky's activities are openly unrolled before our eyes like a long Chinese scroll, they're an open book from beginning to end. What has he achieved in two years' residence here? Let's tick it off point by point. Firstly, he's taught the townsfolk to play bridge—the game was unknown here two years ago, but now everyone plays it morning noon and night, even women and adolescents. Secondly, he's taught the locals to drink beer, which was also unheard of here. They're further indebted to him for information on different brands of vodka, with the result that they can now tell a Koshelev from a Smirnov Number Twenty-one with their eyes blindfolded. Thirdly, men used to sleep with other people's wives surreptitiously from the same motive which makes burglars operate furtively and by stealth. It wasn't the thing to flaunt adultery, they'd have been ashamed to. But Layevsky has pioneered this practice by living openly with another man's wife. Fourthly——'

Quickly finishing his cold soup, Von Koren gave the orderly his bowl.

'I rumbled Layevsky's game before I'd known him a month,' he went on, addressing the deacon. 'We arrived here at the same time. His sort are great on friendship, intimacy, solidarity and all that stuff because they always need someone to make up a rubber of bridge, or join them in a drink and a snack. Being talkative, what's more, they need listeners. We became friendly—in other words, he'd slope along to my place every day, interrupt my work and unburden himself on the subject of his concubine. He was so bogus, he simply made me sick—that's what struck me first. Being his "friend", I nagged him. Why did he drink too much? Live above his means? Fall into debt? Why didn't he do anything? Or read anything? Why was he so uncultured, such an ignoramus? At every question I asked he would give a bitter smile and sigh. "I'm a failure," he'd say. "I'm a Superfluous Man." Or: "What else do you expect from us, old boy, when we're the waste products of the serf system?" Or: "We're going to seed." Or he'd embark on some great palaver about Onegin, Pechorin, Byron's Cain and Bazarov. "Our fathers in flesh and spirit," he'd call them. Do you catch his drift? It's no fault of his, see, if official packages lie around unopened for weeks, and if he drinks and gets others drunk. It's all because of Onegin and Pechorin—and Turgenev for inventing failures and the Superfluous Man. Why is he so utterly degenerate, so repulsive? The reason isn't in himself, see—it's somewhere outside him in space. And then—and this is the cunning of it—he's not the only one who's debauched, bogus and odious. There is always *We*. "We men of the eighties." "We, the debilitated, neurotic offspring of the serf system." "Civilization has crippled us."

'One is to take it, in other words, that a great man like Layevsky is great even in his fall. His dissipation, his lack of education, his dirty habits are an evolutionary phenomenon hallowed by inevitability and based on premises so earth-shaking and elemental that we should all bow down and worship the man as a doomed victim of an era, of trends, of heredity and all that stuff. The local officials and their ladies all drooled and slobbered over him when he spoke, and I couldn't tell for ages whether I was dealing with a cynic or a wily crook. Types like that, resembling intellectuals with their smattering of education, and always going on about how noble they are—they can pass themselves off as extremely complex natures.'

'Shut up!' blazed Samoylenko. 'No one shall run down such a thoroughly decent chap in my presence.'

'You keep out of this, Alexander,' Von Koren said coldly. 'I'll be through in a moment. Layevsky's a fairly simple organism. His moral framework is as follows. Early morning: slippers, bathing, coffee. Till lunch-time: slippers, strolling, conversation. Two o'clock: slippers, lunch, liquor. Five o'clock: bathing, tea, liquor—then bridge and bare-faced lying. Ten o'clock: slippers, liquor. After midnight: bed and *la femme*. His existence is encased in this narrow timetable, like an egg in its shell. Whether he walks, sits, loses his temper, writes or enjoys himself—it all boils down to wine, cards, slippers, woman. Woman plays a fatal and overwhelming part in his life. He was already in love at the age of thirteen, as he'll tell you himself. As a first-year student he lived with a lady who influenced him for the good and gave him his musical education. In his second year at university he bought a prostitute from a brothel and raised her to his own level—made her his mistress in other words. She lived with him for six months and then ran back to her madame, an escape which caused him no little spiritual anguish. So much did he suffer, alas, that he had to leave the university and spend two years at home in idleness. But it all worked out for the best. At home he took up with a widow who advised him to drop law and read an arts subject, so he did. On completing his studies, he fell passionately in love with this married woman, whatever she's called, and had to rush off here with her to the Caucasus—out of idealism, we're told.

'He'll lose interest in her any day now and trot back to St. Petersburg—and that, too, will be idealism.'

'How can you tell?' grumbled Samoylenko, glaring at the zoologist. 'Better eat your lunch.'

They served boiled grey mullet *à la polonaise*, and Samoylenko gave both his guests a whole fish, pouring the sauce himself. Some two minutes passed in silence.

'Woman plays a crucial part in every man's life,' said the deacon. 'You can't get away from that.'

'Yes, but it's a matter of degree. To each of us woman is our mother, sister, wife or friend. But to Layevsky she's the whole of existence, yet no more than his mistress. She—cohabitation with her, rather—is his bliss, his goal in life. If he's gay, sad, bored, disillusioned, that's woman's doing. If he's tired of life, it's a woman's fault. The dawn of a new life glows, ideals have appeared on the scene—and once again there must be a woman somewhere about.

'Only those writings or pictures satisfy him which feature a woman. Ours is a bad period in his view—worse than the forties and the sixties —just because we don't know how to abandon ourselves utterly to love's ecstasy and passion. These voluptuaries must have some special growth in their heads, a tumour which has crushed the brain and controls the whole nervous system. Try watching Layevsky when he's in company. See what happens if you raise some general topic in his presence—cells or instincts, say. He sits on one side, he says nothing, he doesn't hear. He looks limp and blasé. Nothing interests him, it's all stale and trivial. But you start talking about male and female—about the female spider's habit of eating the male after mating, say—and his eyes light up with curiosity, his face brightens. The fellow comes to life, in short. All his ideas, be they never so exalted, lofty or disinterested, have this one focal point. You might walk down the street with him and meet a donkey, say.

'"Do tell me," says he. "What would happen if you crossed a donkey with a camel?"

'And his dreams! Has he told you about those? They're priceless! First he dreams he's being married to the moon, then he's summoned to a police station and ordered to cohabit with a guitar——'

The deacon gave a ringing chortle. Samoylenko's brow clouded and he frowned angrily to stop himself laughing, but he could not keep it up and burst out laughing all the same.

'What rubbish,' he said, wiping away his tears. 'God, what rubbish!'

IV

The deacon was easily amused. Any trifle made him laugh till he had a stitch in his side and nearly fell over. He only seemed to enjoy company because people had their funny side and he could give them absurd nicknames. He called Samoylenko 'the Tarantula', his orderly was 'Drake', and he was tickled pink when Von Koren once referred to Layevsky and Nadezhda as a couple of baboons. He stared eagerly into people's faces, listened without blinking, and one could see his eyes fill with laughter and his face grow tense as he waited till he could let himself go and roar with laughter.

'He's a corrupt, perverted individual,' went on the zoologist, while the deacon gaped at him, anticipating some amusing remark. 'You don't often meet such a nonentity. Physically he's flabby, feeble and senile. Intellectually he's the exact equal of a fat woman—a shopkeeper's wife who does nothing but guzzle food and drink, sleeps on a feather bed, and takes her coachman as a lover.'

The deacon again burst out laughing.

'Don't laugh, Deacon, that's just silly,' said Von Koren. 'I'd overlook the man's insignificance,' he went on, after waiting for the deacon to stop. 'I'd ignore him were he less pernicious and dangerous. His most noxious feature is his success with women, which means that he threatens to have descendants, thus presenting the world with a dozen Layevskys as puny and perverted as himself. Secondly, he's highly contagious—I've already mentioned the bridge and beer business. In a couple of years he'll conquer the whole Caucasian coastline. You know how the masses, especially their middle strata, believe in intellectualism, university education, good manners and speaking correctly. Whatever filthy trick he plays, everyone thinks it's perfectly right and proper because he's an intellectual, a liberal, a university man. He's also a failure, a Superfluous Man, a neurotic, a victim of the age— which means he can do as he pleases. He's a nice chap, a good sort, and so genuinely tolerant of human weakness. He's accommodating, easy-going, adaptable and free from pride. You can share a drink with him, swap the occasional dirty story or bit of scandal.

'The masses always tend towards anthropomorphism in religion and morals, and they prefer their idols to share their own weaknesses. So you can see how wide a field he has to blight. Besides, he's a fair actor, a smart operator—oh yes, he has things pretty well sized up. You take his twists and turns—his attitude to civilization, say. He never so much as caught a whiff of civilization, but you listen to him! "Oh, how civilization has crippled us!" "Oh, how I envy savages—children of nature untouched by civilization!" We're to take it that he was once heart and soul for civilization in the old days, see? He served it, he knew it inside out, but it wearied him—disillusioned and cheated him. He's a Faust, get it? A second Tolstoy.

'As for Schopenhauer and Spencer, they're just schoolboys to him. He patronizes them, claps them on the shoulder. "How is everything, Spencer, old bean?" He's never read Spencer, of course, but how charming he is when he says with that casual air, that nonchalant irony, that his lady friend "has read her Spencer"! And people listen to him. And no one will see that this charlatan has no right to kiss the sole of Spencer's foot, let alone speak about him in that tone. The subversion of civilization, authority and other people's idols, the mud-slinging, the jocular wink designed solely to justify and conceal your own spinelessness and moral bankruptcy—only an animal, a selfish, base, foul animal, could do such things.'

'I don't know what you want out of him, Nicholas,' said Samoylenko, now looking at the zoologist more guiltily than in anger. 'He's just like anyone else. He has his faults, of course, but he is abreast of the times, he does do a job, and he's a useful citizen. Ten years ago we had an old shipping-agent here, a highly intellectual chap. Well, he used to say——'

'Oh, come off it, really!' the zoologist broke in. 'You say he does a job. But how does he do it? Has his arrival on the scene improved things? Has it made officials more punctilious, honest and courteous? Far from that, Layevsky has only sanctioned their slovenliness with the authority of an intellectual, a university man. Only on the twentieth of the month, when he collects his salary, is he punctual. On other days he merely shuffles about in his slippers at home and cultivates the expression of one conferring a great favour on the Russian government by residing in the Caucasus. No, Alexander, don't you stick up for him. You're insincere all the way through. The great thing is this— if you really liked him and considered him your neighbour, you wouldn't be so lukewarm about his faults. You wouldn't be so lenient towards them, you'd try to render him harmless for his own good.'

'Meaning what?'

'Neutralize him. Since he's incurable, there's only one way to do that.'

And Von Koren drew a finger across his throat.

'Or else one might drown him,' he added. 'For humanity's sake—and for their own sake too—such people should be exterminated, make no mistake about it.'

'What talk is this?' muttered Samoylenko, standing up and gaping at the zoologist's calm, cold face. 'What is he saying, Deacon? Are you in your right mind?'

'I won't insist on the death penalty,' said Von Koren. 'If that's been discredited, devise something else. If Layevsky can't be exterminated, then isolate him, deprive him of his individuality, put him to work for the community.'

'What talk is this?' Samoylenko was outraged. 'With pepper, with pepper!' he shouted desperately, seeing that the deacon was eating his stuffed marrows without pepper. 'You're a highly intelligent chap, but what are you saying? This is our friend, a proud man, an intellectual, and you want to make him do forced labour!'

'Yes, and if he's so proud that he won't knuckle under, then throw him in irons.'

Samoylenko was past all speech, and could only twiddle his fingers. Glancing at his bewildered face, which certainly did look funny, the deacon burst out laughing.

'Let's change the subject,' said the zoologist. 'But just bear one thing in mind, Alexander—primitive man was protected from types like Layevsky by the struggle for existence and by natural selection. Now that modern civilization has rendered the struggle and the natural selection process considerably less intense, we must attend to the extermination of the sickly and unfit ourselves. Otherwise, once the Layevskys multiply, civilization will perish, mankind will degenerate utterly—and it will all be our fault.'

'If we're going to drown and hang people, then to blazes with your civilization, and to blazes with mankind!' said Samoylenko. 'To hell with them! You're a highly learned, highly intelligent chap, and your country can be proud of you, but you've been ruined by Germans, I'd have you know. By Germans, sir, by Germans!'

Since leaving Dorpat, where he had studied medicine, Samoylenko had rarely set eyes on a German and had not read a single German book. Yet Germany was the root of all evil in politics and science, to his way of thinking. Even he couldn't say where he had picked up the idea, but he held it tenaciously.

'Yes indeed, Germans!' he repeated. 'Come and have tea.'

The three men stood up, put on their hats, went into the little garden and sat down in the shade of some pale maples, pear-trees and a chestnut. Zoologist and deacon took a bench near the table, while Samoylenko sank into a wicker arm-chair with a wide, sloping back. The orderly served tea, preserves and a bottle of syrup.

It was very hot, about ninety in the shade. The air was sweltering, stagnant, sluggish. From the chestnut a long spider's web hung to the ground, drooping limp and inert.

The deacon picked up a guitar—always to be found on the ground near the table—and tuned it.

'Around ye olde hostelry
Did stand ye college lads,'

—he began singing in a soft, reedy voice.

But it was so hot that he stopped at once, mopped his brow and glanced up at the blazing blue sky.

Samoylenko dozed off. He felt weak and drunk from the heat, the quiet and the sweet afternoon drowsiness which rapidly overpowered all his limbs. His arms dangled, his eyes grew small, his head sank on his chest, and he gazed at Von Koren and the deacon with maudlin sentimentality.

'The younger generation,' he muttered. 'A scientific notability and an ecclesiastical luminary. This long-skirted hierophant will very likely shoot up to become metropolitan, and we'll have to kiss his hand. And why not? Good luck to——'

Soon he was heard snoring. Von Koren and the deacon finished their tea and went out in the street.

'Going back to the harbour to catch gobies?' asked the zoologist.

'No, it's on the hot side.'

'Come round to my place then. You can make up a parcel for me, copy one or two things. And we can discuss what you might be doing while we're about it. You must work, Deacon, this will never do.'

'That's very fair and reasonable,' said the deacon. 'But my sloth finds its justification in my present living conditions. As you know, uncertainty about one's situation does much to promote a state of apathy. Am I here temporarily? Or for ever? God alone knows. I live here in ignorance, while my wife pines away at her father's, feeling lonely. And this heat has addled my brain, I must admit.'

'Rubbish,' said the zoologist. 'You can get used to the heat and to living without your lady deacon. Don't be so spoilt—you must take yourself in hand.'

V

Nadezhda went for a morning bathe, followed by her cook Olga who carried a jug, a copper bowl, towels and a sponge. Two strange steamers with dirty white smoke-stacks were anchored in the roads—foreign freighters, obviously. Some men in white, wearing white boots, were walking on the quay, shouting loudly in French, and people were shouting back from the steamers. From the town's small church came a brisk peal of bells.

'It's Sunday,' Nadezhda remembered delightedly.

She felt very healthy, and was in gay, festive mood, thinking herself most fetching in her loose new dress of coarse tussore and large straw hat with its brim bent sharp forward over her ears, so that her face seemed to peep out of a little box. There was only one young, beautiful, intellectual woman in the town, she reflected—herself. She alone had the knack of dressing inexpensively, elegantly and tastefully. This dress, for instance, had cost only twenty-two roubles, yet it was charming. She was the one attractive woman in a town full of men, so they were all bound to envy Layevsky, like it or not.

She was glad that Layevsky had been cold and icily polite to her of late—and at times brusque and rough, even. Her response to his outbursts and cold, contemptuous—or odd and mysterious—glances would once have been tears, reproaches and threats to leave him or starve herself to death. But now she only reacted by blushing, looking guilty and welcoming his lack of affection. Had he sworn at her, threatened her—that would have been even better, even more delightful, for where he was concerned she felt herself hopelessly in the wrong. In the first place, it was her fault, she felt, that she lacked sympathy for his dreams about a life of toil—dreams which had made him give up St. Petersburg and come out here to the Caucasus. This was the real reason why he had been so angry with her lately, she was sure of that. On her way out to the Caucasus she had felt certain of discovering some secluded seaside spot on her very first day there—some cosy, shady, little garden with birds and brooks, where you could plant flowers and vegetables, keep ducks and chickens, ask the neighbours in, dose poor peasants and give them books to read. But the Caucasus turned out to consist of bald mountains, forests and huge valleys—a place where you must be forever making choices, stirring things up, building things. There *were* no neighbours, it was all very hot, you were liable to be burgled. Layevsky had been in no hurry to acquire his plot of land, and she was glad of that—there might have been an unspoken pact between them never to mention that life of honest toil. He said nothing of it—in other words, he was angry with *her* for saying nothing of it, she thought.

The second point was this. She had, without Layevsky's knowledge, picked up during these two years various trifles to the tune of three hundred roubles in Achmianov's shop. Cloth, silk, a parasol—she had taken the stuff piecemeal, and the debt had piled up unnoticed.

'I'll tell him today,' she decided, but at once realized that with Layevsky in his present mood this was hardly the best of times to tell him of his debts.

Thirdly, she had, in Layevsky's absence, twice entertained Inspector Kirilin of the local police force—once on a morning when Layevsky had gone for a bathe, once at midnight when he had been playing cards. Remembering this, Nadezhda flushed and glanced at the cook, as if afraid of the woman reading her mind. These long, intolerable, sweltering, irksome days, these superb, languid evenings, these stifling nights, this whole existence when time hung on your hands from dawn to dusk and you couldn't think what to do with it, this obsession with being the youngest and loveliest woman in town, this feeling of frittering away her youth, and Layevsky himself—a decent, idealistic but humdrum person for ever shuffling about in his slippers, biting his nails and annoying her with his tantrums... all these things gradually made her a prey to desire, until, like some madwoman, she could think of only one thing morning noon and night. In her breathing, in her way of looking, speaking and walking, she was obsessed by desire. The wash of waves spoke to her of the need to love, the darkness of evening carried the same message—as did the mountains too.

So when Kirilin had begun making up to her, she had been unable and unwilling to resist—it was beyond her powers—and had given herself to him.

These foreign steamers and white-clad people somehow reminded her of a huge ballroom. French conversation mingled in her ears with the strains of a waltz, and her breast trembled with instinctive delight. She felt like dancing and speaking French. There was nothing so very terrible in being unfaithful, she was happy to think, nor had her heart been involved in that betrayal. She still loved Layevsky—witness her jealousy of him, her fondness for him, and the fact that she missed him when he was away. As for Kirilin, he had been nothing special, as it turned out—a bit common, good-looking as he was. She had already

broken with him and it wouldn't happen again. It was over and done
with, it was no one else's business, and if it came to Layevsky's ears
he wouldn't believe it.

On the beach there was only one bathing-house—for ladies. The
men swam out in the open. Going into the bathing-house, Nadezhda
encountered a middle-aged woman, Mary Bityugov—a civil servant's
wife—and her fifteen-year-old schoolgirl daughter Katya. They sat on
a bench undressing. Mary Bityugov was a kind, effusive, genteel
person who spoke with a drawl, and tended to over-dramatize things.
She had been a governess up to the age of thirty-two, when she had
married Bityugov, a small, bald official of extreme docility who
brushed his hair over his temples. She was still in love with him, was
still jealous, still blushed at the word love, and told everyone how
happy she was.

'My dear,' she said effusively, seeing Nadezhda and assuming an
expression termed sugary by all her friends. 'My dear, how very nice
to see you! We'll bathe together—how perfectly sweet!'

Olga quickly threw off her own dress and blouse and began undressing her mistress.

'Not quite so hot today, is it?' said Nadezhda, shrinking at the crude
touch of her naked cook. 'It was sweltering yesterday, I nearly died.'

'Yes, dear. I could hardly breathe myself. Do you know, I bathed
three times yesterday—three, can you believe it? Even Mr. Bityugov
was worried.'

'How can people be so ugly?' thought Nadezhda, as she looked at
Olga and Bityugov's wife. She glanced at Katya. 'That girl's figure
isn't bad,' she thought.

'Your husband's terribly nice,' she told Mary Bityugov. 'I'm quite
crazy about him.'

Mary Bityugov uttered a hollow laugh. 'Ha! ha! ha! How sweet!'

Released from her clothes, Nadezhda felt that she wanted to fly, felt
that she had only to beat her arms to become air-borne. In her undress,
she noticed Olga observing her white body with distaste. Olga, a
young soldier's wife, lived with her lawful husband, and so thought
herself a cut above Nadezhda. Nadezhda also sensed that Mary Bityugov
and Katya feared her and looked down on her. This was disagreeable,
and she decided to raise her standing in their eyes.

'At home in St. Petersburg the holiday season's in full swing just
now,' she said. 'My husband and I know so many people, we really
should pop over and see them.'

'Your husband's an engineer, isn't he?' asked Mary Bityugov timidly.

'I mean Layevsky. He knows a lot of people, but his mother's no end of a snob, unluckily, and not quite all there——'

Without finishing what she was saying, Nadezhda plunged into the water followed by Mary Bityugov and Katya.

'Society's so prejudiced, we find,' Nadezhda went on. 'People aren't as easy to get on with as you might think.'

Having been a governess in upper-class families, Mary Bityugov knew the ways of the world.

'Yes, indeed,' she said. 'Now, can you believe it, dear, at the Garatynskys' you had to dress for lunch *and* dinner, so I was paid a special dress allowance like an actress.'

She stood between Nadezhda and Katya as if protecting her daughter from the water which lapped Nadezhda. Through the open doorway to the sea someone could be seen swimming about a hundred yards from the bathing-house.

'It's Kostya, Mother,' said Katya.

'Dear, oh dear!' clucked the horrorstruck Mary Bityugov. 'Kostya!' she shouted. 'Come back! Come back, Kostya!'

Kostya, a boy of about fourteen, plunged and swam on further to show off in front of his mother and sister, but then tired and hurried back. His earnest, strained expression showed that he did not trust his own strength.

'Boys are so much trouble, dear,' said Mary, relieved. 'He always seems about to break his neck. Oh, how nice to be a mother, dear— but how worrying too. One is afraid of everything.'

Putting on her straw hat, Nadezhda plunged out to sea. She swam about ten yards, then floated on her back. She could see the sea as far as the horizon, the steamers, the people on the beach, the town—all of which, combined with heat and the caress of translucent waves, aroused her, whispering that she needed a bit of life and excitement.

Past her sped a sailing boat, vigorously cleaving waves and air. The helmsman looked at her—how nice to be looked at, she felt.

After their bathe the ladies dressed and went off together.

'I run a temperature every other day, but I don't lose weight,' said Nadezhda, licking lips salty after her bathe, and greeting acquaintances' bows with a smile. 'I always was plump, and now I'm even more so, I think.'

'It's a matter of disposition, dear. If someone isn't disposed to plumpness—like me, say—no amount of food makes any difference. But your hat's sopping wet, dear.'

'Never mind, it'll dry.'

Once again Nadezhda saw the white-clad, French-speaking strollers on the promenade, and again felt happiness vaguely stirring within her as she dimly remembered some huge ballroom where she had once danced—or had she dreamt it? And something whispered from the depths of her being in blurred, muted tones that she was a petty, vulgar, worthless, insignificant woman.

Stopping by her gate, Mary Bityugov asked Nadezhda to come in and sit down.

'Come in, dear,' she pleaded, looking anxiously at Nadezhda—and expecting her to refuse, with any luck.

'I'd love to,' Nadezhda agreed. 'You know I like visiting you.'

She went in, and Mary asked her to sit down. She gave her coffee, fed her on milk rolls, then showed her snapshots of her former charges—the Garatynsky girls, who were married now. She also displayed Katya's and Kostya's examination marks. They were excellent, but to make them seem better still she sighed about how difficult school work was nowadays.

She made her guest welcome—yet pitied her, while worrying lest her presence have an adverse effect on Kostya's and Katya's morals. She was glad that her Nicodemus was not at home. All men fell in love with women *of that type*, she thought, and so Nadezhda might adversely affect Mr. Bityugov too.

While talking to her guest, Mary Bityugov kept remembering that they were going picnicking that evening, and that Von Koren had particularly asked her not to mention the fact to the 'baboons'—to Layevsky and Nadezhda, that is. But she accidentally let it out, and blushed to the roots of her hair.

'I do hope you'll come,' she said awkwardly.

VI

They had arranged to drive about five miles out of town on the road south and stop by the inn at the junction of two streams, Black Brook and Yellow Brook, where they would cook a fish stew. They left just after five o'clock, Samoylenko and Layevsky leading the way in a cabriolet followed by Mary Bityugov, Nadezhda, Katya and Kostya in a carriage drawn by three horses—they had the picnic basket and crockery. The next vehicle bore Inspector Kirilin and young Achmianov—son of the shopkeeper to whom Nadezhda owed the three hundred roubles. On the bench opposite them, his feet tucked underneath him, cringed Nicodemus Bityugov, a dapper little person with his hair brushed over the temples. Von Koren and the deacon brought up the rear, and the deacon had a basket of fish at his feet.

'Drive on the r-r-right, can't you?' Samoylenko shouted at the top of his voice whenever they encountered a native cart or an Abkhazian on his donkey.

'In two years, when I've got the resources and people together, I'll set off on my expedition,' Von Koren told the deacon. 'I'll follow the coast from Vladivostok to the Bering Straits, then go on to the mouth of the Yenisey. We'll make a map, study wild life, conduct detailed geographical, anthropological and ethnographical investigations. Whether you come along or not is up to you.'

'I can't,' the deacon said.

'Why not?'

'I'm not my own master, I'm married.'

'Your wife will let you go—we'll see she's looked after. Or better still, why not persuade her to become a nun as a matter of social duty? Then you could be a monk and join the expedition in that capacity. I can fix it.'

The deacon did not answer.

'How's your theology? Pretty good?' asked the zoologist.

'Anything but.'

'H'm. I can't give you any wrinkles in that line myself, not being much versed in the subject. You make out a list of the books you need, and I'll send them from St. Petersburg next winter. You'll also need to read missionaries' memoirs—they've thrown up quite a few good ethnologists and oriental linguists. You'll find it easier to tackle the job when you're familiar with their approach. Now, there's no need to waste time while you're waiting for the books. Come round to my place—we'll study the compass, and do meteorology. It's all essential stuff.'

'Very well then,' muttered the deacon and laughed. 'I asked for a place in the midlands, and my uncle, who's a superintendent priest, has promised to help me. If I go with you I'll have troubled him for nothing.'

'I can't understand this shilly-shallying. As an ordinary deacon, obliged to conduct service only on Sundays and saints' days and to rest from his labours at other times, you'll be just the same in ten years' time—plus whiskers and a beard, maybe—whereas the expedition will make another man of you ten years from now . . . one enriched by knowing that he's achieved a thing or two!'

From the ladies' carriage shrieks of horror and delight were heard. The vehicles were now on a road scooped out of a sheer cliff, and all had the sensation of careering along a shelf tacked to a high wall. The carriages seemed ready to fall into the gorge any moment. To their right spread the sea, on their left was a rough brown wall with black blotches, red veins and creeping roots. From above gazed frizzy conifers as if in fear and curiosity. A minute later they were shrieking and laughing again as they had to drive under a huge, over-hanging rock.

'I don't know what the hell I'm doing here,' said Layevsky. 'This is so stupid and trivial. I ought to go back north, break free, get away. But I'm taking part in this imbecile picnic instead, heaven knows why.'

'Now, just look at that view,' said Samoylenko when the carriages had made a left turn, to reveal Yellow Brook Valley where the brook itself flashed—yellow, muddied, demented.

'I see nothing good about it, Alexander,' answered Layevsky. 'To keep on gushing about scenery is only to reveal the poverty of your own imagination. Now, compared to the fruits of *my* imagination, all these ditches and rocks are no more than a load of trash.'

The carriages were already skirting the brook. Gradually the towering banks converged, and the valley narrowed, looming canyon-like ahead of them. They were passing a great crag assembled by nature from huge rocks exerting on each other pressure so fantastic that the mere sight always drew a grunt from Samoylenko. The superb, gloomy mountainside was criss-crossed by narrow crevasses and chines exhaling an air of damp and mystery on passers-by. Through clefts loomed other mountains, brown, pink and mauve, hazy or bathed in brilliance. Passing the gullies, they sometimes heard water cascading from a height and splashing on the rocks.

'Bloody mountains,' sighed Layevsky. 'What a bore.'

At the point where Black Brook fell into Yellow, where ink-black water stained yellow and fought it, there stood, away from the road, Kerbalay's Tatar inn with a Russian flag aloft and chalked signboard: 'Good Inn'. Near by was a small garden with a wattle fence. It contained tables and benches, and from a wretched thorn thicket ascended a lone cypress, beautiful and dark.

Kerbalay, a small, agile Tatar, stood in the road, blue-shirted and white-aproned. He clutched his stomach and made a deep obeisance to the approaching carriages, flashing his white teeth in a brilliant grin.

'Hallo, Kerbalay, old man,' shouted Samoylenko. 'We're going on a bit farther. You bring a samovar and some chairs, will you? And look slippy!'

Kerbalay nodded his shaven head and muttered. Only those in the last carriage could make out the words: 'There's trout today, General.'

'Then let's have 'em,' said Von Koren.

The carriages stopped about five hundred yards past the inn. Samoylenko picked a small meadow dotted with stones for sitting on. Felled by a storm, a tree lay there with matted roots exposed and dry yellow pine-needles. A rickety wooden bridge crossed the brook, and on the far bank just opposite there stood a little shack on four low posts—a barn for drying maize, it looked like something out of a fairy tale. A ladder led down from the door.

What struck them first was that there seemed no way out of the place. On all sides mountains loomed glowering wherever one looked, and from the inn and dark cypress evening shadows swiftly advanced, making Black Brook's narrow, twisted gorge seem narrower still and the mountains tower yet higher. The brook gurgled, cicadas kept up their ceaseless chatter.

'How perfectly sweet!' said Mary Bityugov, sucking in her breath rapturously. 'Now, isn't that nice, children? And how quiet it is!'

'Yes, very nice indeed,' agreed Layevsky, who liked the view. Looking at the sky, and then at blue smoke issuing from the inn's chimney, he suddenly felt sad for some reason. 'Yes, very nice,' he repeated.

'Do describe the view for us, Mr. Layevsky,' Mary Bityugov asked plaintively.

'Now, why should I?' replied Layevsky. 'The impact beggars all description. This wealth of colour and sound which we all receive from nature through our senses—writers only make a hideous, distorted mess of it.'

'Think so?' asked Von Koren coldly, choosing the largest rock near the water and trying to climb up and sit on it.

'Think so, do you?' he repeated, staring at Layevsky. 'What of *Romeo and Juliet*? Or Pushkin's "Ukrainian Night", say? Nature should come and do homage to them.'

'Perhaps,' Layevsky agreed, too lazy to think of a rejoinder.

'What are Romeo and Juliet, anyway?' he added a little later.

'Romantic, poetical, sacred love—that's really only roses strewn over corruption to hide it. Romeo's an animal like anyone else.'

'Whatever one discusses with you, you always bring it down to——'

Von Koren looked at Katya and left his remark unfinished.

'What do I bring it down to?' asked Layevsky.

'One remarks "What a fine bunch of grapes," say. "Yes," say you. "But how ugly when they've been chewed up and digested in people's stomachs." Why say it? It's not original, and—it's a pretty odd way to talk, anyway.'

Layevsky feared Von Koren, aware as he was of the other man's dislike. In Von Koren's presence people seemed inhibited, he felt, as if each had someone breathing down his neck. Layevsky walked away without answering, and regretted having come.

'Quick march, everyone! Fetch wood for the fire!' commanded Samoylenko.

All went off this way and that, only Kirilin, Achmianov and Mr. Bityugov remaining behind. Kerbalay brought some chairs, spread a rug on the ground, and set down several bottles of wine. Inspector Kirilin, a tall, imposing man, who wore a cloak over his tunic in all weathers, resembled a young provincial chief constable in his self-important bearing, dignified gait and thick, rather raucous voice. He looked dejected and sleepy, as if he had just been woken up against his will.

'What's that you've brought, you swine?' he asked Kerbalay, enunciating each word slowly. 'I told you to serve *Kvarel*, but what have you brought, you Tatar bastard? Eh? What?'

'We have plenty of wine of our own, Mr. Kirilin,' Mr. Bityugov observed nervously and politely.

'What of it? I want you to have some of *my* wine. I'm one of the party, and I presume I'm fully entitled to contribute my whack. I presume so, sir! Bring ten bottles of *Kvarel*!'

'But why so many?' wondered Mr. Bityugov, knowing that Kirilin had no money.

'Twenty bottles! Thirty!' shouted Kirilin.

'Never mind, let him do it,' Achmianov whispered to Bityugov. 'I'll pay.'

Nadezhda was in gay, skittish mood. She felt like skipping, laughing, shouting, teasing, flirting. In her cheap cotton dress with blue polka dots, red shoes and the same straw hat, she felt tiny, artless, light and airy as a butterfly. Running over the rickety little bridge, she looked at the water for a minute to make herself dizzy, then shrieked and ran laughing towards the barn on the far bank, feeling that all the men, even Kerbalay, could not take their eyes off her. When the rapid onset of dusk had merged trees and mountains, horses and carriages, while a gleam of light showed in the windows of the inn, she climbed a winding path between rocks and thorns up the hillside, and sat on a rock. Down below the fire was already ablaze.

The deacon pottered near it, his sleeves rolled up and his long black shadow moving in a radius round the flames. He added brushwood and stirred the pot with a spoon tied to a long stick. Samoylenko, his face copper-red, was bustling about near the fire as if in his own kitchen.

'Where's the salt, you people?' he shouted. 'Forgot it, eh? Why loll around? Think you're the lords of creation? Am I to do all the work?'

Layevsky and Nicodemus Bityugov sat side by side on the fallen tree, gazing pensively at the fire. Mary Bityugov, Katya and Kostya took the tea things and the bowls out of the baskets. Folding his arms and putting one foot on a rock, Von Koren stood wrapped in thought on the bank near the very edge of the water. Shadows and red patches thrown by the bonfire flickered on the ground near the dark shapes of people and quivered on mountain, trees, bridge and barn. The precipitous, rutted, opposite bank was brightly lit, its glimmerings reflected in the water, but cut to shreds by the churning torrent.

The deacon went to fetch the fish which Kerbalay was cleaning and washing on the bank, but stopped half-way to look around.

'God, how wonderful!' he thought. 'People, rocks, fire, dusk, misshapen tree—that's all, but isn't it beautiful!'

A group of strangers appeared near the barn on the far bank. The flickering of the light and the bonfire smoke blown across the brook blurred the group as a whole, but details of it could be discerned—here a shaggy fur cap and a grey beard, there a navy-blue skirt, elsewhere rags from shoulder to knee, and a dagger across the stomach, or a young swarthy face with black brows thick and sharp as if drawn in charcoal. About five people sat down in a circle on the ground, and another half dozen went into the barn. Hands thrust behind him, one man stood in the doorway with his back to the fire, and began to tell a story. That it was a fascinating tale was shown when Samoylenko added wood to the fire and it flared up, flashing sparks and casting a bright light on the barn—whereupon two faces, calm but expressing rapt attention, were seen looking through the door, while those sitting in the circle had turned round and were listening too. A little later the sitters quietly intoned a leisurely, tuneful song like the chanting at a church service in Lent.

As he listened, the deacon imagined himself returning from the expedition in about ten years' time. He is a young monk, a missionary, a celebrated author with a glorious past. He is made archimandrite, then bishop. He conducts a cathedral service in his golden mitre with his bishop's insignia worn on a chain round his neck, stepping forward to the ambo and making the sign of the cross over the assembled people with his triple and his double candelabrum.

'O God, look down from heaven,' he proclaims. 'Behold and visit this vineyard which Thy right hand hath planted.' In angelic voices children sing the response: 'Holy God——'

'Where's that fish, Deacon?' Samoylenko was heard to say.

Returning to the fire, the deacon pictured a church procession on a dusty road on a hot July day, led by peasants carrying banners, followed by women and girls with icons, and then by choir-boys and the church clerk, with his cheek bandaged and straw in his hair. He is followed in due order by the deacon himself and the priest with his velvet cap and cross, while a throng of peasants—men, women and boys—raises the dust behind them. There, in the crowd, is the priest's wife and the deacon's own wife, both in kerchiefs. The choir sings, children bawl, quails shriek, a lark carols.

Now they stop to sprinkle the herd with holy water.

They move on and pray for rain on bended knee. Food and conversation follow.

'Not such a bad prospect either,' the deacon reflected.

VII

Kirilin and Achmianov climbed the path up the mountainside. Achmianov lagged behind and stopped, but Kirilin went up to Nadezhda.

'Good evening,' he said, saluting.

'Good evening.'

'Yes indeed,' said Kirilin, thoughtfully gazing at the sky.

'And what does that signify?' asked Nadezhda after a brief silence, noticing that Achmianov was observing them both.

'It signifies,' the police officer slowly enunciated, 'that our love has withered—without even flowering, so to speak. What am I to make of that, pray? Some brand of flirtatiousness on your part? Or do you take me for a booby whom you can treat as you like?'

'It was a mistake. Leave me alone,' Nadezhda said sharply, looking at him panic-stricken on this wonderful, magical evening, and wondering in bewilderment whether there could really have been a moment when this person had attracted her and seemed close to her.

'Yes indeed,' said Kirilin, and stood in silence for a while.

'Never mind,' he said after a moment's thought. 'Let's wait till you're in a better mood. In the meantime, I am a man of honour, as I venture to assure you, and I shall permit no doubts to arise on that score. No one trifles with me, madam. I bid you a very good day!'

He saluted and withdrew, threading his way between bushes. A little later Achmianov made a hesitant approach.

'Nice evening,' he said with a slight Armenian accent.

He was not bad-looking, he dressed smartly and had a well-bred youth's ease of manner, but Nadezhda disliked him because she owed his father three hundred roubles. She was also displeased that this shopkeeper had been invited on the picnic—displeased, too, that he should accost her on the very evening when she felt so pure in heart.

'The picnic's rather a success,' he said after a while.

'Isn't it?' she agreed.

'Oh yes,' she went on casually, as if she had just remembered her debt, 'will you tell them in your shop that Mr. Layevsky will look in within a day or two and pay that three hundred roubles or whatever it was?'

'I'd be glad to lend you another three hundred just to stop you bringing up that debt every day. Why so prosaic?'

Nadezhda laughed. The absurd idea had occurred to her that she could discharge that debt in one minute if she so desired and was sufficiently immoral. How about making this handsome young imbecile infatuated with her? How amusing and ridiculous, actually—how crazy!

And she suddenly wanted to make him love her—then rob him, cast him aside and await the sequel.

'May I give you some advice?' Achmianov asked nervously. 'Do beware of Kirilin, I beg you. He's going round saying horrible things about you.'

'I don't care to know what every idiot says about me,' remarked Nadezhda coldly. She was seized with anxiety and the amusing thought of having some sport with this pretty boy Achmianov suddenly lost its charm.

'We must go down,' she said. 'They're calling us.'

Down below the fish stew was now cooked. They poured it into bowls and ate with that ritual air peculiar to picnics. Everyone found the stew very tasty, saying that they had never eaten anything so delicious at home. As happens on picnics, they floundered in a welter of napkins, bundles and surplus bits of greasy paper drifting about in the wind, they didn't know whose glass or piece of bread was where, they spilt wine on the rug and their knees, they scattered salt about. Meanwhile it had grown dark around them, the fire was dying down, and everyone was too lazy to get up and put on more wood. They all drank wine, and they gave half a glass to Kostya and Katya. Drinking one glass after another, Nadezhda became intoxicated and forgot Kirilin.

'Grand picnic, enchanting evening,' said Layevsky, waxing merry in his cups. 'But I'd rather have a good winter than all this.

> "His beaver collar sparkles silver
> And coruscates with frosty dust."'

'That's a matter of taste,' observed Von Koren.

Layevsky felt a certain unease. The heat of the fire beat into his back, while Von Koren's hatred assailed his chest and face. He felt humiliated and enfeebled by this decent, intelligent man's loathing—based, probably, on some sound, hidden reason. Powerless to withstand it, he spoke in a wheedling voice.

'I'm crazy about nature,' said he. 'I'm only sorry that I'm not a scientist myself. I envy you.'

'Well, I'm not sorry or envious,' said Nadezhda. 'I don't see how one can seriously study bugs and beetles while the common people are suffering.'

Layevsky shared her view. Totally ignorant of the natural sciences himself, he could not abide the authoritative tone and air of erudite profundity affected by those who study ants' whiskers and cockroaches' legs. And it had always annoyed him that such people used these whiskers, legs and a thing called protoplasm—somehow he pictured it resembling an oyster—as a basis for solving problems embracing man's origin and life. But Nadezhda's words rang false to him, and he spoke only in order to contradict her.

'It's not the bugs that matter—it's what you deduce from them.'

VIII

It was late—after ten o'clock—when they began climbing into their carriages to drive home. All took their seats, the only defaulters being Nadezhda and Achmianov who were dashing about on the other side of the brook, chasing each other and laughing.

'Hey there, hurry up!' Samoylenko shouted.

'One shouldn't offer ladies wine,' said Von Koren softly.

Exhausted by the picnic, by Von Koren's hatred and by his own thoughts, Layevsky went to meet gay, merry Nadezhda, who felt light as thistledown, breathless and roaring with laughter as she seized him by both hands and placed her head on his chest. He took a step backwards.

'You're behaving like a cheap tart,' he said harshly.

The effect was so very rude that he even felt sorry for her. On his angry, weary face she saw hatred, pity, annoyance with himself—and suddenly her heart sank. She realized that she had gone too far, her behaviour had been too free and easy. Feeling saddened, cumbrous, fat, coarse, drunk, she mounted the first empty carriage along with Achmianov. Layevsky got in with Kirilin, the zoologist with Samoylenko, the deacon with the ladies—and the convoy moved off.

'How typical of the baboons,' began Von Koren, wrapping his cloak around him and shutting his eyes. 'You heard what she said—she wouldn't want to study bugs and beetles because of the common people's sufferings. That's how all baboons judge my kind of person. They're a servile, sly breed, and they've been terrorized by knoutings and punchings for ten generations. They cower, they gush, they fawn —but only under the spur of violence. Now, you let your baboon loose somewhere where no one's going to take him by the scruff of the neck —and you just watch him let himself go and throw his weight about! Watch how bold he is at painting exhibitions, in museums and theatres, or when he passes judgement on science. He rears up, stands on his hind legs, censures, criticizes. Above all, he criticizes—the mark of a slave, that! You just listen, and you'll find that members of the liberal professions are more vilified than any criminal. And why? Because three quarters of society consists of slaves—of baboons like these. Never would such a slave shake hands with you and thank you sincerely for your work.'

'I don't know what you expect,' said Samoylenko, yawning. 'The poor girl is naïve enough to want to talk to you seriously and you jump to these conclusions. You have it in for him for some reason, so you drag her in for good measure. But she's a fine person.'

'Oh, come off it. She's just an ordinary debauched, vulgar, kept woman. Look here, Alexander, if you met a common peasant woman who wouldn't live with her husband and did nothing but giggle and titter, you'd tell her to go and do a job. Then why be so timid now, so mealy-mouthed? Can it be just because Nadezhda's a civil servant's mistress, not a sailor's?'

'Well, what am I to do about her—beat her?' asked Samoylenko angrily.

'Don't flatter vice. We only condemn vice when its back is turned, which is like putting your tongue out at someone when he isn't looking. I'm a zoologist—or a sociologist, which is exactly the same thing—and you're a doctor. Society trusts us, and it's our job to draw society's attention to the fearful threat to its welfare—and to that of future generations—posed by the existence of these Nadezhda Ivanovnas.'

'Nadezhda Fyodorovna,' Samoylenko corrected. 'But what should society do?'

'Do? That's up to society. But if you ask me, the surest and most straightforward means is force. She should be sent back to her husband under military escort. And if the husband won't have her, she should be sentenced to penal servitude, or be put in some house of correction.'

'Whew!' Samoylenko sighed, and was silent for a moment. 'You were saying the other day that people like Layevsky should be exterminated,' he remarked gently. 'Tell me, if, er, the state or society, say, gave you the job of exterminating him, could you—bring yourself to?'

'I wouldn't hesitate for one second.'

IX

Layevsky and Nadezhda arrived home and went into their dark, stuffy, depressing rooms. Neither spoke. Layevsky lit a candle, while Nadezhda sat down and raised her mournful, guilty eyes to him without taking off her coat and hat.

He knew that she wanted to have things out with him, but that would have been so tedious, so pointless, so fatiguing, and he felt depressed because he had lost his temper and spoken to her roughly.

He chanced to feel in his pocket the letter which he had been meaning to read to her for days, and it occurred to him that he could distract her attention by showing it to her now.

'It's time we clarified our relations,' he thought. 'I'll give it to her, come what may.'

He took out the letter and gave it to her. 'Read this. It concerns you.'

With these words he went into his study, and lay on the sofa in the dark without a pillow. Nadezhda read the letter, and felt as if the ceiling had fallen and the walls had closed in on her. She suddenly felt hemmed in by darkness, by fear—and rapidly crossed herself three times.

'May he rest in peace,' she said. 'May he rest in peace.'

She burst into tears.

'Ivan!' she called. 'Ivan!'

There was no answer. Thinking that Layevsky had come in and was standing behind her chair, she sobbed like a child.

'Why didn't you tell me of his death before?' she asked. 'I wouldn't have gone on that picnic, wouldn't have laughed in that awful way. The men made vulgar remarks to me. What a sinful thing to do. Save me, Ivan, save me, I'm out of my mind, I'm ruined——'

Layevsky heard her sobbing. He felt ready to choke, and his heart pounded. In his anguish he rose, stood in the middle of the room, groped about in the darkness for the arm-chair near the table, and sat down.

'This is like prison,' he thought. 'I must go away, can't stand any more——'

It was too late to go and play cards, and there were no restaurants in town. He lay down again, and blocked his ears to shut out the sobs—then suddenly remembered that he could call on Samoylenko. To avoid passing Nadezhda, he climbed through the window into the garden, scaled the fence and set off down the street.

It was dark, and some steamer—a big passenger ship, judging by her lights—had just put in.

The anchor-chain clattered, and a red light sped from shore to ship—the customs boat.

'The passengers are asleep in their cabins,' thought Layevsky, envying the strangers their rest.

The windows were open in Samoylenko's house, and Layevsky peered through one, and then another. The house was dark and quiet inside.

'Are you asleep, Alexander?' he called. 'Alexander Samoylenko!'

A cough was heard, and an anxious cry.

'Who's there? What the blazes?'

'It's me, Alexander—forgive me.'

A little later the door opened. A lamp flashed its soft light, and Samoylenko's bulk appeared, all in white including a white night-cap.

'What is it?' he asked, half asleep, breathing heavily and scratching himself. 'Wait, I'll open up in a second.'

'Don't bother, I'll come through the window.'

Layevsky climbed through a window, went up to Samoylenko and gripped him by the hand.

'Alexander,' he said shakily, 'you must save me! I beg you, I implore you—try to understand me! My situation's sheer agony. If it lasts even a day or two longer I'll hang myself like—like a dog.'

'One moment—what exactly are you on about?'

'Light a candle.'

'Ah me,' sighed Samoylenko, lighting one. 'Oh, God—it's turned one o'clock, old man.'

'Forgive me, but I can't stay at home,' said Layevsky, much relieved by the light and by Samoylenko's presence. 'You're my best friend, Alexander, the only one I have. You're my only hope. Whether you want to or not, for God's sake rescue me. I must leave here at all costs, so lend me some money.'

'Oh, my God,' sighed Samoylenko, scratching himself. 'I'm falling asleep, then I hear the whistle of the steamer putting in, and now you come. Do you need much?'

'Three hundred roubles at least. I must leave her a hundred, and I need two hundred for the journey. I owe you about four hundred already, but I'll send you it all, every bit of it——'

Samoylenko clutched both his side-whiskers in one hand, straddled his legs and pondered.

'Yes,' he muttered pensively. 'Three hundred—. Very well. But I haven't got that much, I'll have to borrow.'

'Then borrow, in God's name!' said Layevsky, who could tell from Samoylenko's expression that he wished to—and definitely would—make the loan. 'Borrow. I'll pay you back without fail—I'll send it you from St. Petersburg as soon as I arrive, don't worry. Tell you what, Alexander,' he said, cheering up. 'Let's have some wine.'

'Well—all right then.'

They went into the dining-room.

'But what about Nadezhda?' asked Samoylenko, placing three bottles and a dish of peaches on the table. 'She won't stay on here, surely?'

'I'll fix all that, don't worry,' said Layevsky in a sudden transport of delight. 'I'll send her money later, and she'll join me. Then we'll clarify our relations. Your health, old pal.'

'Just a second,' said Samoylenko. 'Try this first, it's from my own vineyard. That bottle's from Navaridze's and this other's from Akhatulov. Try all three, and give me your honest opinion. Mine seems a bit on the sour side, eh? What do you think?'

'Yes. You've cheered me up, Alexander. Thank you. I feel a new man.'

'On the sour side, eh?'

'Hell, I don't know, but you're a marvellous, splendid fellow.'

Looking at Layevsky's pale, troubled, amiable face, Samoylenko recalled Von Koren's view that such people should be exterminated, and Layevsky struck him as a weak, defenceless child whom anyone could injure or destroy.

'And when you do go, you must make your peace with your mother,' he said. 'That's a bad business.'

'Oh yes. Without fail.'

There was a brief pause.

'You might patch things up with Von Koren too,' said Samoylenko when they had finished the first bottle. 'You're both grand, highly intelligent chaps, but you always seem to be at loggerheads.'

'Yes, he is a grand, highly intelligent chap,' agreed Layevsky, now ready to praise and forgive everyone. 'He's a splendid fellow, but I can't get on terms with him, indeed I can't. Our characters are too dissimilar. Mine is a sluggish, feeble, submissive nature. I might hold out my hand to him at some auspicious moment, but he'd turn his back on me—with contempt.'

Layevsky sipped his wine and paced up and down.

'I understand Von Koren very well indeed,' he went on, standing in the middle of the room. 'He's a hard, strong man, a tyrant. You've heard all his talk about that expedition, and those are no empty words. He requires a wilderness, a moonlit night. All around, in tents and under the open sky, sleep his hungry, sick Cossacks, worn out by punishing marches—his guides, his bearers, his doctor, his priest. He alone shuns sleep, sitting on his camp stool like Stanley, feeling lord of the waste land and master of these people. On, on, on he presses. His people groan and die one after the other, but he still drives on until he himself perishes in the end—yet still remains the tyrant, the lord of the waste land because the cross on his grave can be seen by caravans thirty or forty miles away, dominating the desert. I'm sorry the man isn't in the army, he'd have made a first-rate general, a military genius. He could have drowned his cavalry in a river, built bridges of corpses—and such boldness is more important in war than all your fortifications and tactics. Oh, I understand him through and through. But tell me—why is he kicking his heels around here? What is he after?'

'He's studying marine life.'

'No, no, that's not it, old man,' sighed Layevsky. 'From what I gathered from a passenger on the steamer, a scientist, the Black Sea's poor in fauna, and organic life can't exist in its depths owing to the excess of hydrogen sulphide. All serious students of the subject work in the biological stations of Naples or Villefranche. But Von Koren's independent and stubborn. He works on the Black Sea because no one else does. He has broken with the university, and will have nothing to do with scientists and colleagues because he's first and foremost a tyrant, and only secondly a zoologist. And he'll go far, you'll find. He sees himself smoking all intrigues and mediocrity out of our universities when he gets back from his expedition—dreams of making mincemeat of those academics. Tyranny is just as potent in the academic world as it is in war. But he's now spending his second summer in this stinking dump, because it's better to be first man in a village than play second fiddle in town. Here he's monarch of all he surveys. He keeps a tight rein on all the locals, crushing them with his authority. He has taken everyone in hand, he meddles in other people's affairs, he makes everything his own concern, and he has everyone scared of him. I'm now slipping out of his clutches—he senses that and hates me. Hasn't he told you that I should be exterminated or made to do forced labour for the community?'

'Yes,' laughed Samoylenko.

Layevsky also laughed and drank some wine.

'His ideals are tyrannical too,' he said, laughing and nibbling a peach. 'When ordinary mortals work for the common weal, they're thinking of their neighbour—me, you . . . human beings, in a word. But for Von Koren people are small fry, nobodies—creatures too petty to form his purpose in life. His work, this expedition on which he'll break his neck—these things aren't done out of love for his neighbour, but in the name of abstractions like mankind, future generations, an ideal race of men. His job is to improve the human breed, in which context we're no more than slaves in his eyes—cannon-fodder, beasts of burden. Some of us he'd exterminate, or put to hard labour, on others he'd impose rigid discipline, making them get up and go to bed to drum rolls like Arakcheyev. He'd post eunuchs to guard our chastity and morality, and give orders to fire at anyone who stepped outside the circle of our narrow, conservative morality—all this in the name of bettering the human race. But what *is* the human race? An illusion, a mirage. Tyrants have always been illusionists. I understand him through and through, old man. I appreciate him, I don't deny his importance. The world depends on such people. Were it handed over entirely to our sort, we'd make as big a hash of it as the flies are making of that picture, for all our kindness and good intentions. Yes indeed.'

Layevsky sat down by Samoylenko's side.

'I'm a paltry, trivial wreck of a man,' he said with real feeling. 'The air I breathe, this wine, love—the whole of life, in sum—I have so far purchased these things with lies, laziness and cowardice. So far I've been cheating others and myself, and I've suffered in consequence. But my very sufferings have been cheap and second-rate. I meekly bow my head to Von Koren's hatred because there are times when I hate and despise myself.'

Layevsky again paced the room excitedly.

'I'm glad I see my own faults so clearly and admit them,' he said. 'This will help me to be born anew and make a fresh start. If you knew how ardently, with what yearning I long to be transformed, old man. I shall be a proper person, I shall—I swear it! I don't know whether it's the effect of the wine, or whether it really is so, but it's ages since I remember having moments as bright and pure as I'm now enjoying here with you.'

'It's bed-time, old boy,' said Samoylenko.

'Yes, yes—forgive me, I'll only be a moment.'

Layevsky bustled round the furniture and windows looking for his cap.

'Thanks,' he muttered with a sigh. 'Thank you. Affection and kind words—there's no better charity than those. You've made me a new man.'

He found his cap, paused and looked guiltily at Samoylenko.

'Alexander!' he implored.

'What is it?'

'May I spend the night here, old man?'

'You're most welcome—certainly.'

Layevsky lay down to sleep on the sofa, and his conversation with the doctor continued for some time.

X

Three days after the picnic, Mary Bityugov unexpectedly called on Nadezhda Fyodorovna. Without uttering a word of greeting or removing her hat, she seized Nadezhda by both hands and pressed them to her bosom.

'My dear, I'm so excited, I'm thunderstruck,' she said with tremendous emotion. 'Yesterday our nice, kind doctor told my Nicodemus that your husband has died. Tell me, tell me, dear—is this true?'

'Yes, it's true,' answered Nadezhda. 'He died.'

'How simply frightful, darling! But every cloud has its silver lining. Your husband was probably a wonderful, splendid, saintly person, but such are more needed in heaven than on earth.'

Every point and feature on Mary Bityugov's face quivered, as if tiny needles were leaping under her skin. She gave her sugary smile.

'This means you're free, dear,' she said in breathless ecstasy. 'Now you can hold your head up and look people in the eye. Henceforward God and man will bless your union with Ivan Layevsky. How perfectly sweet! I'm trembling with joy, I'm lost for words. I shall arrange your wedding, dear. Nicodemus and I have always been so fond of you, you must allow us to bless your lawful, chaste union. When, oh when is the wedding day?'

'I haven't given it a thought,' said Nadezhda, freeing her hands.

'That can't be so, dear. You *have* thought, now haven't you?'

'I haven't, honestly,' laughed Nadezhda. 'Why should we marry? I see no need—we'll carry on as we have so far.'

'What words are these?' Mary Bityugov was horrified. 'What are you saying, in God's name?'

'Marrying won't improve things—far from it. It would make them worse, actually—we'd lose our freedom.'

'How can you talk like that, dearest?' cried Mary Bityugov, stepping backwards and flinging up her arms. 'You're quite outrageous! Think what you're saying! Compose yourself!'

'Compose myself? I haven't lived yet, and you want me to compose myself!'

Nadezhda reflected that she really hadn't had much of a life so far. She had been to a girls' boarding school, and married a man whom she didn't love. Then she had gone off with Layevsky, and spent her time with him on this boring, deserted coast in hopes of something better. Could you call that living?

'We should get married, though,' she thought—but then remembered Kirilin and Achmianov and blushed.

'No, it's impossible,' she said. 'Even if Ivan asked me on bended knee, I'd still refuse.'

Mary Bityugov sat sadly and solemnly on the sofa for a minute without speaking, staring fixedly at one point. Then she stood up.

'Good-bye, dear,' she said coldly. 'I'm sorry I bothered you. Now, this isn't easy for me to say, but I must tell you that all is over between us from now on. Despite my great respect for Mr. Layevsky, the door of my home is closed to you.'

She brought this out solemnly, herself overcome by her own earnestness. Then her face quivered again, adopting its soft, sugary expression, and she stretched out her hands to the terrified, embarrassed Nadezhda.

'My dear,' she implored, 'permit me to speak to you for a minute as your mother or elder sister. I'll be as outspoken as a mother.'

Nadezhda felt warmth, joy and self-pity in her breast, as if her mother actually had risen from the dead and stood before her. She embraced Mary Bityugov impetuously, burying her face in Mary's shoulder. Both wept, sitting on the sofa and sobbing for several minutes —not looking at each other, bereft of speech.

'My dear child,' began Mary. 'I'm going to tell you some home truths without sparing you.'

'Yes, do, for God's sake do!'

'Trust me, dear. I'm the only one of the ladies here, you'll remember, who has asked you to her home. I was terribly shocked by you from your first day here, but I hadn't the heart to look down on you like the others. I suffered for dear, kind Mr. Layevsky as for my own son. A young man in a strange country, inexperienced, weak, without his mother—I endured agonies. My husband was against the acquaintance, but I convinced him, won him over. So we began to invite Mr. Layevsky—and you too, of course, or else he'd have been offended. I have a daughter and a son—. A child's tender mind, you know, its pure heart—"Whosoever shall offend one of these little ones" and all that. I received you—but trembled for my children. Oh yes, you'll understand my fears when you're a mother yourself. Now, everyone was surprised at my receiving you—forgive me—like a respectable woman. They hinted as much—and there was gossip and conjecture, of course. In my innermost self I condemned you, but you were so wretched and pathetic, your behaviour was so monstrous, that my heart bled for you.'

'But why?' asked Nadezhda Fyodorovna, trembling all over. 'Why? What have I done to anyone?'

'You committed a fearful sin. You broke the vow made to your husband at the altar. You seduced a fine young man who would perhaps have taken a lawful spouse from a good family in his own station, had he never met you, and would now be living a normal life. You have wrecked his youth. Now, don't say anything—don't speak, dear. I can't believe any man has ever been to blame for our sins, it's always the woman's fault. Men are so frivolous about family life, they live by their minds, not by the heart—they understand precious little. But the woman understands everything. It all depends on her. Much has been given her, and much shall be asked of her. You know, dear, if the woman was sillier or weaker than the man in these matters, God would never have entrusted her with the upbringing of little boys and girls. And then you trod the path of vice, dear, you lost all sense of shame. In your place any other woman would have hidden her face and stayed at home behind locked doors, never seen but in the Lord's temple—pale, in mourning dress, weeping. "Lord, this fallen angel hath returned to Thee," all would have cried, sincerely mortified. But you threw off all discretion, my sweet, you lived openly, outrageously—as if flaunting your sin. You frolicked and made merry while I shuddered with horror as I watched, fearing lest thunder from heaven strike our house during one of your visits.

'Don't say anything, dear—please!' shouted Mary, seeing that Nadezhda was about to speak. 'Trust me, I won't deceive you, and I won't hide one single truth from your inner eyes. Now, listen, dear. God puts His mark on great sinners and you bear His mark. Remember what appalling clothes you've always worn!'

Nadezhda, who had always thought her clothes particularly good, stopped crying and looked at Mary Bityugov in amazement.

'Yes, appalling!' went on Mary Bityugov. 'Those grotesque, gaudy dresses—people can judge your behaviour by them. Everyone sniggered when they saw you, and shrugged their shoulders—but *I* suffered agonies. Then forgive me, dear, but you're a bit careless in your personal habits. When we met in the bathing-house, you had me in quite a dither. Your top clothes aren't all that bad, but your petticoat and chemise—I can only blush, dear. Besides, no one ever ties Mr. Layevsky's tie properly, and look at the poor man's linen and boots—one can see he's not being looked after at home. Then you never give him enough to eat, darling. And if there's no one at home to see to the samovar and

coffee, you know. one's bound to run through half one's salary in the
Pavilion. And your house is frightful—ghastly! No one else in town
has flies, but your place is crawling with them—the plates and saucers
are all black. And just look at your window-sills and tables! The dust,
the dead flies, the glasses! Why leave glasses *there*? And you still haven't
cleared the table, my sweet. As for your bedroom, one's ashamed to
go in there, what with your underwear scattered all over the place,
your various rubber things hanging on the walls, and an, er, utensil
standing about—*really*, my dear! The husband must know nothing and
the wife must be as pure as a dear little angel in his sight. I wake up
every morning at dawn and wash my face in cold water so that
Nicodemus shan't see me looking sleepy.'

'These are all trivialities,' sobbed Nadezhda. 'If only I was happy—
but I'm so wretched!'

'Yes, yes, you indeed are wretched,' sighed Mary Bityugov, hardly
able to hold back her own tears. 'And great grief awaits you in the
future—a lonely old age, illnesses, and then you must answer at the
Day of Judgement. It's appalling, appalling. And now the very fates
hold out a helping hand, you foolishly reject it. You must get married
—and quickly!'

'Yes, yes, I should,' said Nadezhda. 'But it's out of the question.'

'Oh. Why?'

'It's impossible—ah, if you did but know!'

Nadezhda wanted to tell her about Kirilin, about meeting that
good-looking young Achmianov by the harbour on the previous
evening, about her mad, absurd idea of discharging her three-hundred-
rouble debt, about how funny it had all seemed, and about how she had
arrived home late at night feeling like one irretrievably ruined—a whore,
in fact. She herself didn't know how it had come about. Now she wanted
to swear to Mary Bityugov that she would pay the debt without fail,
but could not speak because she was sobbing so—and felt so ashamed.

'I'll leave this place,' she said. 'Ivan can stay, but I'll go.'

'Go where?'

'To central Russia.'

'But what will you live on? You have no money, have you?'

'I'll do some translating, or—open a little library——'

'Don't be absurd, dear. You need money to run a library. Ah well,
I'll leave you now. Now, you calm down and think things over, then
come and see me tomorrow in a happy little mood. That will be
perfectly sweet. Well, good-bye, cherub. Let me kiss you.'

Mary Bityugov kissed Nadezhda on the forehead, made the sign of the cross over her, and quietly left. It was already growing dark, and Olga had lit the kitchen lamp. Still crying, Nadezhda went into the bedroom and lay on the bed. She was running a high fever. She undressed in a lying position, crumpling her dress down to her feet and curling up under the blanket. She was thirsty, but there was no one to bring her a drink.

'I'll pay it back,' she told herself, imagining in her delirious state that she was sitting beside some sick woman in whom she recognized herself. 'I'll pay. How silly to think that for money I would——. I'll leave here and send him the money from St. Petersburg. First one hundred, then another hundred, then another——'

Layevsky came in later that night.

'First a hundred,' Nadezhda told him. 'Then another hundred——'

'You should take quinine,' he said.

'Tomorrow's Wednesday,' he thought, 'and the boat will sail without me. That means I'm stuck here till Saturday.'

Nadezhda knelt up in bed.

'Did I say anything just now?' she asked, smiling and screwing up her eyes in the candle-light.

'No. We'll have to send for the doctor tomorrow morning. You go to sleep.'

He picked up a pillow and made for the door. Having taken the definite decision to depart and desert Nadezhda, he now found that she stirred his pity and remorse. He felt a certain compunction in her presence, as if she were a horse which was to be put down because of sickness or old age. He stopped in the doorway and glanced back at her.

'I was annoyed at the picnic and spoke rudely to you. Forgive me, for God's sake.'

Saying this, he went into his study and lay down, but was unable to sleep for some time.

On the following morning Samoylenko—sporting full parade uniform, epaulettes and medals since today was an official holiday—felt Nadezhda's pulse and looked at her tongue. When he came out of the bedroom, Layevsky was standing by the door.

'Well now, how about it?' he asked anxiously, his expression a mixture of fear, extreme unease and hope.

'Don't worry, it's nothing serious,' Samoylenko said. 'Just the usual chill.'

'That's not what I meant.' Layevsky frowned impatiently. 'Did you get the money?'

'Forgive me, dear old boy,' whispered Samoylenko, glancing at the door and betraying embarrassment. 'Forgive me, for heaven's sake. No one has any spare cash, and so far I could only pick up five or ten roubles here and there—a hundred and ten altogether. I'll speak to one or two more people today. Be patient.'

'But Saturday's the final date,' whispered Layevsky, quivering with impatience. 'Get it by Saturday—in the name of all that's holy! If I can't leave then you needn't bother, because I shan't want it. How a doctor can be without money—that's what I don't see.'

'Oh Lord, have it your own way,' hissed Samoylenko so rapidly and with such urgency that his throat actually squeaked. 'I've been robbed left right and centre, I'm owed seven thousand and I'm in debt all round myself. Can I help that?'

'You'll have the money by Saturday then?'

'I'll do my best.'

'Please do, old man. Just see that I have that money in my hands by Friday morning.'

Samoylenko sat down and prescribed a solution of quinine, *kalium bromatum*, infusion of rhubarb, tincture of gentian and *aqua foeniculi*— all in one mixture. He added rose syrup to sweeten it, and left.

XI

'You look as if you've come to arrest me,' said Von Koren when he saw Samoylenko come into the place in full parade uniform.

'I was just passing,' said Samoylenko, 'and I thought, why don't I pop in and see how zoology's doing.' He sat down at the big table which the zoologist had knocked together himself out of plain boards.

'Greetings, your reverence,' he nodded to the deacon who sat by the window copying. 'I'll stay a moment, then dash home to arrange lunch. It's already time—. I do hope I'm not disturbing you?'

'Not at all,' answered the zoologist, spreading out some papers covered with fine handwriting on the table. 'We're busy copying.'

'I see—. Oh, good grief!' sighed Samoylenko, cautiously pulling from the table a dusty book with a dead, dry, spider-like insect on it.

'Well, really!' he said. 'Imagine you're some little green beetle going about your business—and you suddenly run into this monstrosity. That must be terrifying, I should think.'

'Oh, I suppose so.'

'Is it equipped with poison to defend itself from its enemies?'

'Yes, for self-defence—and also for attack.'

'Well, well, well,' sighed Samoylenko. 'So everything in nature is functional and rational, is it then, boys? But there's one thing I don't see. You're a highly intelligent chap, so explain it, won't you? There exist certain small creatures—no larger than a rat, you know, pretty-looking little things . . . but vicious and immoral in the ultimate degree, believe you me. One such little beast might be walking through a wood, say. He sees a bird. So he catches it and eats it. He moves on and sees a nest full of eggs in the grass. He's no longer hungry—he's had plenty to eat—still, he chews up an egg and knocks the others out of the nest with his paw. Then he meets a frog and has some sport with that. After torturing the frog he moves on, licking his lips—and meets a beetle. One blow of his paw, and that beetle—. Whatever he meets he maims and exterminates. He pushes into other beasts' lairs, wrecks ant-hills for the hell of it, cracks open snails. If he meets a rat he starts a fight, if he sees a small snake or mouse, he has to strangle it. And so it goes on all day. Now, tell me—what's the purpose of such a creature? Why was it created?'

'I don't know what creature you mean,' Von Koren said. 'It must be one of the insectivores. Very well then. The bird was caught because it was careless. The nest of eggs was destroyed because the bird wasn't clever enough—made its nest badly and didn't succeed in disguising it. The frog probably had some defect in its colouring, or else it wouldn't have been seen—and so on. Your beast destroys only the weak, the clumsy and the careless—in a word, creatures possessing defects which nature holds it unnecessary to transmit to posterity. Only the fittest, the most cautious, powerful and developed survive. Thus your little beast unconsciously serves the great aim of perfecting the species.'

'Yes, yes, I see. By the way, old man,' Samoylenko said casually, 'could you lend me a hundred roubles?'

'Very well. Now, there are some most interesting specimens among the insectivores. Take the mole. It's said to be useful because it destroys insect pests, and there's a story that some German once sent Kaiser Wilhelm I a moleskin coat—but that the Kaiser gave orders to reprimand him for destroying so many valuable animals. Still, the mole is every bit as cruel as your creature, and it's a great pest too—does enormous damage to the fields.'

Von Koren opened a cashbox and took out a hundred-rouble note.

'The mole has a powerful thorax—like the bat,' he went on, locking the box. 'It has frightfully well-developed bones and muscles, and an exceptionally powerful mouth. If it were as big as an elephant, there'd be no stopping it, it would trample everything underfoot. It's interesting that when two moles meet underground, both start digging a platform, as if by common consent—they need it as a convenient place to fight. When it's finished, they join battle fiercely and fight till the weaker drops. Well, take your hundred roubles,' said Von Koren, lowering his voice, 'but only on condition that you don't want it for Layevsky.'

'Suppose it is for Layevsky?' exploded Samoylenko. 'What business is that of yours?'

'I can't provide money for Layevsky's benefit. I know you like lending money—you'd make a loan to some notorious highwayman if he asked you. But I can't help you in that direction, sorry.'

'Yes, it is for Layevsky, sir,' said Samoylenko, standing up and brandishing his right hand. 'Yes, sir, it's for Layevsky. Hell and damnation—no one has the right to tell me how to dispose of my own money! So you won't lend it me, eh?'

The deacon burst out laughing.

'Don't get so worked up—use your brain,' said the zoologist. 'Conferring favours on friend Layevsky—in my view, that makes about as much sense as watering weeds or feeding locusts.'

'Well, in my view it's our duty to help our neighbours,' shouted Samoylenko.

'Then why not help that starving Turk who lies beneath the fence? He's a worker, he's more valuable and useful than friend Layevsky. Why not give him that hundred roubles? Or put a hundred towards my expedition?'

'Look here, are you making me that loan or aren't you?'

'Tell me frankly—what does he need it for?'

'There's no secret about it, he has to go to St. Petersburg on Saturday.'

'So that's it,' said Von Koren slowly. 'Well, well, well! I see. Will she be going with him then?'

'She stays here for the time being. He'll settle his affairs in St. Petersburg and send her money, and then she'll go too.'

'Very neat,' said the zoologist, and gave a short, high-pitched laugh. 'Neat indeed—a very bright idea.'

He went quickly up to Samoylenko, stood facing him and stared into his eyes.

'Tell me frankly,' he said. 'Has he got tired of her, eh? He has, hasn't he?'

'Yes,' said Samoylenko, and broke out in a sweat.

'How nauseating!' said Von Koren, disgust written on his face. 'Now, there are two possibilities, Alexander. Either you and he have cooked this up together, or else you're a half-wit, if you'll pardon my saying so. Can't you see he's making a fool of you—treating you like a child, and in the most unscrupulous way? He wants to get rid of her, abandon her here—why, it sticks out a mile. She'll be left on your hands, and then you'll have to send her to St. Petersburg at your own expense—that's as clear as daylight. Surely your good friend hasn't so dazzled you with his virtues that you can't see what's staring you in the face!'

'But these are merest conjectures,' said Samoylenko, sitting down.

'Oh, are they? Then why is he travelling alone? Why isn't she going with him? And why, you might ask him, shouldn't she go on ahead? And he come on afterwards? Cunning bastard!'

Overwhelmed by sudden doubts and suspicions of his friend, Samoylenko immediately lost heart and lowered his voice.

'But this is impossible,' he said, remembering the night which Layevsky had passed in his house. 'The man suffers so.'

'What of it? Burglars and fire-raisers also suffer.'

'Let's suppose you're right,' Samoylenko said pensively. 'Even so, he's still a young fellow in a strange country, a university man. We were students ourselves once, and there's no one to stand up for him here besides us.'

'To abet his filthy tricks just because you both attended university at different periods, and both wasted your time there—what utter nonsense!'

'Wait, let's reason this out coolly. We might do it this way, I think,' calculated Samoylenko, flicking his fingers. 'I'll make him the loan, see? But I'll insist he gives his word of honour to send Nadezhda her travelling expenses within one week.'

'Oh, he'll give you his word of honour all right, he'll throw in a few tears, even—and he'll mean every bit of it. But what's his word worth? He won't keep it, and when you meet him on the Nevsky Prospekt in a couple of years with his new mistress on his arm, he'll make the excuse that civilization has crippled him, and that he's a chip off the same block as Turgenev's Rudin. For God's sake drop him! Leave that muck alone—don't wallow in it!'

Samoylenko thought for a moment.

'I'll still lend him the money,' he said resolutely. 'Say what you like, but I can't refuse a man on the basis of mere conjecture.'

'Fine. And you can go and slobber all over him for all I care.'

'So let me have that hundred roubles,' Samoylenko said nervously.

'Not likely.'

Silence ensued. Samoylenko felt utterly crestfallen. He assumed a guilty, shamefaced, wheedling expression, and it was strange somehow to see this huge man with his epaulettes and medals looking so pathetic and embarrassed, like a small child.

'The local bishop tours his diocese on horseback, not by carriage,' said the deacon, laying down his pen. 'He looks extraordinarily moving on horseback—the very picture of simplicity and modesty infused with biblical grandeur.'

'Is he a good man?' asked Von Koren, welcoming the change of subject.

'Obviously yes. Would he have been consecrated bishop otherwise?'

'There are some very fine bishops—most able men,' said Von Koren. 'The trouble is, though, a lot of them have this foible of posing as pillars of the state. One tries to spread the Russian way of life, another criticizes science. What has that to do with them? They should pay more attention to diocesan affairs.'

'Laymen may not judge bishops.'

'Why not though, Deacon? A bishop's a man like me.'

'Yes and no,' said the deacon, taking umbrage and picking up his pen. 'Had you been such a man, God's grace would have alighted upon you—you'd be a bishop yourself. Since you aren't one, you can't be such a man.'

'Don't burble, Deacon,' said Samoylenko, much distressed and turning to Von Koren. 'I have an idea,' he went on. 'No need for you to lend me that hundred. You'll be eating at my place for another three months more before winter, so pay me a quarter in advance.'

'No.'

Samoylenko blinked and flushed crimson. Automatically reaching for the book with the spider on it, he gave it a glance, then stood up and took his cap. Von Koren felt sorry for him.

'Fancy having to live and work with such people,' he said, kicking a piece of paper into the corner in his indignation. 'This isn't kindness or love, can't you see? It's craven corruption—sheer poison, it is! What reason builds up, your futile, debilitated emotions pull down. I contracted enteric fever as a schoolboy, and my aunt felt so sorry for me that she stuffed me with pickled mushrooms till I nearly died. Can't you and dear auntie get it into your heads that love of mankind mustn't be located in the heart, nor in the pit of the stomach, nor yet in the small of the back? It should be up here!' And Von Koren slapped his forehead.

'Take the thing!' he said, and tossed over a hundred-rouble note.

'No need to lose your temper, Nicholas,' said Samoylenko meekly, folding the note. 'I know what you mean all right, but—put yourself in my position.'

'You're an old woman, that's what it comes to.'

The deacon guffawed.

'Listen, Alexander, I have one last request,' said Von Koren heatedly. 'When you give that twister the money, make one proviso—he either takes his mistress with him, or he sends her on ahead. Don't let him have it otherwise. You make no bones about it! You tell him that, and if you don't I'll go to his office and throw him downstairs, by God I will, and I'll have nothing more to do with you either—and that's flat!'

'All right then. If he takes her with him or sends her ahead, it'll actually suit him better,' said Samoylenko. 'He'll be glad to, even. Good-bye then.'

He took a fond farewell and left the room, but looked back at Von Koren before closing the door behind him.

'You've been spoilt by Germans, old man,' he said with a terrifying grimace. 'By Germans, sir!'

XII

On the following day, a Thursday, Mary Bityugov was celebrating her son Kostya's birthday. Everyone had been invited for pie at noon and chocolate in the evening. When Laycvsky and Nadezhda arrived that evening, the zoologist was already in the dining-room drinking chocolate.

'Have you spoken to him?' he asked Samoylenko.

'Not yet.'

'Don't stand on ceremony, mind. But the creatures' impudence—it beats me! They're well aware what the Bityugovs here think of their liaison, yet they still barge in.'

'If one were to truckle to every superstition, one couldn't go anywhere,' said Samoylenko.

'The aversion of the masses to licentiousness and love outside marriage—you call that superstition?'

'Of course I do. Superstition and sheer ill will. Soldiers whistle and cackle when they see a loose woman, but you try asking them a few questions about their own behaviour!'

'They have reason to whistle. Unmarried girls smother their illegitimate babies and go to prison. Anna Karenin threw herself under the train, and in the villages people tar women's gates to show they're immoral. You and I are attracted by Katya's innocence, goodness knows why. And everyone feels a vague need for pure love, though he knows there isn't such a thing. Superstition is it, all this? No, old boy, it's all we have left of natural selection. Were it not for this obscure force regulating relations between the sexes, the Layevskys of this world would soon see you in kingdom come, and humanity would go to the bad in a couple of years.'

Layevsky went into the drawing-room and said good evening to everyone, producing a sickly smile as he shook Von Koren's hand.

'Excuse me, Alexander, I must have a word with you,' he told Samoylenko, after choosing a convenient moment.

Samoylenko stood up and put his arm round Layevsky's waist. They both went into Nicodemus Bityugov's study.

'Tomorrow's Friday,' said Layevsky, biting his nails. 'Have you got me what you promised?'

'I've only managed two hundred and ten. The rest I'll have today or tomorrow, never fear.'

'Thank God,' sighed Layevsky, his hands shaking in his joy. 'You're my salvation, Alexander. As I hope to be happy, I'll send you that money the moment I arrive, by God—I swear by anything you like. And I'll pay off my old debt too.'

'One thing, Ivan,' said Samoylenko with a blush, taking him by a button. 'Excuse my meddling in your private affairs, but—why not take Nadezhda along?'

'Don't be silly, how can I? One of us has got to stay here, or my creditors will raise hell—I do owe seven hundred roubles or more to the shops, you know. But just wait, I'll send them the money. I'll shut their mouths—and then she can leave too.'

'I see—but why not send her on ahead?'

'Good grief, how *can* I?' asked Layevsky in horror. 'She's a woman, isn't she? What can she do there on her own? What does she understand? It would be a sheer waste of time and money.'

'That's reasonable,' Samoylenko thought, but remembered his conversation with Von Koren and dropped his eyes.

'I can't agree,' he said gloomily. 'You must go with her or send her on ahead. Or else—or else I won't give you the money, and that's my last word.'

Retreating, he backed into the door, and entered the drawing-room red in the face and appallingly embarrassed.

'Friday, Friday,' thought Layevsky as he returned to the drawing-room. 'Friday.'

He was handed a cup of chocolate, and burnt his lips and tongue on the hot drink.

'Friday, Friday,' he thought.

He had Friday on the brain somehow, he couldn't get it out of his mind. All he knew—not in his mind, but somewhere deep inside him—was that a Saturday departure was out of the question. He was confronted by dapper little Nicodemus Bityugov, his hair brushed forward on to his temples.

'Help yourself,' he urged. 'Please do.'

Mary Bityugov was showing her guests Katya's school marks.

'School work is so frightfully hard these days,' she drawled. 'They expect so much.'

'Mother!' groaned Katya, not knowing where to hide from praises so embarrassing.

Layevsky also looked at the marks and commended them. Scripture, Russian, conduct—the excellents and goods danced before his eyes. All this—added to his obsession with Friday, plus the hair over Bityugov's temples, plus Katya Bityugov's red cheeks—struck him as such a shattering, crashing, frantic bore that he was ready to shriek.

'Shall I,' he wondered, 'shall I really be unable to get away from here?'

They placed two card-tables side by side and sat down to play Post-office. Layevsky joined them.

'Friday, Friday,' he thought, smiling and taking a pencil from his pocket. 'Friday.'

He wanted to think over his situation—yet feared to do so. It was terrifying to realize that the doctor had caught him out, and in a deception which he had so long, so carefully, hidden even from himself. When thinking about his future, he never gave his imagination full rein. He would just board a train and go, thus solving his problem in life—and that was as far as he allowed his thoughts to stray. The idea occasionally flashed through his mind, like some dim light seen far away in the fields, that somewhere—in a back street of St. Petersburg, in the remote future—he would be driven to some minor prevarication in order to break with Nadezhda and pay his debts. After this one lie, a new life would dawn—and a good thing too because he would gain tremendous integrity at the cost of a single fib.

But now that the doctor had turned him down, thus crudely exposing his duplicity, he realized that the need for lies would arise not only in the remote future, but also today, tomorrow, in a month's time—until his dying day, perhaps. He could not leave town, indeed, without lying to Nadezhda, his creditors and his seniors at the office. Nor could he obtain money in St. Petersburg without lying to his mother by claiming to have left Nadezhda. His mother would give him no more than five hundred roubles, which meant that he already had deceived the doctor since he would be unable to send him any money in the near future. Then, when Nadezhda reached St. Petersburg, he would need a vast stock of new lies, great and small, before he could be rid of her. There would be more weeping, more tedium, more world-weariness, more remorse—and therefore no new life for him. And the whole thing was so utterly bogus. A great mountain of lies towered up in Layevsky's mind. If he was to leap it with one bound, if he was to escape lying by instalments, he must steel himself to stern measures. For instance, he might get up from where he sat, say nothing to anyone, put on his hat and leave at once—with no money, without a word to a soul. But Layevsky felt he couldn't do that.

'Friday, Friday, Friday,' he thought.

Everyone was writing notes, folding them in two and putting them in Nicodemus Bityugov's old top hat. When there were enough of them, Kostya made a round of the table as postman and delivered them. The deacon, Katya and Kostya had all received funny notes and had tried to write as amusingly as possible. They were in raptures.

'We must have a talk,' Nadezhda read in her note. She exchanged glances with Mary Bityugov who gave her sugary smile and nodded.

'What is there to talk about, though?' Nadezhda wondered. 'If one can't say everything, why say anything?'

Before leaving for the party she had tied Layevsky's tie, which trivial act had inspired her with tender melancholy. His anxious face, his distraught glances, his pallor, the mysterious recent change in him, her own monstrous, unsavoury secret which she was keeping from him, her trembling hands as she knotted his tie—these things somehow told her that their life together had not much longer to run. She looked at him with penitential awe, as if gazing at an icon.

'Forgive me,' she thought. 'Forgive me.'

Across the table from her, Achmianov could not keep his black, love-sick eyes off her. She was disturbed by desire and felt ashamed, fearing that even her grief and anguish would not prevent her from yielding to lust some day—fearing too that she was as little capable of self-restraint as a compulsive alcoholic.

Not wishing to continue a life degrading to herself and insulting to Layevsky, she decided that she would go away. She would beg him with tears in her eyes to let her go. Should he refuse, she would leave secretly, not telling him what had happened—let him preserve her memory undefiled.

'I'm in love, love, love,' she read. That must be Achmianov.

She would live in some remote spot where she would take a job and send Layevsky money, embroidered shirts and tobacco anonymously. Only in old age would she return to him, should he fall seriously ill and need a nurse. In old age he would learn why she had refused to be his wife, why she had left him. And he would prize her self-sacrifice, forgiving her.

'You have a long nose.' The deacon or Kostya, that must be.

Nadezhda imagined herself saying good-bye to Layevsky. She would hold him tight, kiss his hand and swear to love him always. Then, living among strangers in that remote spot, she would remember every day that she had a dear friend somewhere, the man she loved—a clean-living, high-minded, superior person who preserved her memory undefiled.

'If you won't meet me tonight I shall take steps, on my word of honour. Gentlemen are not to be treated like this, believe me.'

That was Kirilin.

XIII

Layevsky received two letters. He opened one and read: 'Don't leave, dear boy.'

'Who could have written that?' he wondered. 'Not Samoylenko, of course. Not the deacon either—he doesn't know I want to leave. Von Koren, could it be?'

Von Koren leant over the table, sketching a pyramid. His eyes were smiling, Layevsky thought.

'Samoylenko must have let the cat out of the bag,' he reflected.

The other letter was in the same ragged hand with long tails and curlicues: 'A certain person will not leave here on Saturday.'

'What a stupid sneer,' thought Layevsky. 'Friday, Friday——'

He felt a catch in his throat, and touched his collar, making as if to cough, but erupted in laughter instead.

'Ha! Ha! Ha!' he cachinnated, wondering what it was he found so funny. 'Ha! Ha! Ha!'

Trying to control himself, he covered his mouth with his hand, but mirth choked his chest and neck, and his hand was unable to close his mouth.

'How stupid, though,' he thought, rocking with laughter. 'Have I gone mad, or what?'

Higher, ever higher, soared Layevsky's cackles until they sounded like the yapping of a pekinese. He tried to rise from the table, but his legs would not obey him and his right hand was mysteriously bobbing about on the table as if it had a life of its own, and making frenzied attempts to pick up pieces of paper and crumple them. The astonished glances, Samoylenko's earnest, scared face and a leer of cold disgust from the zoologist—seeing these things Layevsky knew that he was having hysterics.

'What a shame and disgrace,' he thought, feeling warm tears on his face. 'Oh, what a scandal—such a thing has never happened to me before.'

They took his arms and led him off, holding his head from behind. A tumbler flashed before his eyes, and banged on his teeth. Water spilt on his chest. Then came a small room and twin beds in the middle covered with clean, snow-white coverlets. Collapsing on one of them, he burst into tears.

'Never mind,' said Samoylenko. 'It's quite common, this. It happens.'

Nadezhda stood by the bed—scared stiff, trembling from head to foot and a prey to awful forebodings.

'What's wrong?' she asked. 'What is it? Tell me, for God's sake.' She wondered if Kirilin had written to him.

'It's nothing,' said Layevsky, laughing and crying. 'Go away, old girl.'

Since his expression betrayed neither hate nor disgust, he must still be in ignorance. Somewhat reassured, Nadezhda went back to the drawing-room.

'Never mind, dear,' said Mary Bityugov, sitting down by her side and taking her hand. 'It'll pass. Men are weak, like us sinful women. You're both weathering a crisis now, and it's all perfectly natural. Now, dear, I'm waiting for my answer. Let's talk.'

'No, let's not,' said Nadezhda, listening to Layevsky's sobs. 'I feel so miserable, let me go home.'

'How can you say such a thing, dear?' asked Mary Bityugov, horrorstruck. 'Can you think I'd let you go without supper? Let's eat, and you can be on your way then.'

'I feel so miserable,' whispered Nadezhda, gripping the arm of her chair with both hands to stop herself falling.

'He's thrown a fit!' Von Koren said gaily, coming into the drawing-room, but went out disconcerted on seeing Nadezhda.

When the attack was over, Layevsky sat on the strange bed.

'How scandalous,' he thought. 'Breaking down like a hysterical schoolgirl! How absurd and repulsive I must seem. I'll go out the back way—. But no—that would mean taking my hysterics too seriously. I should make a joke of it.'

He looked in the mirror and sat still for a while, then went back to the drawing-room.

'Well, here I am,' he said, smiling. But he suffered agonies of embarrassment, and felt that his presence embarrassed others too.

'These things happen,' he said, taking a seat. 'I'm just sitting here, when suddenly, you know, I feel this ghastly stabbing pain in my side —quite insufferable. My nerves can't cope and, er, play me this idiotic trick. It's a nervous age, this, you can't get away from it.'

At supper he drank wine, talked and occasionally rubbed his side, wincing as if to show that it still hurt. No one was impressed except Nadezhda, he saw.

At about half past nine they went for a stroll on the boulevard. Fearing that Kirilin might accost her, Nadezhda tried to keep close to Mary Bityugov and the children. Faint with fear and misery, she could feel a chill coming on. Her heart sank, and she could scarcely drag one foot after the other, but she did not go home, feeling sure that Kirilin or Achmianov—or both—would follow her. Kirilin was walking behind with Nicodemus Bityugov.

'No one is permitted to take liberties with me!' Kirilin was chanting in an undertone. 'I will not allow it!'

From the boulevard they turned towards the Pavilion and set off along the beach, gazing for some time at the phosphorescent glow on the sea. Von Koren began to explain the cause of the phosphorescence.

XIV

'It's time for bridge, though—I'm keeping them waiting,' said Layevsky. 'Good night, all.'

'Wait, I'll come with you,' said Nadezhda, taking his arm.

They bade farewell to the company and walked on. Kirilin took his leave also, remarking that he was going their way, and set off with them.

'So be it. I don't care,' thought Nadezhda. 'Let it happen.'

She felt as if all her bad memories had left her head and were marching by her side, breathing heavily in the darkness. Meanwhile she, like a fly fallen in an ink-pot, could barely crawl along the road, and was smudging Layevsky's side and arm with black.

If Kirilin did something awful, she thought, it would be all her fault, not his. Why, there had once been a time when no man ever spoke to her like Kirilin, and it was she who had ended that time—snapping it off like a thread and obliterating it utterly. And whose fault was that? Bemused by her own desires, she had taken to smiling at a total stranger—just because he was tall and well-built, very likely. After two meetings she had grown tired of him and dropped him, which surely meant that he had the right to treat her as he pleased—or so she now thought.

'I'll leave you here, old girl,' Layevsky remarked, stopping. 'Kirilin will take you home.'

He bowed to Kirilin and hurried over the boulevard, then crossed the street to Sheshkovsky's house, where the lights were burning, after which he was heard banging the garden gate behind him.

'I want an explanation, if you don't mind,' began Kirilin. 'Not being a boy or one of these Achmi-whatever-it-ises or other young popinjays, I insist on being treated seriously.'

Nadezhda's heart pounded. She made no answer.

'The abrupt change in your attitude to me—I was at first inclined to put it down to flirtatiousness,' went on Kirilin. 'But I now see that you simply don't know how to treat respectable people. You just wanted a bit of sport with me—I might be that Armenian brat. But I am a respectable man and I demand to be treated as such. So I am at your service, madam——'

'Oh, I'm so miserable.' Nadezhda started to cry, turning away to hide her tears.

'Well, I'm miserable too. What of it?'

Kirilin paused for a while, then spoke again.

'I repeat, madam,' he said, distinctly and deliberately. 'If you won't grant me an assignation now, I shall make a scene this very night.'

'Let me off tonight,' Nadezhda said, not recognizing her own voice —so piteously faint was it.

'I must teach you a lesson. I'm sorry to be so blunt, but a lesson I must teach you. Yes, madam, a lesson you must, unfortunately, be taught. I require two meetings—tonight and tomorrow. On the day after that you'll be quite free to go where the blazes you like with whom you like. Tonight and tomorrow.'

Nadezhda went up to her gate and paused.

'Let me go,' she whispered, trembling from head to foot, and seeing nothing in the darkness before her but the man's white tunic. 'You're quite right, I *am* a terrible woman and it *is* all my fault, but let me go— please.' She touched his cold hand and shuddered. 'I beg you——'

'Unhappily, however,' Kirilin sighed, 'I do not propose to let you go. I wish to teach you a lesson, that's all—make you understand. Besides, my faith in women is none too great, madam.'

'I feel so miserable.'

Nadezhda listened to the sea's even booming, glanced up at the star-spangled sky and wanted to make a quick end of it all—rid herself of this damned feel of living with all its seas, stars, men and fevers.

'Not in my house, though,' she said coldly. 'Take me somewhere else.'

'Let's go to Myuridov's then—what could be better?'

'Where's that?'

'Near the old town wall.'

She set off quickly along the street, then turned up a lane leading to the mountains. It was dark. Here and there on the road were pale, bright streaks from the lighted windows, and she felt like a fly which keeps falling in an ink-well, then crawling out again into the light. Kirilin walked behind her. Stumbling at one point, he nearly lost his footing and laughed.

'He's drunk,' Nadezhda thought. 'But what do I care, anyway? So be it.'

Achmianov had also taken a hurried farewell of the company, and had followed Nadezhda to ask her to come boating. Approaching her house, he looked over the garden fence—her windows were wide open and there were no lights.

'Nadezhda Fyodorovna!' he called.

A minute passed. He called again.

'Who's there?' It was Olga's voice.

'Nadezhda Fyodorovna in?'

'No, she's not back yet.'

'Now, that's most strange,' thought Achmianov, beginning to feel very anxious. 'She was coming home when she left.'

He strolled along the boulevard and the street—and then looked into Sheshkovsky's windows. Layevsky had removed his frock-coat, and sat at the table staring at his cards.

'Odd, odd,' Achmianov mumbled—then recalled Layevsky's hysterical fit and felt embarrassed. 'If she's not at home, then where is she?'

He went back to Nadezhda's house and looked at the dark windows.

'There's something underhand about this,' he thought—remembering that she had met him at noon that day at the Bityugovs', and had promised to go boating with him that night.

The windows in Kirilin's dwelling were dark, and a slumbering police constable sat on a bench by the gate. When Achmianov saw windows and policeman, everything became clear. Resolving to go home, he moved off—but then found himself near Nadezhda's house again. He sat on a bench there, and took off his hat—his head afire, it seemed, with jealousy and humiliation.

The local church clock struck only twice in every twenty-four hours—at noon and midnight. Soon after it had tolled midnight, hurried footsteps were heard.

'So we'll meet at Myuridov's again tomorrow night,' Achmianov, heard—and knew Kirilin's voice. 'Eight o'clock. See you then, madam.'

Nadezhda appeared near the garden fence. Not noticing Achmianov on the bench, she flitted past him, opened the gate and went indoors, leaving it ajar. She lit the candle in her room and quickly undressed. But instead of lying on the bed, she sank on her knees in front of a chair, put her arms round it and leant her forehead against it.

At about half past two Layevsky came home.

XV

Having decided to tell his lies by instalments, not at one fell swoop, Layevsky went to see Samoylenko at about half past one on the following afternoon to ask for the money so that he could leave on Saturday without fail. Yesterday's hysterical breakdown had added a further twinge of humiliation to his existing dispiritedness, and there was no question of him staying on in town. Should Samoylenko insist on his conditions, Layevsky could accept them, and take the money, he considered. Then, on the morrow, just as he was about to leave, he would say that Nadezhda had refused to go with him—all in her own best interests, as he could start persuading her that evening. But if Samoylenko—obviously under Von Koren's thumb—should refuse the money outright, or pose new conditions . . . then he, Layevsky, would leave that very day by cargo steamer, or even by sailing boat, for New Athos or Novorossisk, whence he would send his mother an abject telegram, and where he would stay until she remitted his travelling expenses.

Calling on Samoylenko, he found Von Koren in the drawing-room. The zoologist had just come for his lunch, had opened the album as was his wont, and was scrutinizing the top-hatted men and mob-capped ladies.

'How awkward,' thought Layevsky when he saw him. 'He might interfere.'

He wished Von Koren good day.

'Good day,' replied Von Koren, not looking at him.

'Is Samoylenko in?'

'Yes, he's in the kitchen.'

Layevsky made for the kitchen, but seeing Samoylenko through the door preparing salad, came back into the drawing-room and sat down. He always felt uneasy with the zoologist, and now feared having to discuss his hysterical seizure. Over a minute passed in silence, then Von Koren suddenly looked up at him.

'How do you feel after yesterday's occurrence?' he asked.

'Fine,' Layevsky replied with a blush. 'Actually, you know, it was nothing particular——'

'Before yesterday I had assumed that only ladies suffered from hysterics, so my first impression was that you had St. Vitus's dance.'

Layevsky smiled a sickly smile.

'How tactless of him,' he thought, 'because he knows very well I'm feeling rotten.'

'Funny business, that,' he said, still smiling. 'I was laughing all this morning. It's a curious thing about hysterics—you know how silly it all is at the time, you're laughing at it deep down inside you, yet you can't stop crying. We're all the slaves of our nerves in this neurotic age. They're our masters, they treat us as they like—which is one filthy trick civilization has played us!'

Layevsky was irked to find Von Koren listening seriously and attentively to his words with an unwinking stare as if studying a specimen. Layevsky was also vexed with himself because he was quite unable, much as he disliked Von Koren, to wipe that sickly smile off his face.

'But there were, I must also confess,' he went on, 'more immediate reasons for the attack—reasons which cut pretty deep. My health has cracked up rather badly of late. Then there's boredom, being so hard up all the time, having no one to talk to and nothing in common with anyone. I'm in a pretty ghastly pickle.'

'Yes,' Von Koren said. 'Your situation is quite hopeless.'

Layevsky found these calm, cold words insulting—containing as they did something between a gibe and a gratuitous piece of fortune-telling. Remembering the zoologist's sneering, disgusted glance of the previous day, he was silent for a moment. He was no longer smiling.

'And where,' he asked, 'did you learn about my situation?'

'You've just been airing it yourself. Anyway, your friends take such a burning interest in you—one hears of nothing else all day long.'

'Which friends? Samoylenko?'

'Yes, he's one of them.'

'I should be grateful if Alexander Samoylenko and my other friends would concern themselves a little less with my affairs.'

'Here comes Samoylenko. Why not tell him yourself all about how grateful you'd be if he would concern himself a little less with your affairs?'

'I don't like your tone,' muttered Layevsky, as if struck by the sudden realization that the zoologist hated him, despised him and was jeering at him—that the zoologist was his worst, his most implacable enemy.

'Keep that tone for someone else,' he said softly, rendered too weak to speak aloud by the loathing which now constricted his chest and neck, as had his urge to laugh on the previous day.

Samoylenko came in—coatless, sweaty, crimson from the kitchen heat.

'Ah, so it's you,' he said. 'Hallo, old man. Had lunch? Now, don't beat about the bush, tell me if you've lunched.'

'Samoylenko,' said Layevsky, standing up, 'if I happened to approach you with a certain intimate request, that doesn't mean I have relieved you of the obligation to be discreet and respect another's privacy.'

Samoylenko was dumbfounded. 'What's all this?'

'If you're out of funds,' Layevsky went on, raising his voice and excitedly shifting from foot to foot, 'then don't give me a loan, turn me down. But don't make such a song and dance about my situation being hopeless and so on. I can't abide these kindnesses and friendly favours from those who promise you everything and give you practically nothing. You can boast of your good deeds till you're blue in the face, but no one gave you the right to disclose my secrets.'

'What secrets?' asked Samoylenko, puzzled and growing annoyed. 'If you came here for a slanging match, go away again and come back later.'

He remembered the rule of mentally counting a hundred as a means of calming oneself when angry. So he quickly began counting.

'I beg you not to concern yourself with me, sir,' Layevsky went on. 'Pay me no attention. Whose business is it who I am? How I live? True, I want to leave this place. True, I run up debts. I drink. I live with another man's wife. I have hysterics. I'm cheap, I'm less profound than certain persons. But whose business is that? Respect privacy!'

'I'm sorry, old chap,' said Samoylenko, who had now counted to thirty-five. 'But——'

'Respect privacy!' Layevsky broke in. 'This endless running down of other people, all this oohing and ahing, this constant checking up and eavesdropping, and these displays of friendly sympathy—to blazes with them! They offer me a loan and impose conditions! Do they take me for a child? They treat me like God knows what. I don't need a thing!' shouted Layevsky, now reeling with agitation and fearing another bout of hysterics.

*Now he couldn't leave on Saturday, the thought flashed through his mind.

'I don't need a thing,' he went on. 'I only ask you to spare me this tutelage. Being neither a minor nor a lunatic, I beg you to remove your surveillance.'

In came the deacon. Seeing Layevsky pale and waving his arms about while addressing these strange words to the portrait of Prince Vorontsov, he stood near the door as if transfixed.

'These constant probings of my psyche—they insult my dignity as a human being,' Layevsky went on. 'And I must ask these self-appointed snoopers to stop spying on me. Cut it out!'

'What, er, what was that, sir?' Samoylenko asked. Having now reached a hundred, he was growing purple in the face. He went up to Layevsky.

'Cut it out!' Layevsky repeated, choking for breath and picking up his cap.

'I am a Russian gentleman,' Samoylenko enunciated. 'I am a doctor, and I hold the rank of colonel. I have never snooped, sir,' he shouted in a cracked voice, 'and I do not permit *insults*! So you shut up!'

Never having seen the doctor look so grandiose, majestic, purple and awe-inspiring, the deacon clapped his hand over his mouth, ran into the hall and burst out laughing. Like a man in a dream, Layevsky saw Von Koren stand up, place his hands in his trouser pockets, and hold this pose as if awaiting further developments. The calmness of his posture struck Layevsky as impudent and insulting in the ultimate degree.

'Kindly take back your words!' shouted Samoylenko.

But Layevsky could no longer remember what those words had been.

'Leave me alone,' he answered. 'I want nothing. All I want is for you and your German-Jewish friends to leave me in peace. Otherwise I shall take steps. I shall fight, sir!'

'Now we're beginning to understand,' said Von Koren, emerging from the table. 'Mr. Layevsky desires to indulge in a little duelling before he leaves. I can accommodate him. Sir, I accept your challenge.'

'Challenge?' Layevsky quietly articulated, going up to the zoologist and glaring at his dark forehead and curly hair with revulsion. 'Challenge? Very well. I detest and abominate you!'

'That's all right then. Early tomorrow morning, near Kerbalay's place. Suit yourself about the details, and now buzz off.'

'I hate you, I've hated you for ages,' panted Layevsky in a low voice. 'A duel? Certainly, sir.'

'Get him out of here, Samoylenko,' Von Koren said, 'or I'll have to go myself. He's liable to bite.'

Von Koren's calm tone soothed the doctor, who seemed to come to with a start, recovering his senses. Putting both arms round Layevsky's waist, he drew him away from the zoologist.

'My friends, my good, kind friends,' he muttered affectionately, in a voice vibrant with emotion. 'You've had a bit of a dust up, and that's that—quite enough in fact. My friends——'

Hearing the gentle, amiable voice, Layevsky sensed that something fantastic and grotesque had invaded his life—it was like being nearly run over by a train. He almost burst into tears, then made a gesture of resignation and ran out of the room.

'To feel someone hating you and to make such a wretched, despicable, abject exhibition of yourself in front of him—God, how awful!' Such were his thoughts as he sat in the Pavilion a little later, feeling as if the other man's detestation, so recently experienced, had covered his body with rust. 'Ye Gods, how crass!'

Cold water and cognac cheered him somewhat. He clearly pictured Von Koren's calm, supercilious face, his expression of the previous day, his rug-like shirt, his voice, his white hands. And a great hatred, intense and ravening, threshed inside his chest, craving an outlet. He imagined himself knocking Von Koren down and trampling him in the dust. He remembered everything, including the minutest details, astonished that he had found it in him to bestow that sickly smile on such a worm —astonished, too, that he had, on the whole, so prized the opinions of small fry and nonentities living in a rotten little town pretty well off the map . . . for no respectable person in St. Petersburg had so much as heard of it. If this miserable dump should suddenly sink into the earth or burn to the ground, people in central Russia would read the news as indifferently as the advertisement for a second-hand furniture sale. To kill Von Koren tomorrow or leave him alive—it was equally pointless and tedious either way. Better shoot him in the leg or arm, wound him, then laugh at him, and let him lose himself and his dumb anguish in a crowd of similar mediocrities, as an insect vanishes in the grass with its leg bitten off.

Layevsky went to Sheshkovsky, told him what had happened and asked him to be a second. Then both went to the local postmaster, asked him to act as second too, and stayed to lunch. Over the meal they joked and laughed a great deal. Layevsky made fun of himself for being practically incapable of shooting—calling himself a crack marksman and a William Tell.

'That character must be taught a lesson,' he said.

After lunch they sat down to cards. Layevsky played, drank wine and thought what a stupid, senseless thing duelling was, since it didn't settle a problem, only complicated it. Still, there were times when a duel was unavoidable. On the present occasion, for instance, one could hardly take Von Koren to court. The forthcoming duel also had the advantage that he, Layevsky, would be unable to stay on in town when it was over. Slightly drunk, he became absorbed in the card game and felt fine.

After sundown and the onset of darkness, however, anxiety overcame him. It was not fear of death, for while lunching and playing cards, he had somehow been firmly convinced that the duel would come to nothing. It was fear of the unknown—of some event new in his life which was to occur on the morrow, and a fear of the coming night.

That night would be long and sleepless, he knew, and he would find himself not only thinking of Von Koren and his hatred, but also about the mountain of lies over which he had to make his way, and which he lacked the strength and skill to avoid. It was as if he had been suddenly taken ill. He abruptly lost all interest in the cards and the company, fell to fidgeting and asked them to let him go home. He wanted to hurry off to bed and lie still, preparing his thoughts for the night. Sheshkovsky and the postmaster saw him home, then set off for Von Koren's to discuss the duel.

Near his quarters Layevsky met young Achmianov, out of breath and much agitated.

'I've been looking for you, Layevsky,' he said. 'Please come quickly——'

'Come where?'

'A certain gentleman wishes to see you. You do not know him, but he has very urgent business with you. He implores you to come for a minute. He has something to discuss—it's a matter of life and death to him.'

Achmianov brought all this out excitedly, in a strong Armenian accent, somehow making 'life' into a word of two syllables.

'Who is it?' asked Layevsky.

'He asked me not to give his name.'

'Tell him I'm busy. Tomorrow, if he likes——'

'That is impossible!' Achmianov was aghast. 'He have important thing to tell you, very important for you indeed. If you do not go a disaster will occur.'

'This is odd,' muttered Layevsky, not understanding why Achmianov should be so upset, or how such secrets could exist in this dreary, undesirable dump of a town.

'Odd,' he repeated thoughtfully. 'All right, come on then—I don't mind.'

Achmianov went briskly ahead, and Layevsky followed. They walked down the street, then took a lane.

'This is a bore,' Layevsky said.

'We shan't be long, it's quite near.'

Near the old town wall they took the narrow lane between two fenced waste plots, then entered a large yard and approached a small cottage.

'Myuridov's place, isn't it?' asked Layevsky.

'Yes.'

'Then why have we come round the back way, that's what I can't see? We could have taken the main road, it's nearer.'

'Never mind that.'

Layevsky was also perplexed because Achmianov was taking him to the back door, with a gesture which seemed to ask him to step quietly and make no noise.

'Come on, this way,' said Achmianov, opening the door cautiously and tip-toeing into the lobby. 'Quiet, please—they might hear.'

He pricked up his ears for a moment and drew a deep breath.

'Open that door and go in,' he whispered. 'Never fear.'

Bewildered, Layevsky opened the door and entered a low-ceilinged room with curtained windows and a candle on the table.

'Who do you want?' someone asked in the next room. 'Is that you, Myuridov, old man?'

Layevsky went in and saw Kirilin with Nadezhda by his side.

Not hearing what they said, he backed away and found himself in the street without knowing how he had got there. His hatred of Von Koren and his anxiety—all that had vanished from his mind. On his way home he swung his right arm awkwardly and looked carefully beneath his feet, trying to walk on level ground. Once back in his study he rubbed his hands, awkwardly twisting his shoulders and neck as if his coat and shirt were too tight, paced up and down the room—then lit a candle and sat at his desk.

XVI

'The humane studies of which you speak—they'll only satisfy man's mind when their path converges and runs parallel with that of the exact sciences. Whether these paths will meet under the microscope, in the soliloquies of a new Hamlet or in some new religion, I can't tell, but I do think a new ice age will cover the whole earth before it happens. Of all the humane studies the most stable and vital is, of course, Christ's teaching. But even that—look at the different interpretations it gives rise to! Some teach us to love our neighbours—but make exceptions of soldiers, criminals and lunatics. The first may legitimately be killed in war, the second may be isolated or executed, and the third are forbidden to marry. Other interpreters teach us to love all our neighbours without exception, without awarding plus and minus signs. If a consumptive, a murderer or epileptic seeks your daughter's hand, then let him marry her, say they. If cretins make war on the physically and mentally normal, then normal people should simply throw up the sponge. Should it come into force, this doctrine of love for love's sake—like art for art's sake—would end in mankind's total extinction . . . the most colossal crime in the world's history. There are masses of doctrines, in view of which no serious mind can be satisfied with any one of them, but hurries to add its individual gloss to the pile of others. So never base an issue on what you call philosophical or so-called Christian grounds, because that only takes you further from a solution.'

The deacon listened carefully to the zoologist's words and pondered.

'The moral law inherent in all men,' he said, '—is that a philosophers' invention? Or did God create it along with the body?'

'I can't say. But the law is common to all periods and ages—and to such an extent that we must recognize it as an organic part of man's nature, I think. No one invented it—it just is, and will be. I'm not saying we shall ever see it under the microscope, but its organic links are a matter of observation. Serious brain trouble—all the so-called mental diseases—find their chief expression in perversions of the moral law, so far as I know.'

'Very well. So the moral law wants us to love our neighbours in the same way as our stomach wants food, is that your meaning? But our nature, being self-centred, resists the voice of conscience and reason, thus creating many knotty problems. To whom then should we apply for a solution of such problems if you won't let us tackle them philosophically?'

'Apply such little exact knowledge as we possess. Trust plain evidence and the logic of facts. They aren't much to go on, I know, but at least they're less flimsy and nebulous than philosophy. The natural law requires you to love people, say. Now then, love must consist in removing everything which in any way injures people or menaces their present and future. Knowledge and common sense tell us that the morally and physically abnormal constitute a menace to mankind. If so, then you must wage war on these freaks. If you can't raise them to the norm, you at least have the strength and skill to neutralize them— exterminate them, in other words.'

'So love is the victory of the strong over the weak?'

'It most certainly is.'

'But dash it, the strong crucified our Lord Jesus Christ!' said the deacon heatedly.

'It was the weak who crucified Him, not the strong—that's the whole point! Civilization has whittled down the struggle for existence and natural selection—it seeks to eliminate them. Hence the rapid increase of the weak, hence their ascendancy over the strong. Suppose you managed to instil a rough and ready form of humane ideals into bees—where would that lead? The drones, who should be killed, would remain alive. They'd eat up the honey, they'd corrupt and smother the other bees, and the result would be the ascendancy of the weak over the strong, leading to the latter's extinction. That's what is happening to man now—the weak are crushing the strong. Among savages as yet untouched by culture, the stronger, the wiser, the morally superior man forges ahead. He is their chief and master. But we civilized people crucified Christ—we still are crucifying him. So we must lack something. That missing element we must restore, or else these misadventures will go on for ever.'

'But what criterion have you to distinguish strong from weak?'

'Knowledge and common sense. As the consumptive and the scrofulous are known by their symptoms, so are the immoral and insane by their acts.'

'But mistakes can happen, can't they?'

'Yes, but why worry about wet feet with a flood at your door?'

'That's philosophy,' laughed the deacon.

'Not a bit of it. You've been so ruined by philosophy of the theological college brand that you refuse to see anything but fog anywhere. Those abstract studies with which your young brain is crammed—the only reason they're called abstract is that they abstract your thoughts from what's staring you in the face. Look the devil straight in the eye. If he is the devil, say so—don't run off to Kant or Hegel for your explanations.'

The zoologist paused briefly.

'Twice two is four,' he went on. 'And a stone is a stone. Tomorrow we have this duel. We may call it stupid and inept, you and I, we may say the days of duelling are done, we may say there's no real difference between a gentleman's duel and a drunken brawl in an ale-house. Still, that won't stop us, we shall go and fight—which means that there is a force mightier than our deliberations. We scream about war being robbery, barbarism, horror, fratricide. We faint at the sight of blood. But let the French or Germans only insult us, and we at once feel elated, we raise a cheer from the very bottom of our hearts, and we pounce on the enemy. You invoke God's blessing on our arms, while our valour arouses universal—and heartfelt—enthusiasm. So it once again follows that there is a force which is at least stronger—even if no higher—than we and our philosophy. We can't bar its way any more than we can stop that cloud moving in from the sea. Now, don't you be hypocritical about that force, don't mutter defiance at it under your breath, and don't go on about how stupid, outmoded and anti-scriptural it is. You look it straight in the eye, recognizing its validity and rationality. And when, say, it wants to destroy some feeble, scrofulous, degenerate breed, don't try to stop it with your patent medicines and your quotations from the Gospels which you so ill understand. There's a high-minded character in Leskov called Daniel—in the name of love and Christ he feeds and warms a leper whom he's discovered near his town. But if this Daniel had really loved people, he'd have hauled that leper as far out of town as possible, thrown him in a ditch, and gone off to serve the healthy. The love which Christ commanded us is, I should hope, rational, intelligent and useful.'

'Oh, get away with you,' laughed the deacon. 'Why bring Christ in so often when you don't believe in Him?'

'But I do believe—in my own way, of course, not in yours. Oh, Deacon, Deacon,' laughed the zoologist, putting his arm round the deacon's waist. 'How about it?' he went on happily. 'Do we go duelling tomorrow?'

'My cloth does not permit me, or I'd come.'

'Cloth? What cloth?'

'I'm ordained, by God's grace.'

'Oh, Deacon, Deacon,' said Von Koren again, laughing. 'I do like talking to you.'

'You say you have faith,' said the deacon. 'But what kind of faith is it? Now, I have an uncle, an ordinary parish priest, and such is his faith that in time of drought he takes his umbrella and leather top-coat with him when he goes into the fields to pray for rain—to avoid being caught by the shower on the way home. There's faith for you. When he talks about Christ you can see a halo round his head, and all the peasants, men and women, weep torrents of tears. He could stop that cloud and put any of your "forces" to flight. Yes sir, faith moves mountains.'

The deacon laughed and clapped the zoologist on the shoulder.

'Yes indeed,' he went on. 'Here are you for ever teaching, plumbing the depths of the sea, dividing the weak from the strong, writing pamphlets and issuing challenges to duels. And you change nothing.

But one day some little old man may mumble one single word in the name of the Holy Ghost—or a new Mohammed will gallop up from Arabia brandishing his scimitar—and the whole bag of tricks will go up in smoke, and not one stone will be left on another in Europe, see?'

'Now, that's just a lot of hot air, Deacon.'

'Faith without deeds is dead, and deeds without faith are still worse—they're no more than a waste of time.'

The doctor appeared on the sea front. Seeing deacon and zoologist, he went up to them.

'It all seems to be fixed up,' he panted. 'Govorovsky and Boyko will be seconds. They'll come along at five a.m. I say, isn't it cloudy!' he went on, looking at the sky. 'Can't see a thing. We're in for a shower.'

'You'll come along too, I trust,' Von Koren added.

'God forbid. I'm absolutely done in, anyway. Ustimovich will go in my place, I've already had a word with him.'

Far over the sea lightning flashed and the hollow rumbling of thunder was heard.

'Stifling, isn't it, before a storm?' Von Koren said. 'I bet you've already been round to Layevsky's and wept on his shoulder.'

'Why should I?' answered the doctor, disconcerted. 'What nonsense!'

He had walked up and down the boulevard and street several times before sundown, hoping to meet Layevsky and feeling ashamed—both of his outburst and of its sequel, his sudden impulse of kind-heartedness. He wanted to make Layevsky a jocular apology, tell him off a bit, put his mind at rest, and say that duelling was a survival from medieval barbarism—but that this duel was a means of reconciliation devised by Providence itself. On the morrow these two most excellent, highly intelligent chaps would exchange shots, recognize each other's nobility of character and become friends. However, he had not run across Layevsky.

'Why should I go and see him?' Samoylenko repeated. 'I didn't insult him, it was he insulted me. But what made him jump on me like that, in heaven's name? What harm have I done him? I go into the drawing-room, and he suddenly flies off the handle and calls me a snooper. Tell me, what started him off? What did you say to him?'

'I told him his situation was hopeless, and I was right. It's only an honest man or a scoundrel who can extricate himself from any situation whatever. For someone who wants to be an honest scoundrel—

both things at the same time—there's no escape. Well, gentlemen, it's eleven o'clock, and we have to be up early in the morning.'

A sudden squall arose. It whipped up the dust of the sea-front in a whirl, and howled, drowning the sea's roar.

'A storm,' said the deacon. 'We must go, there's dust in my eyes.'

They moved off.

'This means no sleep for me tonight,' Samoylenko sighed, holding his cap.

'Don't take it so much to heart,' laughed the zoologist. 'You can rest easy, this will come to nothing. Layevsky will be generous and shoot into the air—what else can he do? And I shan't fire at all, obviously. To find myself in the dock, wasting my time on Layevsky's account— it's just not worth the powder and shot. And by the way, what is the penalty for duelling?'

'Arrest, and—should your opponent die—up to three years' imprisonment in a fortress.'

'In the Peter and Paul dungeons?'

'No—in a military fortress, I think.'

'I ought to teach that young cub a lesson, though.'

Lightning flashed on the sea behind them, briefly illuminating house roofs and mountains. Near the boulevard the friends parted. The doctor had vanished into the darkness, his steps already sounding faint, when Von Koren shouted after him. 'I hope the weather won't spoil things tomorrow.'

'I shouldn't be surprised. God grant it may.'

'Good night.'

'Eh? What do you say?'

The howling gale and thunder-claps made his voice barely audible.

'Never mind,' the zoologist shouted, and hurried off home.

XVII

. . . In my oppressed and anguished mind
Swarms of unhappy thoughts arise,
While silent memories unwind
Their endless scroll before my eyes.
Reading, appalled, my life's sad tale,
I tremble, curse the waste of days.
But naught my bitter tears avail
The gloomy record to erase.

                                        Pushkin

Tomorrow morning they might kill him. Or they might make a laughing-stock of him—let him live, in other words. In either case he was done for. That degraded female might commit suicide in her despair and shame, or she might drag out a miserable existence—in either case she too was finished.

Such were Layevsky's thoughts as he sat at his desk late that night, still rubbing his hands together. Suddenly his window banged open, the gale swept into the room, and papers flew from the desk. Layevsky closed the window and bent down to pick them off the floor. He felt a new physical sensation, an awkward feeling never experienced before, and his movements seemed alien to him. He walked timorously, thrusting his elbows to each side, twitching his shoulders, and when he sat down at the desk he started rubbing his hands again. His body had lost its suppleness.

On the brink of death one writes to one's dear ones, remembering which Layevsky took up his pen.

'Dear Mother,' he wrote in a shaky hand.

He wanted to urge his mother by the merciful God of her faith to shelter and welcome kindly the unhappy woman whom he had dishonoured—lonely, destitute and weak as she was. His mother should forget him. She should forgive all—atoning, at least in part, by her sacrifice for her son's grievous sin. But then he remembered his mother —a portly, massive old woman in her lace mob-cap—issuing into her garden from the house in the morning followed by her companion with a lap-dog. She had a way of hectoring gardener and servants, and her face was proudly supercilious—remembering which, he crossed out what he had written.

Bright lightning flashed in all three windows. Followed a deafening, pealing roll of thunder—at first dull, but then growling and crackling with such violence that the windows rattled. Layevsky stood up, went over to a window and laid his forehead against the pane. A mighty storm raged outside. It was superb. On the horizon sheet lightning flashed from clouds to sea in white ribbons, illuminating the high black waves far out. Lightning also flashed to right and left, and probably above the house too.

'Thunder, good old thunder,' whispered Layevsky, feeling an urge to pray to someone or something—if only to lightning or clouds.

When he was a boy, he remembered, a storm would send him rushing into the garden, his head uncovered, with two fair-haired, blue-eyed little girls pelting after him. Soaked by rain, they laughed in sheer ecstasy. But then a loud thunder-clap sent the girls huddling trustfully against the little boy, while he crossed himself and quickly recited a 'Holy, holy, holy'.

Where, oh where have you vanished, you intimations of splendid innocence? What sea has drowned you? No longer did he fear thunder. He disliked nature, he had no God. He and his fellows had long ago debauched all the trustful girls of his acquaintance, and not once in his life had he planted a tree in the garden of his home, or grown a single blade of grass. Never in all his born days had he rescued so much as a fly, he had dealt solely in destruction, ruin and lies, lies, lies.

'Is there anything in my past but sheer depravity?' he asked himself, trying to cling to some bright memory as one falling over a precipice may clutch at bushes.

What of his high school days? The university? All sham. He had studied badly, forgetting what he had been taught. What of his service to society? That was bogus too, for he had served without working— he had been paid a salary for doing nothing, his 'service' being only an odious form of embezzlement from public funds in a manner not liable to prosecution.

He had failed to cultivate integrity, having no need for it. His conscience, mesmerized by depravity and pretence, had slept or remained silent. Like some stranger or hireling—like one from another planet— he had shirked collective social life, caring nothing for the sufferings of others, nothing for their ideas and religions, nothing for what they knew, nothing for their quests and struggles. He had never uttered a single kind word, every line he had written was cheap and useless. He had not done a thing for his fellows but eat their bread, drink their wine, steal their wives and borrow their ideas, while seeking to justify his despicable, parasitical existence in the world's eyes and his own by passing himself off as a higher form of life. It was all lies, lies, lies.

He clearly remembered what he had seen at Myuridov's earlier that night, and the anguish of nauseated revulsion overwhelmed him. Foul as Kirilin and Achmianov were, they were only carrying on where he had left off, after all—they were his accomplices and pupils. A weak young woman, who had trusted him more than her own brother—he had taken her from her husband, her circle of friends and her homeland. He had carried her off to this sweltering, fever-ridden dump, and day after day she had inevitably come to mirror his own idleness, depravity and spuriousness, the whole of her feeble, listless, wretched existence being utterly abandoned to these things. Then he had wearied of her and come to hate her. But not having the guts to leave her, he had tried to enmesh her ever more tightly in the web of his lies.

Achmianov and Kirilin had completed the job.

Layevsky now sat at his desk, now moved to his window, sometimes putting out his candle, sometimes lighting it again. He cursed himself aloud, wept, lamented, begged forgiveness. Several times he rushed to the desk in his despair, and wrote: 'Dear Mother——'

His mother apart, he had no near and dear ones. But how could his mother help him? And where was she? He wanted to run to Nadezhda, fall down before her, kiss her hands and feet, beg her to forgive him. But she was his victim, and he feared her as if she were dead.

'My life is in ruins,' he muttered, rubbing his hands. 'Ye gods, why do I still go on?'

He had cast his own dim star from the skies and it had plummeted down, its trace lost in the mists of night. Never would it reappear in the heavens, for life is given only once—it never comes round a second time. Were it possible to relive past days and years, Layevsky would exchange his lies for truth, his idleness for industry, his boredom for joy, he would restore innocence to those whose innocence he had stolen, he would find God, discover righteousness. But these things were no more possible than putting that fallen star back in the sky, and the sheer hopelessness of it filled him with despair.

When the storm had blown over, he sat by the open window calmly surveying his future. Probably Von Koren would kill him. The man's clear, cold view-point permitted the liquidation of weaklings and good-for-nothings. And if his philosophy should waver at the last moment, there was always his hatred and disgust with Layevsky to help him out. But were Von Koren to miss, were he to mock his hated opponent by just wounding him, or shooting into the air—what then? Where could Layevsky go?

'To St. Petersburg?' he wondered. 'But that would mean resuming my old life which I so execrate. To seek redemption in changes of scenery, like a migrating bird—that means finding nothing because one part of the world's the same as any other to someone like that. Should I seek salvation in people? But with whom? How? Samoylenko's kindness and generosity are of no more avail than the deacon's ready laugh or Von Koren's hatred. Seek deliverance in yourself alone. If you can't find it, why waste your time? Kill yourself and have done with it.'

Day was breaking and a carriage whirred past, turned and stopped near the house, its wheels grating on wet sand. There were two people in it.

'I'll just be a moment,' Layevsky told them through the window.
'I wasn't asleep. Can it be time already?'

'Yes, it's four o'clock. By the time we arrive——'

Layevsky donned overcoat and cap, put cigarettes in his pocket and
paused for thought. There must be something else that needed doing,
he felt. His seconds were talking quietly in the street, the horses snorted.
In the damp of early morning, when everyone was still asleep and
barely a streak of light marked the sky, these sounds filled Layevsky's
heart with despondency akin to a premonition of evil. He stood for a
moment in thought, then went into the bedroom.

Nadezhda was stretched out in bed with a rug round her head. She
lay motionless, and her head in particular reminded him of an Egyptian
mummy. Looking at her without a word, Layevsky mentally implored
her to forgive him. If the heavens are not void, he thought, if there
really is a God up there, He will protect her. But if there is no God, she
may as well go to her doom, there's no point in her living.

She suddenly started and sat up in bed, lifting her pale face and
gazing horrorstruck at Layevsky.

'Is it you?' she said. 'Is the storm over?'

'Yes.'

Then memory returned and she put both hands on her head,
shuddering in every limb.

'I feel so awful,' she said. 'So awful, if you did but know.'

'I thought you'd kill me,' she went on, frowning, 'or throw me out
in the rain and storm. But you don't do anything, you just——'

On an impulse he clutched her tightly to him, covering her knees and
hands with kisses. Then, when she muttered something, shuddering at
her memories, he stroked her hair, gazing into her face—and knew
that this unhappy, immoral woman was the one person in his life. She
was near to him, dear to him. She was the only one.

He left the house and took his seat in the carriage. Now he wanted
to come home alive.

XVIII

The deacon rose, dressed, took his thick, knobbly walking-stick and
went quietly out of doors. It was so dark that during the first few
minutes of his walk along the street he could not even see the white
stick. No star shone in the sky, and it looked like rain again. There was
a smell of wet sand and sea.

'Let's hope there won't be a Chechen raid,' thought the deacon, listening to the thump of his stick on the road and to the resonance of that lonely sound in the silent darkness.

After leaving town, he found that he could see his path and his stick. Blurred patches appeared here and there in the black sky, and soon a single star peeped out and timidly winked. The deacon was walking along a high, rocky cliff from which he could not see the sea drowsing below as its unseen waves broke, lazily ponderous—and with sighs, as it seemed—on the beach. How slow they were. After one wave had broken, the deacon counted eight paces before the next. Then came a third, six paces later. It must have been just like this when God floated over chaos—no visibility, the lazy, sleepy sound of the sea in the darkness, a sense of time immemorially remote and unimaginable.

The deacon felt uneasy, believing that God might punish him for consorting with unbelievers, and even going to watch them fight a duel. The duel would be a trivial, bloodless, farcical affair. Still, it was a pagan spectacle all the same, and for it to be graced by a member of the clergy was quite unseemly. He stopped and thought of going back, but a powerful, restless curiosity overcame his doubts and he went on.

'Unbelievers they may be, but they're good people, and they'll be saved,' he consoled himself.

'They'll definitely be saved,' he said aloud, lighting a cigarette.

By what standard should one measure people's virtues? How does one assess them rightly? The deacon remembered his old enemy, the inspector at his old school—an institution for clergy's sons—a believer in God, no duellist, and a man of chaste life, but one who had fed the deacon on bread mixed with sand, and had once come near to pulling his ear off. If human life had assumed so foolish a shape that this cruel, dishonest inspector, this stealer of government-issue flour, enjoyed general respect, while prayers were said at school for his health and salvation—could it really be right to shun men like Von Koren and Layevsky solely because they were unbelievers? The deacon tried to resolve this question, but then remembered how funny Samoylenko had looked on the previous day—which broke his flow of thought. What a good laugh they would have later in the day! The deacon pictured himself hiding under a bush and watching. Then, at lunch, when Von Koren started boasting, he, the deacon, would laugh and tell him every detail of the duel.

'How can you know all that?' the zoologist would inquire.

'Well may you ask. I stayed at home, but I know all the same.'

It would be nice to do a comic description of the duel. It would amuse his father-in-law, who was ready to forgo food and drink so long as someone told or wrote him funny stories.

Yellow Brook Valley opened up ahead. The rain had made the stream wider and angrier—it no longer grumbled, as before, but roared. Dawn began to break—a dull, grey morning with clouds scurrying westwards in the wake of the thunderheads, mountains ringed with mist, damp trees, all seeming ugly and bad-tempered to the deacon. He washed in the stream, said his morning prayers, and longed for tea and hot rolls with sour cream, the regular breakfast at his father-in-law's. He thought of his wife, remembered her playing Gone Beyond Recall on the piano. What sort of woman was she? The deacon had been introduced, engaged and married to her all in one week, and he had lived with her less than a month before being transferred to his present post, so that he had not yet discovered what she was like. He did rather miss her, though.

'Must write her a long letter,' he thought.

The flag on the inn was rain-soaked and hung limp, while the inn itself looked darker and lower than before with its wet roof. Near the door stood a native cart. Kerbalay, a couple of Abkhazians and a Tatar girl in baggy trousers—she must be Kerbalay's wife or daughter—were carrying full sacks out of the inn and packing them on maize straw in the cart. Near the cart stood a pair of donkeys with lowered heads. After loading the sacks, the Abkhazians and the Tatar girl began putting straw on top, and Kerbalay hurried to harness the donkeys to the cart.

'Smuggling, perhaps,' thought the deacon.

Now he came to the fallen tree with its dry needles, and over there was the black patch from the bonfire. He remembered the picnic in every detail—the fire, the Abkhazians singing, his sweet dreams about being a bishop and about the church procession.

The rain had made Black Brook blacker and broader. The deacon circumspectly crossed by the rickety bridge, now lapped by dirty wave-crests, and climbed the ladder into the drying-barn.

'He has a good head on his shoulders,' he thought, stretching out on the straw and thinking of Von Koren. 'A fine brain, that—and best of luck to him! But there is this cruelty about him——'

Why did Von Koren hate Layevsky? Why did Layevsky hate Von Koren? Why were they fighting this duel? Unlike the deacon, they had not suffered dire penury from their earliest years. Nor had they been brought up by a lot of thick-skinned, money-grubbing oafs who grudged them every mouthful of food—rough-mannered louts who spat on the floor and belched after dinner or during prayers. They had been spoilt from boyhood onwards by living among an élite in a good environment. Had this been otherwise, how they would now cleave to each other! How gladly they would forgive each other's faults and prize each other's good qualities! Why, there are so few people in this world who even have decent manners! Layevsky was mischievous, dissolute, eccentric—true. But at least he wouldn't steal, spit loudly on the floor or curse his wife. ('Guzzles her food, but not a hand's turn will she do!') He wouldn't whip a child with harness reins, or feed his servants putrid salt beef. Surely these things entitled him to some consideration? Moreover, was he not himself his own worst enemy? Did he not suffer—as an injured man suffers from his wounds? Instead of such people giving way to boredom and mistakenly inspecting each other for signs of degeneracy, decline and bad breeding, which made precious little sense, would they not do better to stoop lower? Why not vent their hatred and anger on whole streets where the welkin groans with barbarism, ignorance, greed, quarrels, filth, foul oaths and women's screams?

The deacon's thoughts were interrupted by the clatter of a carriage. Peeping through the door, he saw three men in the vehicle—Layevsky, Sheshkovsky and the postmaster.

'Halt!' said Sheshkovsky.

All three climbed down and looked at each other.

'They're not here yet,' Sheshkovsky said, shaking off the dust. Ah, well. Let's look for a site while we're waiting for proceedings to begin. There's no room to move here.'

They went off up-stream and soon vanished from view. The Tatar coachman climbed inside the carriage, laid his head on his shoulder and fell asleep. The deacon waited ten minutes, then came out of the barn, removing his black hat to make himself inconspicuous. Crouching and looking around him, he threaded his way along the bank among bushes and strips of maize while heavy drops fell on him from trees and bushes. Grass and maize were wet.

'Scandalous,' he muttered, gathering up his wet, muddy skirts. 'I'd never have come if I'd known.'

Soon he heard voices and saw people. Layevsky had his hands inside his sleeves, and was rapidly pacing back and forth in a small clearing, his head bowed. Near the bank stood his seconds, rolling cigarettes.

'How odd,' the deacon thought, not recognizing Layevsky's walk. 'He looks positively senile.'

'Most discourteous of them,' said the postal official, glancing at his watch. 'These academics may think it good form to turn up late, but it's damn bad manners if you ask me.'

Sheshkovsky, a fat man with a black beard, pricked up his ears. 'Here they are.'

XIX

'I've never seen anything like it—how fabulous!' said Von Koren, appearing in the glade and holding out both hands to the east. 'Look—green light!'

In the east two green beams stretched from the mountains, and beautiful they indeed were. The sun was rising.

'Good day,' the zoologist continued, nodding to Layevsky's seconds. 'I trust I'm not late?'

He was followed by his own seconds, Boyko and Govorovsky—two very young officers of identical height in white tunics—and the gaunt, unsociable Dr. Ustimovich who carried a bag in one hand and had the other behind him. He held his cane behind his back as usual. Putting his bag on the ground without a word of greeting, he placed his other hand behind his back as well and took to pacing the clearing.

Layevsky felt the weariness and awkwardness of one who might be just about to die, and was therefore the object of general attention. He wanted them to get the killing over quickly or take him home.

This was the first time he had ever seen the sun rise. The early morning, the green rays, the damp, the men in their wet riding-boots—he found it all a bit too much. What good were these things to him? They only hampered him, and none of them had any bearing on his experiences of the night before—on his thoughts, his feeling of guilt—and so he would have been glad to leave without waiting for the duel.

Visibly nervous but trying to hide it, Von Koren pretended to be absorbed in the green sunbeams. The seconds were embarrassed, and exchanged glances as if to ask why they were there and what they were to do.

'I don't think we need proceed further, gentlemen,' said Sheshkovsky. 'This will do.'

'Yes, of course,' Von Koren agreed.

Silence ensued. Ustimovich suddenly turned in his tracks.

'I don't suppose they've had time to inform you of my terms,' he told Layevsky in an undertone, breathing into his face. 'Each side pays me fifteen roubles. Should one of the parties die, the survivor pays the whole thirty.'

Layevsky had met him before, but only now did he first clearly discern the man's dull eyes, bristling whiskers and gaunt, wasted neck. This was no doctor—a usurer, more like! His breath smelt unpleasantly of beef.

'It takes all sorts to make a world,' thought Layevsky.

'All right then,' he replied.

The doctor nodded and strode off again.

He didn't need the money at all, that was obvious—he had simply asked for it out of hatred.

Everyone felt that it was now time to start, or to end what had already been started, but they did neither—they only walked about or stood and smoked. As for the young officers, it was their first duel, and by now they had little faith in a civilian encounter for which there was no necessity in their view. They carefully scrutinized their tunics and smoothed down their sleeves.

'Gentlemen,' said Sheshkovsky, going up to them and speaking softly. 'We must do our best to stop this duel. We must reconcile them.'

'Kirilin came to see me last night,' he went on, blushing. 'He complained that Layevsky found him with Nadezhda Fyodorovna last night, and all that.'

'Yes, we'd heard,' said Boyko.

'Now, look here—Layevsky's hands are shaking and all that. He's in no state to pick up his pistol, even. To fight him would be like fighting a drunk or someone with typhus—sheer inhumanity. If they won't be reconciled, gentlemen, we'd better postpone the duel, hadn't we? This is crazy, I feel terrible about it.'

'Then speak to Von Koren.'

'I don't know the rules of duelling, damn it, and I don't want to know them. He might think Layevsky sent me over because he has the wind up. Oh, let him think what he likes, I'll see him anyway.'

Hesitantly and limping slightly as if from leg cramp, Sheshkovsky approached Von Koren, the very picture of indolence as he walked over, clearing his throat.

'A word with you, sir,' he began, studying the flowers on the zoologist's shirt. 'This is confidential. I don't know the rules of duelling, blast it, and I don't want to know them. I'm not talking as a second and all that, but as a man and so on.'

'Yes? Well?'

'When seconds propose reconciliation, they're not usually listened to because it's thought a formality. Just their conceit and so on. But you look at Ivan Layevsky, I most humbly beg you. He's not normal today, he's not himself, so to speak—he's in a pathetic state. He's had a terrible experience. I can't stand scandal,'—Sheshkovsky blushed and looked round—'but in view of this duel I find it necessary to tell you this. Last night he found his lady friend at Myuridov's place with, er, a certain person.'

'Ugh, sickening!' muttered the zoologist. He blenched, frowned and spat noisily.

His lower lip quivered. He moved away from Sheshkovsky, not wishing to hear more, and again spat noisily as if he had accidentally tasted something bitter. With loathing he now looked at Layevsky for the first time that morning. His nervousness and awkwardness had passed, and he tossed his head.

'But what are we waiting for, gentlemen, that's the question?' he said in a loud voice. 'Why don't we get on with it?'

Sheshkovsky exchanged glances with the officers, and shrugged his shoulders.

'Gentlemen,' he shouted, not addressing anyone in particular. 'Gentlemen, we call on you to compose your differences.'

'Let's hurry up and get the formalities over,' said Von Koren. 'Reconciliation has already been discussed. Now, what's the next procedure? Quickly, gentlemen, we've no time to waste.'

'Nevertheless, we still insist you make it up,' said Sheshkovsky in the guilty tone of one obliged to meddle in others' business.

'Gentlemen,' he continued, blushing and putting his hand against his heart, 'we fail to see any causal connection between insult and duel. Affronts, such as we sometimes offer one another through human frailty—they have nothing to do with duelling. You've been to university, you're educated men, and you yourselves naturally see nothing in a duel but outmoded empty ritual, and all that. Such must be our view, or we shouldn't have come here, for we can't permit people to shoot each other in our presence, and so on.'

Sheshkovsky mopped the sweat off his face. 'So compose your differences, sirs,' he went on. 'Shake hands, and let's go home for a friendly drink—honestly, gentlemen.'

Von Koren said nothing. Seeing people looking at him, Layevsky spoke.

'I have nothing against Nicholas Von Koren,' he said. 'If he finds me to blame, I'm ready to apologize.'

Von Koren was offended.

'Obviously, gentlemen,' said he, 'it suits you to have Mr. Layevsky ride home as a paragon of knightly chivalry, but I can't give you and him that satisfaction. Nor was there any need to get up early and drive six miles out of town just to drink and be friends, have a bite to eat and explain to me about duels being outmoded ritual. Duels are duels. And there's no need to make them more of a silly farce than they already are. I wish to fight.'

Silence followed. Boyko took the two pistols out of the case. One was given to Von Koren and the other to Layevsky, but then a hitch occurred, affording zoologist and seconds some passing amusement. It transpired that none of those present had ever attended a duel in his life, and no one knew exactly how they should stand, or what the seconds should say and do. Then Boyko remembered, and began to explain with a smile.

'Any of you remember Lermontov's description?' Von Koren asked with a laugh. 'Turgenev's Bazarov also exchanged shots with someone or other——'

'Why go into all that?' Ustimovich asked impatiently, halting in his tracks. 'Measure off your distance, that's all.'

And he took three steps, as if to show how measuring is done. Boyko counted out the paces, while his comrade unsheathed his sabre and scratched the ground at each end to mark the barrier.

The adversaries took their places amid general silence.

'Those moles!' remembered the deacon where he sat in the bushes.

Sheshkovsky made some remark, and Boyko gave some further explanation, but Layevsky did not hear. More probably he heard, but did not understand. When the time came, he cocked the cold, heavy pistol and raised it barrel upwards. He had forgotten to unbutton his overcoat, and felt tightly constricted about shoulder and armpit, while he raised his arm as awkwardly as if his sleeve was made of metal. He remembered how he had hated that swarthy forehead and curly hair on the previous day, and realized that even then, at the climax of his hatred and rage, he could never have shot a man. Afraid of his bullet somehow hitting Von Koren by accident, he kept raising the pistol higher and higher, feeling that this display of excessive magnanimity was tactless—and anything but magnanimous—yet physically and morally incapable of acting otherwise. Looking at the pale, sneering, smiling face of Von Koren—obviously certain from the start that his adversary would fire into the air—Layevsky thought that it would all be over any moment now, thank God, and that he only had to squeeze the trigger hard.

He felt a heavy jolt against his shoulder, the shot rang out, and the echo from the mountains replied with a double thud.

Von Koren cocked his pistol and looked towards Ustimovich—still pacing up and down with his hands behind his back and ignoring the proceedings.

'Doctor,' said the zoologist, 'would you mind not walking up and down like that, you're putting me off.'

The doctor stood still, and Von Koren began to take aim at Layevsky.

'It's all over now,' Layevsky thought.

The pistol barrel levelled straight at Layevsky's face, Von Koren's posture, his whole figure so expressive of hatred and contempt, this decent man about to commit daylight murder in front of other decent men, the hush, the strange force which made Layevsky hold his ground and stopped him running away—how mysterious, incomprehensible and terrible it all was! Von Koren seemed to take so long aiming— longer than an entire night, Layevsky felt. He glanced imploringly at the seconds. They did not move, and were pale.

'Oh, hurry up and shoot,' thought Layevsky, sensing that his white, trembling, pathetic face must make Von Koren hate him even more.

'I'll kill him now,' thought Von Koren, aiming at the forehead, and already fingering the trigger. 'Yes, of course I will.'

'He'll kill him!'

The despairing cry was suddenly heard somewhere quite near.

And then the shot rang out.

Seeing Layevsky stand his ground, still upright, everyone looked towards the cry—and saw the deacon. Pale, his wet hair plastered over brow and cheeks, thoroughly soaked and muddy, he stood in the maize on the far bank, smiling strangely and waving his wet hat. Sheshkovsky laughed with joy, burst into tears and withdrew to one side.

XX

A little later Von Koren and the deacon met near the bridge. The deacon was upset, breathing heavily and avoiding people's eyes. He was ashamed of his panic and his wet, muddy clothes.

'I thought you meant to kill him,' he muttered. 'How contrary to human nature! How very unnatural!'

'But where did you spring from?' the zoologist said.

'Don't ask me!' The deacon made a gesture of disgust. 'The foul fiend tempted me—lured me on and on. So on and on I went, and nearly died of fright in the maize. But now, thank God, thank God—. I'm very pleased with you,' muttered the deacon. 'And old Grandfather Tarantula will be pleased too. What a lark, I must say! Only don't tell anyone I was here, I beg you most urgently, or else I may catch it in the neck from the authorities. They'll say a deacon acted as second.'

'Gentlemen,' said Von Koren. 'The deacon asks you not to tell anyone you saw him here. It could lead to unpleasantness.'

'How contrary to human nature,' sighed the deacon. 'Be generous, forgive me—but looking at your face I thought you definitely meant to kill him.'

'I did feel strongly tempted to do the swine in,' said Von Koren. 'But your shout put me off, and I missed. This whole procedure is repulsive if you're not used to it, I must say. It's tired me out, Deacon, I feel terribly exhausted. Let's drive home.'

'No, let me walk. I must dry out. I'm wet through and frozen.'

'All right, do as you like,' said the weary zoologist in a tired voice, climbing into his carriage and closing his eyes. 'Suit yourself.'

While they were coming and going near the carriages and taking their seats, Kerbalay stood by the road clutching his stomach with both hands, bowing low and showing his teeth. He thought the gentlemen had come out to enjoy the view and have tea—why they should be getting into their carriages, he could not think.

The convoy moved off amid general silence, leaving only the deacon near the inn.

'Me go inn. Me drink tea,' he told Kerbalay. 'Me want eat.'

Kerbalay spoke good Russian, but the deacon thought the Tatar would understand him more easily if he addressed him in pidgin.

'You make omelette, you bring cheese.'

'Come, come, priest,' said Kerbalay, bowing. 'I give you everything. Is cheese, is wine. Eat all you want.'

'What's the Tatar word for God?' asked the deacon, entering the inn.

'Your God and my God are same,' said Kerbalay, not understanding. 'God is same for all, only peoples is different. Is Russians, is Turks, is English, is many peoples, but God is one.'

'Very well, then—if all peoples worship one God, why do you Moslems look on Christians as your eternal enemies?'

'Why you angry?' asked Kerbalay, seizing his belly in both hands. 'You are priest—I am Moslem. You say you hungry—I give you food. Only rich men make difference which God is his and which mine. For poor man is no difference. Come and eat please.'

While this theological discussion proceeded in the inn, Layevsky was on his way home, remembering the eerie sensation of driving along at dawn when road, cliffs and mountains were wet and dark, and the future had loomed ahead unknown and terrifying as a bottomless pit. But now raindrops hung on grass and stones, glittering diamond-like in the sun, nature smiled happily and that terrifying future seemed a thing of the past. He glanced at Sheshkovsky's grim, tear-stained face, then looked ahead at the two carriages conveying Von Koren, his seconds and the doctor, and he felt as if they were all on their way home from a cemetery where they had just buried some abysmal bore who had made everyone's life a misery.

'It's all over,' he thought, with reference to his past, carefully stroking his neck with his fingers.

A small swelling about as long and as wide as his little finger had come up on the right of his neck near the collar, and it hurt as if someone had passed a hot iron over it. It was a weal made by the bullet.

Once arrived home, he found the long, strange, sweet day stretching out in front of him, vague as oblivion. As if released from prison or hospital, he gazed at objects long familiar, amazed that tables, windows, chairs, light and sea should evoke this vivid, childlike joy to which he had all too long been a stranger. Pale and wan, Nadezhda did not understand his tender voice, his strange walk. She hastened to tell him everything that had happened to her.

He must be unable to hear her properly or make her out, she felt— for if he knew all about it, he would curse her, kill her. But he listened, stroked her face and hair, looked into her eyes.

'I have no one but you,' he said.

Then they sat for a long time in the garden, clinging to each other in silence. Or they mused aloud about their happy future, speaking in short, broken sentences, and he felt as if he had never spoken at such length or so eloquently before.

XXI

Over three months had passed.

The day of Von Koren's scheduled departure broke. A cold, drenching rain set in at dawn, a north-easterly gale blew up, and the sea roughened. The steamer could hardly get into the roadstead in such weather, it was said. It should have arrived before ten in the morning according to the timetable, but going on to the beach at midday and in the afternoon, Von Koren saw nothing through his binoculars except grey waves and rain veiling the horizon.

By the end of the day it had stopped raining and the wind had dropped considerably. Now reconciled to the impossibility of leaving that day, Von Koren had settled down to a game of chess with Samoylenko, but after nightfall the orderly announced that lights had appeared out at sea, and a rocket had been seen.

Von Koren made haste. Throwing a knapsack over one shoulder, he kissed Samoylenko and the deacon, made a quite unnecessary tour of the house, said good-bye to orderly and cook—and went out of doors, feeling as if he had left something behind at the doctor's or in his own quarters. He walked down the street beside Samoylenko, with the deacon behind him carrying a chest, and the orderly bringing up the rear with two suitcases. Only Samoylenko and the deacon could discern the dim lights out at sea, the others stared unseeing into blackness. The steamer had anchored far from shore.

'Hurry up,' Von Koren urged. 'I'm afraid of missing it.'

As he passed the cottage—it had only three windows—into which Layevsky had moved soon after the duel, Von Koren could not resist glancing through the window. Layevsky sat hunched over a table with his back to the window, writing.

'Wonderful how he's pulled himself together,' said the zoologist quietly.

'Well may you wonder,' Samoylenko sighed. 'He stays like that from dawn to dusk, just sits there working. He wants to pay off his debts. And he lives in direst poverty, old boy.'

Half a minute passed in silence. Zoologist, doctor and deacon all stood at the window, watching Layevsky.

'So the poor chap never got away after all,' Samoylenko said. 'Remember the trouble he went to?'

'Yes, he really has pulled himself together,' Von Koren repeated. 'His marriage, this day-long grind to earn his living, that new look on his face, his walk, even—it's all so out of the ordinary, I don't know what name to give it.'

The zoologist took Samoylenko by the sleeve and continued in an unsteady voice. 'Do tell him and his wife that I left here admiring him and wishing him all the best—and ask him not to think too badly of me if possible. He knows me. He knows I might have been his best friend could I have foreseen this change.'

'Then go in and say good-bye yourself.'

'No, it would be too awkward.'

'Why? God knows, you'll never see him again, perhaps.'

The zoologist thought for a moment, 'That's true.'

Samoylenko tapped a finger on the window, and Layevsky looked round with a start.

'Nicholas Von Koren wants to bid you good-bye, Ivan,' said Samoylenko. 'He's just leaving.'

Layevsky stood up from the table, and went into the lobby to open the door. Samoylenko, Von Koren and the deacon entered the house.

'I only looked in for a moment,' began the zoologist, taking off his galoshes in the lobby and already regretting his sentimentality in calling here uninvited.

'I feel as if I'm butting in,' he thought. 'A stupid thing to do.'

'Excuse me disturbing you,' he said, following Layevsky into his room. 'But I'm just leaving and I felt I had to see you. God knows if we'll ever meet again.'

'Delighted. Do come in,' said Layevsky, placing chairs for his guests awkwardly as if trying to bar their way. He paused in the middle of the room, rubbing his hands.

'I wish I'd left the others in the street,' Von Koren thought.

'Don't think too badly of me, Layevsky,' he said in a steady voice. 'One can't forget the past, of course, for it was too lamentable, and I didn't come in here to apologize or tell you I wasn't to blame. I acted sincerely, nor have I changed my views in the meantime. Admittedly, I was wrong about you, as I'm now only too delighted to see. But even the most sure-footed of us can come an occasional cropper. And if you don't err in essentials, then you'll trip up over the details—it's only human nature. None of us knows the real truth.'

'Yes indeed, no one knows the truth,' said Layevsky.

'Well, good-bye. God speed and good luck.'

Von Koren held out his hand to Layevsky, who pressed it and bowed.

'No hard feelings, then,' said Von Koren. 'My regards to your wife, and tell her how sorry I was not to be able to say good-bye.'

'But she's at home.'

Layevsky went to the door and spoke into the next room.

'Nadezhda dear, Nicholas Von Koren wants to say good-bye.'

Nadezhda came in and stood by the door, timidly glancing at the guests. Her expression was guilty and fearful, and she held her arms like a schoolgirl under reprimand.

'I'm just leaving, Mrs. Layevsky,' said Von Koren. 'And I've come to say good-bye.'

She stretched out her hand timidly, and Layevsky bowed.

'How pathetic they both are, though,' Von Koren thought. 'This life is quite a struggle for them.'

'I shall be in Moscow and St. Petersburg,' he said. 'Is there anything I could send you?'

'Oh,' said Nadezhda, exchanging a worried glance with her husband. 'I don't think so.'

'No, it's all right,' Layevsky said, rubbing his hands. 'Give them our regards.'

Von Koren did not know what else he could or should say, though when entering the house he had supposed himself about to utter a great many edifying, cheering and significant statements. He shook hands with Layevsky and his wife in silence, and left, feeling downcast.

'What wonderful people,' said the deacon in a low voice, following behind. 'Dear God, what people. Verily the Lord's right hand hath planted this vine. Lord, Lord, one hath conquered thousands and another tens of thousands. Von Koren,' he went on solemnly, 'know that you have this day conquered man's greatest enemy—pride.'

'Oh, come off it, Deacon. What sort of conquerors are we, Layevsky and I? Conquerors look as if they were on top of the world, but he's pathetic, timid, down-trodden. He bobs up and down like one of those Chinese mandarin-dolls, and I—I feel sad.'

Steps were heard behind them—it was Layevsky running after them to see them off. At the quayside the orderly was standing with the two suitcases, and there were four ferrymen a little way off.

'I say, it isn't half blowing!' said Samoylenko. 'There must be a tidy storm out there at sea. Phew! What a time to leave, Nicholas!'

'I'm not afraid of being sea-sick.'

'That's not what I mean. I only hope these idiots don't capsize you. You should have taken the agent's dinghy. Where's the agent's dinghy?' he shouted to the ferrymen.

'It's already left, General.'

'And the customs boat?'

'She's gone too.'

'Then why didn't you tell me?' Samoylenko asked angrily. 'Imbeciles!'

'Don't let it upset you, anyway,' Von Koren said. 'Good-bye then, God preserve you.'

Samoylenko embraced Von Koren and made the sign of the cross over him three times.

'Now don't forget us, Nicholas. Be sure to write. We'll expect you next spring.'

'Good-bye, Deacon,' said Von Koren, shaking hands with the deacon. 'Thanks for your company and all the good talk. Think about the expedition.'

'Oh Lord yes—to the ends of the earth if you like,' laughed the deacon. 'I've nothing against it.'

Recognizing Layevsky in the darkness, Von Koren silently held out his hand. The ferrymen were already standing below, holding the boat as it made to crash into the breakwater, though protected from the real swell by the quay. Von Koren went down the ladder, jumped aboard and took the helm.

'Don't forget to write,' Samoylenko shouted after him. 'And look after yourself.'

'No one knows the real truth,' thought Layevsky, pulling up his overcoat collar and thrusting his hands into his sleeves.

Briskly rounding the quay, the boat emerged in the open sea. It vanished in the waves and then straightway swooped up from a deep pit to a high crest, so that men, and even oars, could be distinguished. For every six yards which the boat made, she was thrown back about four.

'Mind you write,' shouted Samoylenko. 'But what the hell possessed you to leave in such weather?'

'Yes, no one knows the real truth,' thought Layevsky, looking sadly at the rough, dark sea.

'The boat is thrown back,' he thought. 'She makes two paces forward and one back. But the rowers are persistent, they ply their oars untiringly, they aren't afraid of the high waves. The boat keeps advancing. Now it's out of sight, but in half an hour's time the rowers will see the steamer lights clearly, and within an hour they'll be along-side her ladder. Such is life.

'When seeking truth, people take two steps forward to one step back. Sufferings, mistakes and world-weariness throw them back, but passion for truth and stubborn will-power drive them onwards, ever onwards. And—who knows?—perhaps they will reach real truth in the end.'

'Good-bye,' shouted Samoylenko.

'Out of sight and out of hearing,' said the deacon. 'Happy journey!' It began to drizzle.

A HARD CASE

AT the edge of Mironositskoye village, in Prokofy's—the village elder's—barn, two men were bivouacking after a long day's hunting: Ivan Ivanovich, a veterinary surgeon, and Burkin, a grammar-school teacher.

The vet had a rather odd and quite unsuitable double-barrelled surname (Chimsha-Gimalaysky), but answered to plain Ivan Ivanovich in the neighbourhood. He lived at a suburban stud farm and had made this hunting trip just for the sake of an outing—whereas Burkin, the schoolmaster, was the regular summer guest of a local county family, being very much at home in these parts.

They were still awake. Ivan Ivanovich—a tall, thin old man with a long moustache—sat outside the doorway smoking his pipe in the moonlight, while Burkin lay inside on the hay, invisible in the gloom.

They talked about this and that, incidentally remarking that the elder's wife—a healthy, intelligent woman called Mavra—had never been outside her native village in her life, had never seen a town or railway, had spent the last ten years sitting over her stove, and would venture out of doors only at night.

'What's so odd about that?' asked Burkin.

These solitary types (Burkin continued), these snails, these hermit crabs who seek refuge inside their own shells ... there are plenty of them about. Perhaps such types represent throw-backs to an epoch when man's ancestors hadn't yet become social animals, but lived alone in their lairs. Or perhaps it's just a quirk of human nature. Who knows? I'm not a scientist myself, that sort of thing isn't my line. All I say is, the Mavras aren't all that rare. Well, you take an instance close at hand: someone who died in town a couple of months ago—one Belikov, classics master at my own school. You've heard of him of course. His great feat was to sport galoshes and an umbrella even on the finest days, and he always wore a warm, padded greatcoat. He kept his umbrella in a holder, his watch in a grey chamois-leather bag. When he took out a penknife to sharpen a pencil, that knife was also in a little holder. His face seemed to be encapsulated, too, because he kept it hidden behind an upturned collar. He wore dark glasses and a

pullover, he kept cotton wool in his ears, and when he took a cab he
always had the top put up. The man evinced, in short, a persistent
obsessive drive to envelop himself in a membrane, creating a sort of
carapace to isolate him and protect him from outside influences. The
real world irritated him, scared him, kept him permanently on edge. It
was to justify this nervousness, perhaps—this abhorrence of the
actual—that he always praised things past, things which have never
existed. The ancient languages which he taught were, in effect, the
same old galoshes and umbrella in another form: his refuge from real
life.

'The Greek language . . . oh, how melodious, how beautiful it is!'
he would say with a sugary expression. And, as if to prove his words,
he would screw up his eyes, hold up a finger and pronounce the word
anthropos.

His thoughts also Belikov tried to confine within a framework.
Nothing made sense to him except official regulations and newspaper
articles condemning something or other. A school rule forbidding
pupils to appear in the streets after nine in the evening, an article
censuring sexual intercourse . . . he found clarity and precision in such
matters. The thing was banned. That was that. In permissions and
concessions, though, he always sensed a lurking sinister quality: something incomplete and vague. When a town drama club was licensed—
or a reading room, or a tea-shop—he would shake his head.

'That's all very well of course and so on,' he would say. 'But what of
the repercussions?'

All offences, all deviations, all infringements of the rules made him
despondent—one might have wondered, though, what business they
were of his. If a colleague was late for church, if rumour reached him of
some schoolboy prank, if a schoolmistress was seen out late at night
with an officer, he would take it very much to heart and keep worrying
about those repercussions. At staff meetings he really depressed
us with his misgivings, his pernicketiness, his utterly hidebound
observations on how badly the boys and girls behaved in school, on
their rowdiness in class. ('Dear, oh dear, what if the authorities get
wind of it? Oh dear, what of the repercussions? And what a good idea
it would be to expel Petrov of the Second Form and Yegorov of the
Fourth.')

Well, what with his moaning and groaning, what with the dark
glasses on his pale and—you know—ferrety little face, he so got us
down that we yielded, we gave Petrov and Yegorov bad conduct

marks, we put them in detention, and in the end we expelled them both.

He had the odd habit of visiting our lodgings. He would call on some teacher, sit down, say nothing, and seem to be on the look-out for something. He would sit there for an hour or two without a word, and then he would go. Maintaining good relations with his colleagues, he called it. This calling and sitting obviously irked him, and he only did it because he felt it his duty to his colleagues. We teachers were afraid of him. So was the headmaster, even. Fantastic, isn't it? Our teachers were all thoroughly decent, right-thinking folk brought up on their Turgenev and their Shchedrin—and yet this little galoshes-and-umbrella man kept the entire school under his thumb for fifteen whole years! And not the school only. The whole town! Our ladies gave up their Saturday amateur theatricals lest he should hear of them. The clergy feared to eat meat and play cards in his presence. Thanks to the Belikovs of this world our townsfolk have begun to fear everything during the last ten or fifteen years. They fear to speak aloud, send letters, meet people, read books. They fear to help the poor, they fear to teach anyone to read.

Wishing to say something, Ivan Ivanovich coughed, then lit his pipe and looked at the moon.

'Yes, they're decent, right-thinking folk,' said he, enunciating carefully. 'They've read their Shchedrin, their Turgenev, their Henry Buckles and all that. But they caved in, you see, they did nothing about it—my point, precisely.'

Belikov and I lived in the same house (Burkin went on). We were on the same floor, his door opposite mine. We often met, and I knew his domestic circumstances. It was just the same at home. Dressing-gown, nightcap, shutters, bolts, a whole gamut of sundry bans and restrictions, and all this what-about-the-repercussions stuff. To diet was bad for the health—but you couldn't eat what you liked, or people might say that Belikov didn't keep his fasts. So he ate fresh-water fish fried in butter: food which was neither one thing nor the other. He kept no female servants in case people got the wrong ideas, but he had a cook: one Afanasy, a tipsy, half-witted old boy of about sixty, who had been an army batman in his time and could put together a meal of sorts. This Afanasy usually stood by the door with his arms folded.

'There's been a lot of *it* about lately,' he was for ever muttering with an oracular sigh.

Belikov's bedroom was like a little box, and he slept in a four-poster. When he went to bed he would pull a blanket over his head. It was hot and stuffy, the wind rattled the closed door and whined in the chimney. Sighs drifted in from the kitchen, sighs of evil portent.

He was scared, too, under that blanket. He was afraid of the repercussions, afraid of Afanasy cutting his throat, afraid of burglars. Then he would have nightmares all night, and when we went to school together in the morning he would be dispirited and pale. The crowded school for which he was bound . . . it terrified him, revolted his whole being, that was obvious. And walking by my side was an ordeal for so solitary a type.

'Our children are too noisy in class,' he would say, as if seeking a reason for his low spirits. 'It's quite disgraceful.'

Yet this teacher of Greek—this hard case—nearly got married, believe it or not.

Ivan Ivanovich glanced into the barn.
'You must be joking,' he said.

Yes, he nearly married, strange as it may seem (continued Burkin). A new history and geography master had been appointed: a Michael Kovalenko, from the Ukraine. He brought his sister Barbara with him. He was a tall, swarthy young man with huge hands. He had the kind of face that goes with a deep bass voice, and that voice really did seem to come boom boom booming at you out of a barrel.

Now, his sister was no longer young—she was about thirty—but she was also tall, well-built, black-browed, rosy-cheeked. She was a real knock-out, in fact: a jolly, hearty girl, for ever singing Ukrainian songs, for ever roaring with laughter. She was always ready to launch into a great peal of mirth on the slightest pretext. It was on the headmaster's name-day, I remember, that we first really met the Kovalenkos. There, amid those austere, overwrought, dim pedagogues, who make even party-going a matter of duty . . . behold a new Venus rises from the foam! She walks with arms akimbo, she guffaws, she sings, she dances. She renders a spirited 'Where Southern Breezes Blow', then sings one song after another, and bewitches us all—all, even Belikov.

'The Ukrainian language,' says he with his honeyed smile, sitting down by her side, 'resembles the ancient Greek in its tenderness and agreeable melodiousness.'

This flattered her, and she launched a harangue about how they had their own farm down Gadyach way and how their old mum lived on that farm. What pears they had, what melons, what pumpkins! Pumpkins, pubs, 'pubkins' ... they have their own special words for these things down south, and out of their dear little red little tomatoes and their blue little egg-plants they would brew soup: 'frightfully scrumptious, actually!'

We listened and we listened ... until suddenly the same idea dawned on one and all.

'They'd make a very good match,' the headmaster's wife told me quietly.

For some reason it now struck us all that friend Belikov wasn't married. We wondered why we had never noticed such a thing before, why we had utterly lost sight of so crucial a factor in his biography. What was his attitude to woman? His solution to this basic problem? So far we had taken no interest in the matter. Perhaps we couldn't even see him as capable of love—this four-poster-bed man, this galoshes fiend!

'He's well over forty, and she's thirty,' the headmaster's wife elucidated. 'I think she'd have him.'

Boredom in the provinces ... the things it leads to, the wrong-headedness, the nonsense! And why? Because people somehow just can't get anything right. Well, for instance, why this sudden urge to marry off friend Belikov, who was hardly anyone's idea of a husband? The headmaster's wife, the second master's wife, all the school ladies perk up, they even look prettier, as if they've suddenly glimpsed the purpose of existence. The head's wife takes a box in the theatre—and behold Barbara sitting in that box with some sort of fan, radiant and happy. By her side is Belikov: small, crumpled, looking as if he's been extracted from his house with a pair of pincers. When I give a party the ladies make a point of my inviting both Belikov and Barbara. Things, in short, begin to hum. Barbara, it transpires, doesn't mind getting married. She isn't all that happy living with her brother—they argue and quarrel for days on end by all accounts.

Now, take this for a scene. Kovalenko walks down the street: a tall, lanky brute in his embroidered shirt with a quiff of hair tumbling from cap on to forehead. He has a clutch of books in one hand and a thick knobbly stick in the other. His sister follows, also carrying books.

'But you haven't *read* it, Michael!' she loudly avers. 'I tell you—I *swear*—you haven't read a *word* of it!'

'Well, I say I *have*,' shouts Kovalenko, thumping his stick on the pavement.

'Goodness me, Michael! Why so *angry*? This is only a matter of principle, after all.'

'Well, I say I *have* read it,' Kovalenko shouts in an even louder voice.

Whenever they had visitors they were at it hammer and tongs. It must have been a bore, that kind of life, and she wanted a place of her own. And then there was her age. You couldn't pick and choose any more, you were ready to marry anyone—even a teacher of Greek. And then most of our young ladies don't care who they marry so long as they get themselves a husband. Anyway, be that as it may, Barbara began to show Belikov marked partiality.

And Belikov? He used to call on Kovalenko, just as he would call on us. He would arrive, sit down, say nothing. And while he was saying nothing Barbara would be singing him 'Where Southern Breezes Blow', or looking at him pensively with her dark eyes. Or she would suddenly go off in a peal of noisy laughter.

In love affairs, and not least in marriage, suggestion plays a large part. Everyone—his colleagues, their ladies—began assuring Belikov that he must marry, that there was nothing left for him in life except wedlock. We all congratulated him, we made various trite remarks with solemn faces: 'marriage is a serious step,' and the like. What's more, Barbara wasn't bad looking. Besides being attractive she was the daughter of a senior civil servant and owned a farm. Above all, she was the first woman who had ever been kind and affectionate to Belikov. His head was turned, and he decided that he really must marry.

'Now would have been the time to detach him from his galoshes and umbrella,' pronounced Ivan Ivanovich.

That proved impossible, believe it or not (said Burkin). He put Barbara's portrait on his desk, and he kept calling on me and talking: about Barbara, about family life, about marriage being a serious step. He often visited the Kovalenkos. But he didn't change his way of life one little bit. Far from it, actually—his resolve to marry had a rather debilitating effect on him. He grew thin and pale, he seemed to retreat further and further into his shell.

'Barbara attracts me,' he tells me with a weak, wry little smile. 'And I know that everyone must get married. But, er, all this has been rather sudden, you know. One must, er, give it some thought.'

'Why?' I ask. 'Just marry, that's all.'

'No. Marriage is a serious step. One must first weigh one's impending responsibilities and duties, just in case of repercussions. I'm so worried, I can't sleep a wink. I'm scared, too, frankly. She and her brother have a rather peculiar outlook—they do have an unconventional way of discussing things, you know. And they are a bit on the hearty side. You get married, but before you know where you are you find you've become the subject for gossip.'

So he didn't make her an offer, but kept putting it off: to the great grief of the headmaster's wife and all our ladies. He kept weighing his impending responsibilities and duties while walking out with Barbara almost every day—perhaps he thought that necessary for someone in his position—and coming along to talk to me about family life. He would have proposed in the end, very likely. And the result would have been one of those stupid, unnecessary marriages of which we see thousands: the product of boredom, of having nothing else to do. But then a gigantic scandal suddenly erupted!

The point is, Barbara's brother Kovalenko had taken against Belikov at first sight—simply couldn't stand him.

'It beats me how you put up with the blighter, it really does,' he told us, shrugging his shoulders. 'Horrible little creep! Honestly, gentlemen, how *can* you live here? Your air stifles a man, damn it. Call yourselves teachers, do you? Educators? You're just a lot of little hacks. It's no temple of learning, this isn't—it's more like a suburban police station, and it smells as sour as a sentry-box. Well, that's it, lads. I shall stay here a little longer, and then I'll go to my farm down south to catch crayfish and teach the local kids. I shall be off, while you stay on here with this miserable humbug, blast him.'

Or he'd laugh—now in a deep guffaw, now in a thin, piping tone: laugh until the tears came.

'Why does he sit around my place?' he would ask with a bewildered gesture. 'What does he want? He just sits and stares.'

He even gave Belikov the nickname 'Master Creepy Crawly'. Well, we naturally didn't tell him that his sister Barbara was thinking of marrying Master Crawly. Once, when the headmaster's wife hinted that it would be worth fixing up his sister with some such generally respected worthy as Belikov, he frowned.

'Nothing to do with me,' he muttered. 'Let her marry a rattlesnake if she wants to. I mind my own business.'

Now hear what happened next. Some wag drew a cartoon of Belikov walking in his galoshes, with the bottoms of his trousers rolled up, carrying that great umbrella and arm in arm with Barbara. It was captioned THE LOVESICK ANTHROPOS. And it had just caught his expression to perfection, see? The artist must have worked at it night after night because the teachers at the two grammar schools, the boys' and the girls', all got their copy. So did the lecturers at the theological college, so did our local officials. Belikov got one too. The caricature had a most depressing effect on him.

On the first of May, a Sunday, we had an outing. All of us—teachers, pupils—had arranged to meet at school and then go for a walk to the woods. Well, we set off on this trip, and there's Belikov looking quite green and gloomier than a storm-cloud.

'What nasty, evil people there are,' says he, his lips quivering.

I actually feel sorry for him. Then, as we're walking along, all of a sudden (believe it or not) Kovalenko sails past on his bicycle followed by Barbara, also on a bicycle: flushed and puffed, but good-humoured and happy.

'I say, we're going on ahead,' she shouts. 'What marvellous weather —frightfully marvellous, actually.'

Both vanished from view, while friend Belikov turned from green to white and seemed paralysed. He stopped and looked at me.

'What, pray, is the meaning of this?' he asked. 'Or do my eyes deceive me? Is it proper for grammar-school teachers—for *women*!—to ride bicycles?'

'What's improper about it?' said I. 'Let them cycle away to their heart's content.'

'What do you mean?' he shouted, amazed at my calmness. 'You can't know what you're saying.'

But he was so shaken that he decided not to go on and turned back.

All next day he was nervously rubbing his hands and twitching. He wasn't at all well, his face showed that. He abandoned his classes, too— and that for the first time in his career. He missed his lunch as well. And then, in the late afternoon, he donned warm clothing in spite of the fine summer weather, and off he toddled to the Kovalenkos'. Barbara was out, only the brother was at home.

'Pray be seated,' pronounced Kovalenko coldly. He frowned,

looking sleepy—he'd just been taking an after-lunch nap, and he was in a very bad mood indeed.

Belikov sat for ten minutes without speaking, and then began.

'I have come to you to relieve my mind. I am deeply grieved. Some humorist has drawn a picture ridiculing myself and a certain other individual dear to us both. I am in duty bound to assure you that I am in no way implicated, that I have given no occasion for such witticisms. I have, on the contrary, conducted myself throughout as a person of complete probity.'

Kovalenko sat there fuming and said nothing. Belikov paused.

'I also have something else to tell you,' he went on in a quiet, sad voice. 'I have been in the profession for some time, while you are only a beginner, and I consider it my duty as your senior colleague to give you a warning. You ride a bicycle: a pastime wholly improper in one who instructs the young.'

'Why so?' asked Kovalenko in his deep voice.

'Need I say more, Kovalenko? Are my words not intelligible? If a teacher goes bicycling, then what are we to expect of his pupils? That they will walk on their heads, I presume! There is nothing in the school rules which says that you *can* bicycle. Which means you can't. I was appalled yesterday. When I saw your sister my eyes swam. A woman or a girl on a *bicycle*! An abomination!'

'What, precisely, do you require?'

'I require one thing only: to warn you, Kovalenko. You are young, you have your future before you. You should comport yourself very, very carefully indeed, but you don't toe the line at all, oh dear me no. You wear an embroidered shirt. You're always carrying books in the street. And now we have this bicycling! This bicycling, yours and your sister's, will come to the headmaster's ears, and then it will reach the higher authorities. Not very nice, now, is it?'

'Whether my sister and I do or do not ride bicycles is no one else's business,' said Kovalenko, turning crimson. 'And if anyone meddles in my domestic and family affairs I'll bloody well see him in hell!'

Belikov blenched. He stood up.

'If you take this tone with me I cannot continue,' he said. 'And I must beg you never to use such expressions about the authorities in my presence. You must treat authority with respect.'

'Did I say anything against the authorities?' asked Kovalenko, looking at him angrily. 'Kindly leave me in peace. I am an honest man, and I have no wish to bandy words with an individual of your description. I don't like narks.'

Fidgeting nervously, Belikov quickly put his coat on, horror written on his face—no one had ever been so rude to him in his life.

'You may say what you please,' he remarked as he came out of the lobby on to the landing. 'But I must warn you of this. Someone may have overheard us. Now, in case our conversation might be misinterpreted, in case of possible repercussions, I shall be obliged to inform the headmaster of its substance, er, in general outline. That is my duty.'

'Inform, eh? Carry on then, sneak away!'

Seizing him from behind by the collar, Kovalenko gave him a shove —and Belikov flew downstairs, his galoshes drumming. They were high, steep stairs, but he slid down without mishap, he stood up, and he touched his nose to see if his spectacles were broken. Now, just as he was slithering down those stairs, in came Barbara with two ladies. They stood at the bottom, watching—which, for Belikov, was the last straw. I think he'd rather have broken his neck or both legs than become a laughing-stock. Now the whole town would know, wouldn't it? The Head would hear of it, and so would the higher authorities. There would—alas—be repercussions. There would be another cartoon. And he would end up having to resign.

Barbara recognized him when he was on his feet. Seeing his ludicrous expression, his rumpled coat, his galoshes, not understanding what it was all about—but supposing him to have fallen down by accident—she couldn't help giving a great guffaw.

'Ha, ha, ha!'

It rang through the entire house.

This reverberating peal of laughter was the end of everything for Belikov: of his courtship and also of his life on earth. His ears did not hear what Barbara was saying, his eyes saw nothing. On arriving home he first removed her portrait from his desk, after which he lay down . . . never to rise again.

Three days later Afanasy came in to ask me if we should send for a doctor as there was 'something wrong' with the master. I went to see Belikov. He lay in his four-poster with a blanket over him, not speaking. In answer to questions he would only say yes or no, and that was all. While he lay there Afanasy hovered near by—gloomy, scowling, sighing deeply, stinking of vodka.

Belikov died a month later. We all went to the funeral: both high schools, that is, and the theological college. Now, as he lay in his coffin, his expression was gentle and agreeable—merry, even—as if he was glad to have been placed at last in that ultimate receptacle from which there would be no emerging. Yes, he had attained his ideal. During the funeral the weather was dull and rainy—in his honour, so to speak— and we all sported our galoshes and umbrellas. Barbara was there too, and she sobbed when they lowered the coffin into the grave. Ukrainian girls can only cry or laugh, I've noticed—they have no intermediate mood.

It's a great pleasure, frankly, is burying a Belikov. On our way back from the cemetery we wore modest, sober expressions. No one wanted to show how pleased he felt—it was a pleasure which we had known long, long ago as children when our elders had gone out and we ran about the garden for an hour or two enjoying absolute freedom. Freedom, oh freedom! Even a hint, even the faint hope of its possibility . . . it makes one's spirits soar, doesn't it?

We came back from the cemetery in a good mood. But within a week life was back in its old rut. It was just as austere, wearisome and pointless as before: a life which was neither forbidden in the school rules, nor yet wholly sanctioned either. There was no improvement. We had buried Belikov, admittedly. But what a lot of other men in capsules he had left behind him! And we shall see plenty more of them in the future.

'My point exactly,' said Ivan Ivanovich, and lit his pipe.

'We shall see plenty more of them,' repeated Burkin.

The schoolmaster came out of the barn. He was a short, fat, completely bald man with a black beard almost down to his waist. Two dogs came out with him.

'What a moon!' said he, looking up.

It was midnight. On his right could be seen the whole village, and a long road stretching about three miles into the distance. Everything was plunged in deep, peaceful slumber. There was no movement, no sound—it was incredible, indeed, that nature could be so quiet. When you see a broad village street by moonlight—a street with its huts, ricks and sleeping willows—your heart is at peace, and takes refuge in this calm, in the shadows of the night, from its toils, trials and tribulations. It is gentle, sad, serene. The stars seem to look down with loving kindness, there seems to be no evil in the world—all seems for the best. On the left, at the edge of the village, open country began. It could be

seen stretching away as far as the horizon, and in the entire breadth of
these moonlit fields there was neither movement nor sound.

'My point exactly,' repeated Ivan Ivanovich. 'What about us living
in a stuffy, crowded town, writing our futile papers and playing our
bridge? Isn't all that a kind of capsule? To spend our whole lives among
loafers, mischievous litigants and stupid, idle women, talking and
hearing various forms of nonsense . . . isn't that a capsule too? Now, if
you like I'll tell you an extremely edifying story.'

'No, it's time to sleep,' said Burkin. 'Tell it tomorrow.'

They went into the barn and lay down on the hay. Each had covered
himself up and started dozing, when suddenly the padding of footsteps
was heard.

Someone was walking near the barn. The steps passed and stopped.
Then, a minute later, you would hear the same padding sound.

The dogs whimpered.

'That's Mavra,' Burkin said.

The steps died away.

'People are such liars,' said Ivan Ivanovich, turning over. 'To see
them, to hear them, to put up with their lies . . . and be called a fool
for your pains! The insults, the humiliations, that you suffer! Not
daring to proclaim aloud that you are on the side of honest, free men!
The lies you yourself tell, the smiles you give! And all this to earn your
daily bread and a roof over your head—all for the sake of some miserable little job not worth a farthing! No—one can't go on living like
this!'

'Now, that's another story,' said the teacher. 'Let's go to sleep.'

Ten minutes later Burkin was asleep. But Ivan Ivanovich kept tossing
from side to side and sighing. Then he got up, went outside again, sat
down by the door and lit his pipe.

GOOSEBERRIES

RAIN clouds had filled the whole sky since early morning. It was quiet weather—not hot and tedious as it is on those dull grey days when clouds hang over the countryside for hours on end while you wait for rain which never comes. Ivan Ivanovich the vet and Burkin the schoolmaster were tired of walking, and the fields seemed to go on for ever. Far ahead of them the windmills of Mironositskoye village could just be seen. On their right was a chain of hills which vanished far beyond the village, and which—as they both knew—marked a river bank. There were meadows, green willows and homesteads over there. And if you stood on one of those hills you could see another equally vast expanse of fields, a telegraph line and a train crawling caterpillar-like in the distance. In clear weather you could even see the town. On this calm day, when all nature seemed gentle and pensive, Ivan Ivanovich and Burkin were filled with love of this open landscape, and both thought how vast, how glorious a land it was.

'That time when we stayed in Elder Prokofy's barn . . . you were going to tell me some story,' Burkin said.

'Yes—about my brother.'

Ivan Ivanovich gave a long sigh, and lit a pipe as a prelude to his narrative, but just then the rain began. Five minutes later it was absolutely pelting down—looked as if it would never end. Ivan Ivanovich and Burkin paused, wondering what to do. The dogs—wet, tails between their legs—stood and gazed at them devotedly.

'We must find shelter,' said Burkin. 'Let's go to Alyokhin's, it's quite near.'

'All right.'

They turned off and made across mown fields—now walking straight ahead, now bearing to the right—until they hit the road. Poplars soon appeared, then an orchard and red-roofed barns. There was a gleam of river, and then a view of a wide reach with its mill and white bathing-hut. This was Sofyino, Alyokhin's place.

The mill was working, and drowned the noise of rain. The weir quivered. Wet horses stood with bowed heads by some carts, and men with sacks over their heads moved about. It was damp, muddy, desolate—and that reach of river had a cold, malignant look. Ivan

Ivanovich and Burkin felt wet, unclean and uncomfortable all over. Their feet were heavy with mud. When they had passed the weir and climbed up to the manor barns they were not speaking—and so seemed angry with each other.

From one shed came the noise of a winnowing-fan, and there was a surge of dust through the open door. On the threshold stood the boss —Alyokhin, a man of about forty, tall, stout, long-haired, more like a professor or artist than a landowner. He wore a white shirt which needed washing and a rope for a belt. He had underpants on instead of trousers, and he had mud and straw sticking to his high boots. His eyes and nose were black with dust. He recognized Ivan Ivanovich and Burkin, and was obviously glad to see them.

'Come in, gentlemen, come inside the house,' he smiled. 'Be with you in a moment.'

It was a large, two-storeyed house. Alyokhin lived downstairs in two rooms with vaulted ceilings and small windows—once his bailiffs' quarters. It was all very unpretentious, smelling of rye bread, cheap vodka and harness. His best rooms, upstairs, he used very seldom, only when he had visitors. Ivan Ivanovich and Burkin were received in the house by the maid: a young woman so beautiful that both halted in their tracks and stared at each other.

'You can't imagine how glad I am to see you gentlemen,' said Alyokhin, following them into the hall. 'What a nice surprise!

'Give the guests something to change into, Pelageya,' he told the maid. 'And I'll change too while I'm about it. But I must go and wash first—feel as if I hadn't washed since spring. Would you like to come to the bathing-hut while they get things ready?'

The fair Pelageya—so delicate, so gentle-looking—brought towels and soap, and Alyokhin took his guests to the bathing place.

'Yes, I haven't washed for ages,' he said, undressing. 'I have a good bathing-hut, as you see—my father built it—but somehow I never have time for a bathe.'

He sat on the step soaping his long hair and neck, while the water round him turned brown.

'Yes, I see what you mean,' said Ivan Ivanovich with a meaning look at his head.

'I haven't washed for ages,' repeated Alyokhin awkwardly. He soaped himself again and the water round him turned inky.

Ivan Ivanovich came out, plunged in with a loud splash, swam about in the rain with broad sweeps of his arms and sent up waves with white water-lilies tossing on them. He swam to the middle of the reach and dived. A little later he appeared somewhere else and swam on further. He kept plunging and trying to touch bottom.

'By God, this is terrific!' he kept repeating. He was enjoying himself.

He swam up to the mill, spoke to the villagers there, then turned and floated on his back in the middle of the reach, exposing his face to the rain. Burkin and Alyokhin were dressed and ready to leave, but still he swam and dived.

'Ye Gods!' said he. 'Mercy on us!'

'That's enough,' shouted Burkin.

They went back to the house. The lamp was alight in the large drawing-room upstairs. Burkin and Ivan Ivanovich, in silk dressing-gowns and warm slippers, sat in easy chairs, while Squire Alyokhin —washed, combed, wearing a new frock-coat—paced up and down, obviously revelling in the warmth, cleanliness, dry clothing and light footwear. Soundlessly treading the carpet and softly smiling, the fair Pelageya served tea and jam on a tray. And only now did Ivan Ivano-vich embark on his story. His audience seemed to include not only Burkin and Alyokhin, but also the ladies, young and old, and the officers who looked out calmly and severely from the gilt frames on the walls.

There are two of us brothers (he began): myself, Ivan, and Nicholas —two years my junior. I studied to be a vet, while Nicholas had a local government job from the age of nineteen. Our father had been a ranker, and after getting his commission he had bequeathed us the status of gentleman together with a small estate which was sequestrated after his death to pay his debts. Anyway, we lived a free life in the open air as boys. We spent our days and nights in fields and woods like ordinary village children, minding horses, stripping bark, fishing: that kind of thing.

Now, as you know, once you've ever hooked a ruff—or seen migrat-ing thrushes swarm over your village on clear, cold autumn days— you'll never make a townsman after that, you'll yearn for those wide open spaces till your dying day. My brother was miserable at the office. Years passed, but he stayed put: for ever copying the same old docu-ments, for ever obsessed with getting back to the land. Gradually this vague longing crystallized into a specific desire: the dream of buying a nice little country estate beside a river or lake.

He was a gentle, kind man. I was fond of him, but never did I sympathize with his wish to coop himself up for life in a country house. There's a saying that six foot of earth is all a man needs. A man? A corpse, more like! Now, if our professional people want to get back to the land, if they all have their eye on country properties, that's supposed to be a good thing these days. But those little places in the country . . . they're just that same old six foot of earth, really, aren't they? To leave the town, the tumult and the shouting, to skulk in your little place in the country . . . that's no life, that isn't. It's selfishness, it's idleness, it's the monastic discipline—but without the hope of glory! Man needs no six foot of earth, he needs no little place in the country. He needs the whole globe—all nature—so that he can develop, untrammelled, all his potentialities, all the attributes of his free spirit.

At the office brother Nicholas dreamed of eating stew made from his own cabbages and seemed to sniff their savour wafting through his yard. He dreamed of taking his meals on green grass, of sleeping in the sun, of sitting on a bench outside his gate for hours on end gazing at fields and woods. Booklets on agriculture, calendar mottoes and such . . . these were his joy, his favourite spiritual sustenance. He liked newspapers too, but only read advertisements about so many acres of arable land and meadow being up for sale with farmhouse, river, orchard, mill and mill-pond. His imagination pictured garden paths, flowers, fruit, nesting boxes for starlings, carp in ponds—you know the sort of stuff. These fancies varied with the advertisements which came his way, but for some reason the staple feature of them all was . . . the gooseberry. No manor house, no idyllic nook could he picture without that gooseberry patch.

'Country life does have its advantages,' he would say. 'You have tea on your balcony while your ducks swim on the pond. There's a wonderful smell and, er . . . and there are these gooseberries!'

He would sketch a plan of his estate, a plan which always had the same features: (a) manor house; (b) servants' quarters; (c) kitchen-garden; (d) gooseberries. He lived miserably. He went short of food and drink, he dressed any old how—like a tramp—and he kept saving money and putting it in the bank. He was a fearful miser. It pained me to see him, and I used to give him one or two things—send them on special occasions. But those things too he used to put away. Once a man's obsessed by an idea there's nothing you can do about it.

The years pass, he is transferred to a different county, he is now in his forties, but he is still reading those newspaper advertisements and saving money. Then I hear he's got married. Still aiming to buy that estate with the gooseberry patch, he has married an ugly old widow for whom he has no feelings—just because she's well-heeled. He leads her a miserable life too, keeping her half starved and putting her money in his own bank account. Before that she has been a post-master's wife, and as such she's been used to cakes and home-made wines, but with her second husband she even goes short of black bread. This routine sends her into a decline, and three years later she duly gives up the ghost! Not, of course, that my brother for one moment feels responsible for her death. Money's like strong drink, it makes a man act strangely. There was once a merchant of our town, a dying man, who ordered a bowl of honey on his death-bed, mixed in his banknotes and his lottery tickets ... and swallowed the lot, to stop anyone else getting it. Once, when I was inspecting beasts at a railway station, a cattle-dealer was run over by a train. It takes his leg off. We get him to a casualty department, there's blood everywhere: a horrible business! But he keeps begging us to look for that leg—can't stop worrying about the twenty roubles he has in the severed boot, thinks he may lose them.

'That's a bit beside the point,' said Burkin.

After his wife's death (Ivan Ivanovich went on after half a minute's thought) my brother began looking for a country property. Now, of course, you can spend five years hunting and still make the wrong choice, still end up with something quite unlike your dream house. Through an estate agent brother Nicholas bought three hundred acres on a mortgage. There was a manor house, there were servants' quarters, there was a park. But there was no orchard, there were no gooseberries and there were no duck-ponds. He did have a river, but the water was coffee-coloured because of a brickyard on one side of the estate and a bone-ash works on the other. Still, good old Nicholas didn't much care. He ordered twenty gooseberry-bushes, he planted them, and he set up as a squire.

I looked him up last year, thought I'd go and see what he was up to. In his letters my brother called his estate 'Chumbaroklov Patch' or 'Gimalaysky's', and one afternoon I turn up at this 'Gimalaysky's'. It's hot. There are ditches, fences, hedges, rows of little firs all over the place, and there doesn't seem to be any way into the yard or any place to leave your horse. As I approach the house I am met by a fat, ginger-coloured dog which resembles a pig and would like to bark but can't be bothered. From the kitchen emerges a cook—barefoot, fat, also resembling a pig—and says that the master is having his after-lunch nap. I enter my brother's room, and there he is sitting up in bed with a blanket over his lap. He has aged, he has put on weight, he looks positively frowsty. His nose, lips and cheeks jut forward. He seems all set to grunt into his blanket.

We embrace, we shed a tear of joy—and at the sad thought that we were once young but are both grey-haired now, and that our lives are nearly over. He dresses and begins showing me round his estate.

'Well, how's life?' I ask.

'Oh, pretty good, thank God. Can't complain.'

No longer was he the poor, timid little clerk. He was a real squire now, a man of property. He'd settled here, he'd put down his roots, he was in his element. He was eating a lot, taking steam-baths, putting on weight. He was already suing the parish council and both factories, and he took umbrage when the locals wouldn't call him 'sir'. His spiritual welfare . . . that too he cultivated with the dignity befitting a proprietor. He couldn't just do good, he had to be so pompous about it! And what did his charity add up to? He dosed all the villagers with bicarbonate of soda and castor oil, no matter what might be wrong with them. On his name-day he would hold a thanksgiving service in the village, then stand the lads vodka all round because he thought it the done thing. Oh, those awful bumpers of vodka! One day your fat landowner takes the villagers to court for trespass, and on the next day —some festival—he treats them all to vodka. They drink, they cheer him and they make their drunken salaams.

Improving one's living standards, eating too much, laziness . . . these things develop the most blatant arrogance in us Russians. Back at the office Nicholas had been scared even to hold views of his own, but here he was pronouncing eternal verities in magisterial style about education being 'essential, but inopportune for the lower orders', and about corporal punishment being 'detrimental, generally speaking, but in certain cases useful and indispensable'.

'I know the working man, I can get on with him,' he would say. 'I'm popular with the ordinary common chap. I need only move a finger and the lads will do anything for me.'

And all this, mark you, with a good-natured, knowing smile. A score of times he'd say 'we landowners' or 'speaking as one of the gentry'. He'd evidently forgotten that our grandfather had been a farm labourer and our father a private in the army. Even our surname Chimsha-Gimalaysky, so essentially absurd, now seemed to him melodious, illustrious and highly agreeable.

It's not Nicholas I'm concerned with, though, it's myself. I want to tell you how I changed during my few hours on his estate. At tea that afternoon the cook served a full bowl of gooseberries. These were no bought gooseberries, they were his own crop: the first to be picked since the planting. Nicholas chuckled, contemplated the gooseberries for a minute in silence and tears—his feelings too deep for words. Then, placing a lone berry in his mouth, he surveyed me with the glee of a child who has at last been given a longed-for toy.

'Delicious.'

He ate them greedily.

'Ah, delicious indeed,' he kept saying. 'You *must* try them.'

They were sour and unripe. Still,

> To hosts of petty truths man much prefers
> A single edifying lie,

as Pushkin has put it. Before me was a happy man whose most cherished dream had come true for all to see, who had attained his object in life, who had realized his ambitions, who was content with his fate and with himself. In my reflections on human happiness there had always been an element of sadness, but now the spectacle of a happy man plunged me into a despondency akin to despair. I felt particularly low that night. They had made up a bed for me in the room next to my brother's, and I could hear that he was still awake: he was getting up, going to that bowl and taking out one gooseberry at a time. Really, what a lot of contented, happy people there are, I reflected! What a crushing force they represent! What a life, though! Look at the impudence and idleness of the strong, the ignorance and bestiality of the weak, look at the grotesque poverty everywhere, the overcrowding, degeneracy, drunkenness and hypocrisy, the silly talk.

And yet. . . . In all the houses and streets there is peace and quiet. Out of fifty thousand townsfolk there's not one ready to scream or protest aloud. We see people shopping for food in the market, eating by day, sleeping by night, talking their nonsense, marrying their wives, growing old, complacently dragging off their dead to the cemetery. But we have no eyes or ears for those who suffer. Life's real tragedies are enacted off stage. All is peace and quiet, the only protest comes from mute statistics: so many people driven mad, so many gallons of vodka drunk, so many children starved to death.

Oh yes, the need for such a system is obvious. Quite obviously, too, the happy man only feels happy because the *unhappy* man bears his burden in silence. And without that silence happiness would be impossible. It's collective hypnosis, this is. At the door of every contented, happy man there should be someone standing with a little hammer, someone to keep dinning into his head that unhappy people do exist —and that, happy though he may be, life will round on him sooner or later. Disaster will strike in the shape of sickness, poverty or bereavement. And no one will see *him* or hear *him*—just as he now has neither eyes nor ears for others. But there *is* no one with a hammer, and so the happy man lives happily away, while life's petty tribulations stir him gently, as the breeze stirs an aspen. And everything in the garden is lovely.

'That night I realized that I too was happy and contented,' Ivan Ivanovich went on, standing up. 'I too had laid down the law—at dinner, out hunting—about how to live, what to believe, how to handle the lower classes. I too had said that learning is a boon, that education is essential—but that plain reading and writing are enough for the common herd to be going on with. Freedom is a blessing, said I, we need it as the air we breathe—but we must wait for it. Yes, such were my words. But now I want to know what on earth we're waiting *for*?

'What *are* we waiting for, I ask you?' Ivan Ivanovich demanded, glaring at Burkin. 'What are we trying to prove? We can't have everything at once, I'm told, every idea takes shape gradually, in its own good time. But who says so? Where's the evidence that he's right? You refer me to the natural order of things, to the law of cause and effect. But is there any law, any order which says that a vigorous, right-thinking man like me should stand by a ditch and wait for it to become overgrown or covered with mud—when all the time I might be able to jump across it or bridge it? Again I ask, what are we waiting for? To wait while we don't have the guts to live, yet need and long so much to be alive!

'I left my brother's early next morning, since when I've found town life unbearable. The peace and quiet . . . they get me down. I fear to look through windows because I know no spectacle more depressing than a happy family having tea round a table. I'm old, I'm past fighting,

I can't even hate any more. I'm just deeply grieved, I'm exasperated,
I'm indignant. The thoughts which crowd upon me at night . . . they
make my head burn and I can't sleep. Oh, if I were only young!'

Ivan Ivanovich paced up and down excitedly, repeating 'if I were
only young!'

Suddenly going up to Alyokhin, he took him by one hand, and then
by the other.

'Never give up, my dear Alyokhin,' he pleaded. 'Never let them
drug you. While you're still young, strong and in good heart, never
tire of doing good. There's no such thing—there need be no such thing
—as happiness. And if life has any meaning and purpose, that meaning
and purpose certainly aren't in our happiness, but in something higher
and more rational. Do good.'

All this Ivan Ivanovich said with a pathetic, pleading smile, as if
asking a personal favour.

Then all three sat in arm-chairs in different corners of the drawing-
room and said nothing. Ivan Ivanovich's story had satisfied neither
Burkin nor Alyokhin. To hear about an impoverished clerk eating
gooseberries while those generals and ladies looked down from their
gilt frames, seeming alive in the twilight . . . it was a bore. Somehow
one would rather have talked about women, about persons of elegance.
To be sitting in this drawing-room, where the covered chandelier, the
arm-chairs, the carpets under foot, all proclaimed that the watchers in
those frames had once walked, sat and had tea here themselves . . . to
have the fair Pelageya moving noiselessly about—all that was better
than any story.

Alyokhin was terribly sleepy. He had been up about the farm before
three in the morning, and he could hardly keep his eyes open. But he
lingered on, fearing to miss any interesting tale which his guests might
have to tell. As for what Ivan Ivanovich had just said, as for whether
it was wise or true . . . that was beyond him. His guests were not
discussing meal, hay or pitch, but something with no direct bearing on
his life. He liked that, and he wanted them to go on.

'It's bedtime, though,' said Burkin, getting up. 'May I wish you good
night?'

Alyokhin said good night and went down to his own quarters while
his guests remained upstairs. They were sharing a large room containing
two old carved wooden beds and an ivory crucifix in the corner. Their
beds were wide and cool, they had been made by the fair Pelageya, and
the linen smelt agreeably fresh.

Ivan Ivanovich undressed in silence and lay down.

'Lord, forgive us sinners,' said he, pulling the blankets over his head.

His pipe was on the table, reeking strongly of stale tobacco, and Burkin could not sleep for a long time for wondering where the atrocious smell came from.

All night long rain drummed on the windows.

CONCERNING LOVE

FOR lunch next day delicious pasties, crayfish and mutton rissoles were served. During the meal Nikanor the cook came upstairs to ask what the guests wanted for dinner. He was a man of average height with a puffy face and small eyes—and so clean-shaven that his whiskers seemed to have been plucked out rather than cut off.

Alyokhin explained that the fair Pelageya was in love with this cook. He was a drunkard and a bit of a hooligan, so she didn't want to marry him, but she didn't mind 'just living with him'. He was very pious, though, and his religion forbade his just living with her. He insisted on marriage, didn't want her otherwise. He swore at her in his cups, and even beat her. She would hide upstairs, weeping, when he was drunk, while Alyokhin and his servants stayed at home to protect her if necessary.

The conversation turned to love.

'What makes people fall in love?' asked Alyokhin. 'Why couldn't Pelageya love someone else more suited to her intellectually and physically? Why must she love this Nikanor—"Fat-face", everyone calls him round here—seeing that personal happiness is an important factor in love? It's all very mysterious, there are any number of possible interpretations. So far we've only heard one incontrovertible truth about love: the biblical "this is a great mystery". Everything else written and spoken about love has offered no solution, but has just posed questions which have simply remained unanswered. What seems to explain one instance doesn't fit a dozen others. It's best to interpret each instance separately, in my view, without trying to generalize. We must isolate each individual case, as doctors say.'

'Very true,' agreed Burkin.

'Your ordinary decent Russian has a weakness for these unsolved problems. Where other peoples romanticize their love, garnishing it with roses and nightingales, we Russians bedizen ours with dubious profundities—and the most tedious available, at that. Back in my student days in Moscow I had a "friend": a lovely lady who, when I held her in my arms, was always wondering what monthly allowance I would give her, and what was the price of a pound of beef. We're just the same. When we're in love we're for ever questioning ourselves.

Are we being honourable or dishonourable? Wise or stupid? How will it end, this love? And so on. Whether this attitude is right or wrong I don't know, but that it is a nuisance, that it is unsatisfactory and frustrating—that I do know.'

He seemed to have some story he wanted to tell. People who live alone always do have things on their minds that they are keen to talk about. Bachelors deliberately go to the public baths, and to restaurants in town, just to talk, and they sometimes tell bath attendants or waiters the most fascinating tales. In the country, though, it is their guests to whom they usually unbosom themselves. Grey sky and rain-soaked trees could be seen through the windows. There was nowhere to go in such weather—and nothing to do except swap yarns.

I've been living and farming in Sofyino for some time—since I took my degree (Alyokhin began). By upbringing I'm the arm-chair type, my leanings are academic. But this estate was badly in debt when I came here, and since it was partly through spending so much on my education that Father had run up those debts, I decided to stay on and work until I'd paid them off. I made my decision and started working here: not without a certain repugnance, frankly. The land isn't all that productive hereabouts, and if you don't want to farm at a loss you either have to use hired hands—slave labour, practically—or else you have to run the place peasant-fashion: do your own field work, that is, yourself and your family. There's no other way. But I hadn't gone into these subtleties at the time. Not one single plot of earth did I leave in peace, I corralled all the near-by villagers and their women, and I had us all working away like billy-o. I ploughed myself, I sowed and I reaped myself—bored stiff the while, and frowning fastidiously like a village cat eating gherkins in the vegetable patch because it's starving. My body ached, I was nearly dead on my feet. At first I thought I could easily combine this drudgery with the cultured life—all I had to do, thought I, was to observe a certain routine. I moved into the best rooms up here, I arranged for coffee and liqueurs to be served after lunch and dinner, and I read the *European Herald* in bed at night. But one day our priest, Father Ivan, turned up and scoffed my whole stock of liquor at a sitting. The priest also ran off with my *European Heralds*, or rather his daughters did, because I never managed to get as far as my bed in summer, especially during haymaking, but slept in the barn, in a sledge, or in some woodman's hut—hardly conducive to reading, that.

I gradually moved downstairs, I began having my meals with the servants, and there's nothing left of my former gracious living but these same servants who once worked for my father, and whom I hadn't the heart to dismiss.

Quite early on I was elected an honorary justice of the peace, and had to go to town now and then to take part in sessions and sit at the assizes, which I found entertaining. When you've been cooped up here for a couple of months, especially in winter, you end up yearning for a black frock-coat. Now, at the assizes you had your frock-coats, your uniforms, your tail-coats. They were all lawyers there, all educated men. They were the sort of people you could talk to. To sit in an arm-chair wearing clean underwear and light boots with your watch-chain on your chest ... after sleeping in a sledge and eating with servants, that really was the height of luxury.

I was always welcome in town, and I liked meeting new people. Now, among these new friendships the most serious—and, quite honestly, the most pleasant—was with Luganovich, the Deputy Chairman of Assize. You both know him: a most charming individual. This happened just after the famous arson case. The proceedings had lasted two days, we were worn out, and Luganovich looked in my direction.

'How about dinner at my place?'

I was surprised, barely knowing the man, and then only in an official capacity—I had never visited his home. After calling briefly at my hotel to change, I set off. This dinner led to my first meeting with Luganovich's wife, Anne. She was still very young, not more than twenty-two, and her first child had been born six months previously. It all happened so long ago that I'd be hard put to it, now, to define precisely what it was about her that so much attracted me. But at that dinner it was abundantly clear. I saw a woman—young, handsome, kind, intellectual and captivating—unlike any I had ever met before. I at once sensed that this creature was dear to me, I seemed to know her already—rather as if I'd once seen that face, those eager, intelligent eyes, when I was a little boy looking at the album on my mother's chest-of-drawers.

At the arson trial four Jews had been found guilty and it had been made a conspiracy charge: quite indefensibly in my view. I became rather agitated at dinner—most distressed, in fact—and I've forgotten what I said, now, except that Anne kept shaking her head and telling her husband that 'I just can't believe it, Dmitry'.

Luganovich is a good fellow, one of those simple-minded chaps who have got it into their heads that the man in the dock is always guilty, and that a sentence may be challenged only in writing, through the proper channels—most certainly not at a private dinner-table.

'You and I didn't start that fire,' he said gently. 'Which is why you and I aren't being tried and sent to prison.'

Husband and wife both pressed food and drink on me. From several details—the way they made coffee together, the way they understood each other almost without words—I concluded that they lived in peace and harmony, that they were pleased to be entertaining a guest. We played piano duets after dinner. Then it grew dark and I went to my lodgings.

This happened in early spring, after which I was stuck in Sofyino all summer. I didn't even think of town, I was so busy. But I was haunted all along by the memory of that slender, fair-haired woman. Not directly present in my consciousness, she seemed rather to cast a faint shadow over it.

In late autumn a charity performance was staged in town. I went into the Governor's box (having been invited in the interval), and there was Anne Luganovich seated by the Governor's wife. Again I was struck by that same irresistible vibrant beauty, by that charming, friendly expression in her eyes. And again I sensed an intimacy shared.

We sat next to each other, we walked in the foyer, and she told me that I had grown thinner. Had I been ill?

'Yes. I've had a bad shoulder, and I sleep poorly when it rains.'

'You look worn out. When you came to dinner in the spring you seemed younger, more sure of yourself. You were a bit carried away at the time, you talked a lot, you were quite fascinating. I couldn't help being a bit taken with you, actually. I've often thought of you during the summer for some reason, and when I was getting ready for the theatre tonight I felt sure I should see you.'

She laughed. 'But today you look worn out,' she repeated. 'It makes you seem older.'

I lunched at the Luganoviches' next day. Afterwards they drove out to their holiday cottage to put it in shape for the winter. I went with them, I came back to town with them, and at midnight I had tea with them in the peaceful setting of their home: by a blazing fire, with the young mother going out from time to time to see if her little girl was asleep. After that I always made a point of seeing the Luganoviches when I was in town. We got to know each other, and I used to call unannounced. I was just like one of the family.

'Who is that?' I would hear her ask from the back of the house in the slow drawl which I found so attractive.

'It's Mr. Alyokhin,' the maid or nanny would answer, and Anne would appear looking worried. Why hadn't I been to see them sooner? Had anything happened?

Her gaze, the clasp of her fine, delicate hand, the clothes which she wore about the house, the way she did her hair, her voice, her steps ... they always made me feel as if something new and out of the ordinary, something significant, had happened to me. We enjoyed long conversations—and long silences, each wrapt in his own thoughts. Or she would play the piano for me. When there was no one at home I would wait, I'd talk to nanny, play with baby, or lie on the study ottoman reading the newspaper. When Anne came in I would meet her in the hall and take her shopping off her. I always carried that shopping so fondly and triumphantly, somehow—just like a little boy.

It was a bit like the farmer's wife in the story, the one who had no troubles—not, that is, until she went and bought herself a pig! The Luganoviches had no troubles—so they went and chummed up with me! If I hadn't been to town recently, then I must be ill or something must have happened to me, and both would be genuinely alarmed. What worried them was that I—an educated man who knew foreign languages—didn't devote myself to learning or letters, but lived in the country, going round and round the same old treadmill, that I worked so much but was always hard up. I was bound to be unhappy, they felt, and if they saw me talking, laughing or having a meal, I must be doing so merely to conceal my anguish. Even when I was happy and relaxed I could feel them viewing me with concern. They were particularly touching when I really was in a bit of a fix: when some creditor was pressing me, when I couldn't meet some payment on time. Husband and wife would then whisper together by the window, and he would approach me looking very solemn.

'If you're a bit short, Paul, my wife and I would like to lend you something. Please don't hesitate to ask.' His ears would flush with embarrassment.

Or else he would come up with his red ears after one of those whispering sessions by the window, and say that he and his wife 'do most urgently beg you to accept this gift'. He would then present me with some studs, a cigarette-case or a lamp. In return I would send them something from the country: a bird for the table, butter, flowers. Both of them, incidentally, had money of their own. Now, I was always borrowing in the early days, and I wasn't particularly choosy about it—I took my loans where I could get them. But no power on earth would have induced me to borrow from the Luganoviches. Need I say more?

I was unhappy. At home, in my fields and in my barn my thoughts were of her. I tried to plumb the mystery of a young, handsome, intelligent woman, the wife of an unattractive, almost elderly husband (the man was over forty) and the mother of his children. I also tried to plumb the mystery of this same unattractive husband, this good sort, this easy-going fellow with his boring, common-sensical views, who (when attending a party or dance) always cultivated the local fuddy-duddies, this listless misfit with his submissive air of being a spectator or a bale of goods put up for auction . . . of this man who still believed in his right to be happy and to have children by her. Why ever, I kept wondering, had she met him instead of me? To what purpose so drastic an error in our lives?

On my visits to town I could always tell from her eyes that she was expecting me, and she'd admit having had a special feeling all day—she'd guessed I'd be coming. We enjoyed our long conversations and silences, not declaring our love for each other but concealing it fearfully and jealously. We feared anything which might betray our secret to ourselves. Deep and tender though my love was, I tried to be sensible about it, speculating what the upshot might be if we should lack the strength to fight our passions. It seemed incredible that a love so quiet, so sad as mine could suddenly and crudely disrupt the happy tenor of her husband's and children's lives: disrupt an entire household where I was so loved and trusted. Was that the way for a decent man to behave? She would have gone away with me—but where to? Where could I take her? Things would have been different if my life had been romantic and enterprising: if I'd been fighting for my country's freedom, for instance, if I'd been a distinguished scholar, actor or artist. As it was I should be conveying her from one humdrum, colourless milieu into another equally humdrum, or even worse. How long would our happiness last? What would happen to her if I became ill or died? What if we just fell out of love?

Her reflections were evidently similar. She thought about her husband and children, thought about her mother who loved her husband like a son. If she yielded to her passions she would either have to lie or tell the truth, but both courses would be equally alarming and difficult to one in her situation. Would her love bring me happiness, she wondered agonizingly. Wouldn't it complicate my life: irksome enough anyway, and beset with all sorts of tribulations? She felt she was too old for me, that she lacked the drive and energy to start a new life. She often told her husband that I ought to marry some decent, intelligent girl who would be a good housewife and helpmeet—but she would add at once that such a paragon was unlikely to be found anywhere in town.

Meanwhile the years were passing. Anne now had two children. Whenever I visited the family the servants smiled their welcome, the children shouted that Uncle Paul had arrived and clung round my neck, and everyone rejoiced. Not understanding my innermost feelings, they thought I was rejoicing with them. They all saw me as the embodiment of integrity. Adults and children alike, they felt that integrity incarnate was walking about the room—which imparted a special charm to their relations with me, as if my presence made their lives purer and finer. Anne and I used to go to the theatre together, always on foot. We would sit beside each other in the stalls, our shoulders touching, and I'd silently take the opera glasses from her, sensing her nearness to me, sensing that she was mine, that we couldn't live without each other. But through some strange lack of *rapport* we always said good-bye when we left the theatre, and we parted like strangers. People were saying goodness knows what about us in town, but not one word of truth was there in all their gossip.

Anne had begun going away to her mother's and sister's more often in recent years. She had become subject to depressions: moods in which she was conscious that her life was unfulfilled and wasted. She didn't want to see her husband and children at such times. She was under treatment for a nervous condition.

And still we did not speak our minds. In company she would feel curiously exasperated with me. She would disagree with everything I said, and if I became involved in an argument she would take my opponent's side. If I chanced to drop something she would coldly offer her 'congratulations'. If I forgot the opera glasses when we went to the theatre, she'd tell me she had 'known very well I'd forget those'.

Luckily or unluckily, there is nothing in our lives which doesn't end sooner or later. The time had now come for us to part: Luganovich had been appointed to a judgeship in the west country. They had to sell their furniture, horses and cottage. We drove out to the cottage, and as we turned back for one last look at the garden and green roof everyone was sad, and I knew that it was time for me to take my leave of rather more than a mere cottage. It had been decided that we should see Anne off to the Crimea (where her doctors had advised her to stay) at the end of August, and that Luganovich would take the children to the west a little later.

A large crowd of us went to see Anne off. She had already said good-bye to her husband and children, and the train was due to leave at any moment, when I dashed into her compartment to put a basket—which she had nearly left behind—on the luggage rack. It was my turn to say good-bye. Our eyes met there in the compartment, and we could hold back no longer. I put my arms around her, she pressed her face against my breast, and the tears flowed. Kissing her face, her shoulders, her tear-drenched hands—we were both so unhappy—I declared my love. With a burning pain in my heart, I saw how inessential, how trivial, how illusory it was . . . everything which had frustrated our love. I saw that, if you love, you must base your theory of love on something loftier and more significant than happiness or unhappiness, than sin or virtue as they are commonly understood. Better, otherwise, not to theorize at all.

I kissed her for the last time, I clasped her hand, and we parted—for ever. The train had already started. I sat down in the next compartment, which was empty . . . sat there, weeping, until the first stop. Then I walked home to Sofyino.

It had stopped raining while Alyokhin was telling his story, and the sun had peeped out. Burkin and Ivan Ivanovich went on to the balcony, which had a superb view of the garden, and of the river which now gleamed, mirror-like, in the sun. As they admired the view they felt sorry that this man with the kind, intelligent eyes—who had spoken with such sincere feeling—really was going round and round the same old treadmill, doing neither academic work nor anything else capable of making his life more pleasant. And they imagined how stricken that young woman must have looked when he had said good-bye to her in the train, kissing her head and shoulders. Both of them had met her in town. Burkin, indeed, had been a friend of hers and had thought her very good-looking.

PEASANTS

I

NICHOLAS Chikildeyev, a waiter at the Slav Fair Hotel in Moscow, fell ill. There was a numbness in his legs and his walk was so much affected that going down a corridor one day he tripped and fell with a trayful of ham and peas. That meant the end of his job. His own and his wife's savings, such as they were, had gone on treatment and they had nothing to live on. Bored with doing nothing, he decided that he must return to his village. Even illness is not so bad at home and life is cheaper. 'No place like home,' they say, and there is something in it.

He reached his village—Zhukovo—towards evening. Remembering the old place from boyhood as a bright, comfortable, homely spot, he actually took fright when he went inside the hut now and saw how dark, cramped and dirty it was. His wife Olga and daughter Sasha had come with him, and they stared aghast at the huge, clumsy stove, black with soot and flies. It took up nearly half the hut. And what a lot of flies! The stove was lop-sided, the beams were askew and the hut looked just about ready to fall down. In the corner opposite the stove, bottle labels and newspaper cuttings had been stuck near the icons to serve as pictures. This was real poverty and no mistake.

The adults were all out harvesting. On the stove sat a little girl of about eight, fair-haired, unwashed, and so bored that she did not even give the newcomers a glance. A white cat rubbed itself against the fire-irons on the floor.

Sasha beckoned to it. 'Puss, puss! Come here, pussy!'

'She can't hear,' said the little girl. 'Deaf.'

'Why?'

'Oh, someone hit her.'

One glance showed Nicholas and Olga how things were, but they said nothing—just threw down their bundles and went out in the street without a word.

Their hut was third from the end and seemed the poorest and oldest. The second hut along was no better, but the one at the end did have a metal roof and window-curtains. This hut, unfenced and standing a little to one side, was the inn. The huts formed a single row and the whole village, quiet and sleepy, with willow, elder and mountain-ash peeping out of the yards, looked pleasant enough.

Behind the villagers' gardens a steep slope, almost a cliff, fell away down to the river, with bare boulders dotted about in the clay. Paths wound down the slope among the boulders and clay-pits dug by potters, and there were great heaps of brown and red broken pottery piled around. Down at the bottom stretched a bright green meadow, broad and level, already mown, where the village herd strayed. The river was the best part of a mile from the village and meandered between splendid leafy banks. Beyond it was another broad meadow, a herd of cattle, long strings of white geese, and then a steep upward rise, as on the near side. At the top of the rise was a large village, a church with five onion-domes and—a little further off—a manor-house.

'Isn't it lovely here!' said Olga, crossing herself as she saw the church. 'Lord, what an open view!'

Then the bell rang for evensong—it was Saturday evening. Two little girls, carrying a bucket of water down below, looked back at the church to listen to the bells.

'Dinner time at the Slav Fair,' said Nicholas dreamily.

Nicholas and Olga sat on the edge of the cliff and watched the sun go down. The sky, all gold and crimson, glowed in the river, in the church windows and through the whole air, gentle, quiet, incredibly pure as it never is in Moscow. After sunset cows and sheep moved past, lowing and bleating, geese flew over from across the river, and then all was quiet. The soft light faded in the air and the evening darkness swiftly descended.

Meanwhile the old folk—Nicholas's father and mother—had come home. They were gaunt, bent, toothless and both the same height. His brothers' wives came too—Marya and Fyokla, who worked at the squire's place across the river. Marya, his brother Kiryak's wife, had six children, and Fyokla—the wife of his brother Denis, who was away in the army—had two. Nicholas went into the hut and saw the whole family, all these bodies large and small, swarming on the sleeping platform, in cradles and in all the corners. He saw how ravenously the old man and the women ate their black bread, dipping it in water, and he knew that he had been wrong to come here—sick, penniless, and with a family too. A great mistake.

'Where's Kiryak?' he asked, after they had greeted each other.

'Lives in some woods belonging to a merchant. He's the watchman there,' his father answered. 'Not a bad lad, but he can put away the liquor all right.'

'He's no good to us,' said the old woman tearfully. 'A rotten lot, our men are—all spend and no earn. Kiryak drinks and the old man knows his way to the pub too, no use saying he doesn't. The Blessed Virgin's angry with us.'

They put the samovar on in honour of the visitors. The tea smelt of fish, the sugar was grey and looked nibbled, and cockroaches scurried over the bread and crockery. The tea was disgusting. No less disgusting was their talk, all about being ill and hard up. Before they had got through their first cup a loud, long, drunken shout was heard from outside.

'Ma-arya!'

'Sounds like Kiryak,' said the old man. 'Talk of the devil.'

No one spoke. A little later the same shout was heard again. Harsh and prolonged, it seemed to come from underground.

'Ma-arya!'

Marya, the elder sister-in-law, turned pale and pressed against the stove. It was odd somehow to see this broad-shouldered, strong, ugly woman so scared. Her daughter, the little girl who had been sitting on the stove looking bored, burst out sobbing.

'What's up with you, you little pest?' shouted Fyokla, a good-looking woman, also strong and broad-shouldered. 'He won't kill anyone, I reckon.'

The old man told Nicholas that Marya was afraid to live in the woods with Kiryak and that he always came for her when drunk, making a great row about it and beating her cruelly.

The yell rang out right by the door.

'Ma-arya!'

'For the love of Christ don't let him hurt me, please,' stammered Marya, gasping as though plunged into icy water. 'Don't let him hurt me. Please. . . .'

The children in the hut all burst into tears, and seeing this Sasha started up as well. There was a drunken cough and a tall man came into the hut. He had a black beard and wore a fur cap. In the dim light of the lamp his face could not be seen, which made him terrifying. This was Kiryak. He went up to his wife, lashed out and punched her in the face. Stunned by the blow, she made not a sound, but her feet seemed to give way. Her nose started bleeding at once.

'A disgrace! A downright disgrace!' muttered the old man, climbing onto the stove. 'In front of visitors too! Proper wicked, I call it!'

The old woman sat there in silence, hunched up and thoughtful. Fyokla rocked a cradle.

Clearly aware of the fear that he caused and pleased by it, Kiryak seized Marya's arm and dragged her to the door, bellowing like a wild animal to make himself more frightening still. Then he saw the visitors and stopped.

'Oh, look who's come ...' he said, letting go of his wife. 'My dear old brother and family. ...'

He said a prayer before the icon, staggering and opening wide his drunken red eyes.

'My dear brother and family come back to the old home ...' he went on. 'From Moscow, eh? From our great capital city of Moscow, eh? The mother of cities. ... So sorry. ...'

He flopped down on the bench near the samovar and began drinking tea, lapping noisily out of the saucer. No one spoke. He drank a dozen cups, then lay on the bench and started snoring.

They went to bed. Nicholas, being ill, was put on the stove with the old man, Sasha lay on the floor and Olga went to the barn with the women.

'Now then, dearie,' she said, lying on the hay by Marya's side. 'Tears won't do no good. You must just put up with it. The Bible says, "Whosoever shall smite thee on thy right cheek, turn to him the other also. ..." That's how it is, dearie.'

Then she spoke in a low, sing-song voice about Moscow and her life there as a maid in a lodging-house.

'They have big houses in Moscow, made of brick and stone,' she said. 'There are lots of churches, hundreds and hundreds of them, dearie. And there's gentlefolk living in them houses. All nice and pretty, they are.'

Marya said that she had never been as far as the local town, let alone Moscow. She could not read or write and knew no prayers, not even 'Our Father'. She and Fyokla, the other sister-in-law who sat a little way off listening, were both very backward and understood nothing. They both disliked their husbands. Marya was scared of Kiryak. She shook with fear whenever he was with her and felt queer in the head because he smelt so strongly of vodka and tobacco. And when Fyokla was asked if she missed her husband, she answered crossly, 'What—him!'

They talked a little and then grew quiet. ...

It was chilly and near the barn a cock was crowing at the top of his voice, keeping them awake. When the bluish morning light began to peep through the cracks, Fyokla quietly got up and went out. Her bare feet were heard pounding the ground as she ran off.

II

Olga went to church and took Marya with her. On their way down the path to the meadow both felt cheerful. Olga liked the open view and Marya felt that her sister-in-law was very near and dear to her. The sun was rising. A sleepy hawk skimmed over the meadow, the river looked gloomy and there were patches of drifting mist, but a streak of sunlight lay on the hill across the river, the church shone, and in the manor garden rooks cawed furiously.

'The old man's all right,' Marya was saying. 'But Gran's very strict. A proper terror, she is. Our own grain only lasted till Shrovetide so we bought some flour at the pub. Real angry, that made her. She says we eat too much.'

'Now then, dearie, you must put up with things, that's all. As was said, "Come unto me, all ye that labour and are heavy laden."'

Olga spoke in a dignified, sing-song voice and walked like a pilgrim, with quick, bustling steps. She read the Gospels every day aloud, like someone reading the lesson in church, not understanding much of them. But the holy words moved her to tears and she almost swooned with delight as she brought out such things as 'whosoever' or 'until I bring thee word'. She believed in God, the Holy Virgin and the Saints. She believed that no one in the world—whether simple folk, Germans, gipsies or Jews—should be harmed, and woe betide even those who were unkind to animals. She believed that this was what the Scriptures tell us, so when she said words from the Bible, even without understanding them, she looked compassionate, radiant and deeply moved.

'Where are you from?' Marya asked her.

'Vladimir. But I was taken to Moscow long ago when I was about eight.'

They reached the river. A woman stood undressing by the water's edge on the far side.

Marya saw who it was. 'That's our Fyokla. She's been across the river, playing around with the staff at the manor. She's a bad girl and she swears something terrible.'

Black-browed Fyokla with her hair down, still young, and strong as a girl, struck out from the bank and thrashed the water with her legs, sending waves in all directions.

'She's a bad girl,' Marya repeated. 'A real bad lot.'

There was a rickety wooden footbridge across the river and just below it in the clear, limpid water moved shoals of broad-headed chub. Dew sparkled on the green bushes that stared into the water and there was a breath of warmth and cheerfulness in the air. What a lovely morning! And how lovely life on earth might be but for poverty—sheer, grinding poverty that you could not escape from. One glance at the village and yesterday's events came vividly to mind, dispersing in a moment the atmosphere of blissful enchantment.

They reached the church. Marya stopped by the porch and ventured no farther, not even daring to sit down, though the bells were not rung for service till after eight o'clock. She remained standing all the time.

During the reading of the Gospel the congregation suddenly moved to make way for the squire's family. Two girls, wearing white dresses and broad-brimmed hats, came in with a plump, rosy little boy in a sailor suit. Olga was touched by their appearance, and one glance decided her that these were nice, cultivated, fine-looking people. But Marya gave the new arrivals a sullen, morose, glowering look as if they were not human, but monsters that would crush her if she did not get out of their way.

Whenever the priest's deep voice boomed out she fancied she heard the shout of 'Ma-arya!' and shuddered.

III

The village learnt of the visitors' arrival and a crowd gathered in the hut after service. The Leonychevs, the Matveichevs and the Ilichovs came for news of relatives working in Moscow. All the lads from Zhukovo who could read and write were packed off to Moscow to be waiters and hotel servants, just as the boys from the village across the river all went as bakers. This had been going on for some time, since the days of serfdom when a certain Luke—a Zhukovo man, now a legendary figure—had been steward at a Moscow club. He would only take on people from his own village to work under him, and as soon as they found their feet they sent for their own relatives and fixed them up in restaurants and taverns. Ever since then Zhukovo village has been called 'Lower Flunkey' or some such name round those parts. Nicholas had been sent to Moscow when he was eleven and was found a job by Ivan, a Matveichev, then an usher at the Hermitage

Garden Theatre. Meeting the Matveichevs now, Nicholas addressed them authoritatively.

'Mr. Ivan did a lot for me. I must pray for him day and night. It was him that gave me my start.'

'Yes, my friend,' said a tall old woman, Ivan's sister, tearfully. 'But not a word do we hear of the poor dear.'

'Last winter he was working at Aumont's and this season I heard he was out of town somewhere in a garden restaurant. . . . He's looking much older. Time was he brought home his ten roubles a day in the summer season, but things are quieter everywhere now and the old fellow's having a thin time.'

The women looked at Nicholas's feet—he wore felt boots—and his pale face.

'You'll never bring much home, Nicholas, that you won't,' they said sadly. 'No indeed!'

They all made a fuss of Sasha. She was ten, but short for her age and very thin. She did not look more than seven. Fair-haired Sasha, with her huge, dark eyes and the red ribbon in her hair, seemed a bit funny among the other little girls, sunburnt with their crude hair-cuts and long, faded smocks. She was like a small animal caught in the fields and brought into the hut.

'The little pet can even read,' boasted Olga, looking lovingly at her daughter. 'Read something, dear,' she said, fetching the Gospels from the corner. 'You read a bit and these good Christian folk will listen.'

It was a heavy old copy of the Gospels in a leather binding with dog-eared edges. It smelt as if monks had come into the hut. Sasha raised her eyebrows and began intoning loudly.

'And when they were departed, behold, the angel of the Lord . . . appeareth to Joseph in a dream, saying, Arise, and take the young child and his mother. . . .'

'The young child and his mother,' Olga repeated, glowing with excitement.

'And flee into Egypt . . . and be thou there until I bring thee word. . . .'

At this 'bring thee word' Olga broke down and wept. First Marya and then Ivan Matveichev's sister looked at her and sobbed. The old man had a coughing fit and fidgeted about looking for some little present for his granddaughter, but found nothing and gave up with a wave of his hand. After the reading was over the neighbours went home, much moved and delighted with Olga and Sasha.

It was a holiday, so the family stayed at home all day. The old woman—'Gran' to her husband, daughters-in-law and grandchildren alike—tried to do everything herself. She lit the stove, put on the samovar, even took the others their dinner in the fields, and then complained of being worked to death. She was always worrying— someone might eat too much or the old man and her daughters-in-law might sit around doing nothing. Thinking that she heard the inn-keeper's geese getting at her kitchen-garden round the back, she some-times dashed out of the hut with a long stick and screeched for half an hour among cabbages as scraggy and decrepit as herself. Or she would think that a crow was after her chicks and rush at it swearing. She stormed and grumbled from morning to night and the row she made often caused people in the street to halt in their tracks.

She was not very kind to the old man—said he was bone idle and a thorough pest. The man was no good. In fact he was hopeless and might just have sat talking on the stove and never done a stroke of work if she had not kept on at him. He held forth to his son about certain enemies of his and complained of being wronged by the neigh-bours every day. This talk was very tiresome.

'Aye,' he would say, holding his sides. 'Aye. . . . Last week in Sep-tember I sold some hay at a rouble the hundredweight. All my own idea. . . . Aye. . . . And very nice too. . . . Well, I'm carting my hay one morning, pleasing myself and minding my own business, when the gaffer, Antip Sedelnikov, comes out of the inn—worse luck. "Where d'you think you're taking that lot, you so-and-so?" says he and clouts me on the ear.'

Kiryak had a hangover and a shocking headache and could hardly face his brother.

'Look what the vodka does for you. Oh, my God!' he muttered, shaking his aching head. 'Forgive me, dearest brother and sister, for Christ's sake. It's not much fun for me either.'

As it was a holiday they bought herring at the inn and made herring's head broth. At noon they all sat down to drink tea and went on and on till the sweat poured off them. Only when they seemed bloated with tea did they start eating the broth, out of a single pot. As for the herring, Gran hid it.

In the evening a potter was firing pots on the slope. Down on the meadow, girls danced country dances and sang. Someone played an accordion. On the far side of the river another kiln was burning and girls were singing. Their songs sounded gentle and melodious at a distance. In and around the inn rowdy peasants sang in discordant, drunken voices and swore so hard that Olga could only shudder. 'Oh, my goodness . . .!' she said.

She wondered why they never seemed to stop swearing and why old men with one foot in the grave swore loudest and longest of all. Obviously used to it from the cradle, children and girls heard the bad language without being in the least put out.

Midnight passed and the kilns went out on both sides of the river, but the merrymaking continued down on the meadow and at the inn. Kiryak and the old man, both drunk, linked arms, banging into each other's shoulders, and went up to the barn where Olga and Marya were lying.

'Let her be,' urged the old man. 'Let her be. . . . She never did no harm. . . . It's all wrong. . . .'

'Ma-arya!' Kiryak shouted.

'Let her be. . . . It's downright wicked. . . . The woman's all right.' They stood near the barn for a minute, then moved off.

'The flowers that bloom in the field tra la,' the old man suddenly sang in a high, shrill tenor. 'I lo-ove to pi-ick them flowers!'

He spat and went into the hut with a foul oath.

IV

Gran stationed Sasha near her kitchen garden and told her to see that the geese didn't get in. It was a hot August day. The inn-keeper's geese could get at the plot round the back, but just now they were busy pecking oats near the inn and quietly chatting. Only the gander craned his neck as if to see whether the old woman was coming with her stick. Other geese might come up from below, but they were feeding far away on the other side of the river, strung out over the meadow like a long daisy-chain.

Sasha stood about for a while, then grew bored and, seeing that no geese were coming, went off to the cliff.

There she saw Marya's eldest daughter Motka standing quite still on a boulder and looking at the church. Marya had had thirteen children, but only six had lived. They were all girls—not a boy among them—and the eldest was eight. Barefoot, in a long smock, Motka stood with the full glare of the sun beating on her head, but was unaware of that and seemed rooted to the spot. Sasha stood by her looking at the church.

'God lives in church,' she said. 'People have lamps and candles, but God has red, green and blue lamps like little eyes. At night God walks round the church with the Holy Mother of God and St. Nicholas —clump, clump, clump . . . ! And the caretaker gets terribly scared. Now then, dearie,' she added, mimicking her mother. 'At the Day of Judgment the churches will all fly off to heaven.'

'Wha-at, be-ells and a-all?' asked Motka in a deep voice, dragging out each syllable.

'Yes, bells and all. On the Day of Judgment all good people will go to heaven, and angry ones will burn forever in everlasting flames, dearie. "You never harmed anyone so you can go to the right—to heaven," God will tell Mother and Marya. But He'll send Kiryak and Gran to the left—into the fire. And anyone who eats meat or drinks milk in Lent will be burnt too.'

She looked up at the sky with wide open eyes.

'If you look at the sky without blinking you'll see angels,' she said.

Motka looked at the sky too and a minute passed in silence.

'See anything?' asked Sasha.

'I can't see nothing,' said Motka in a deep voice.

'Well, I can. There are tiny angels flying round the sky, flapping their little wings—buzz, buzz, like mosquitoes.'

Motka thought a little, looking at the ground. 'Will Gran burn?' she asked.

'Yes, dearie.'

From the boulder a smooth slope led down to the bottom. It was covered with soft green grass that made you want to touch it or lie on it. Sasha lay down and rolled to the bottom. Motka, looking grave and stern, lay down as well and rolled, puffing and panting, to the bottom and her smock got pulled up to her shoulders.

'That was fun,' said Sasha gleefully.

They went up to the top to roll down again, but then a familiar screeching sound was heard. How horrible! Toothless, bony, doubled up, her short grey hair streaming in the wind, Gran was driving geese out of the vegetables with a long stick.

'Trample me cabbages, would 'ee!' she shouted. 'Drat 'ee, curse 'ee and plague be on 'ee! Want yer necks wrung, do 'ee?'

She saw the little girls, threw down her stick and picked up a switch, then seized Sasha's neck with fingers as hard and dry as a pair of tongs and started whipping her. Sasha cried out with pain and fear, whereupon the gander went up to the old woman, waddling and sticking his neck out, and hissed at her. When he went back to the flock, the geese all greeted him with a cackle of approval. Then Gran pitched into Motka, whose smock rode up again. Frantic, sobbing loudly, Sasha went to the hut to complain, followed by Motka who was crying too, but in a deep roar and not wiping her eyes—her face was wet as if she had plunged it in water.

'Goodness gracious me!' cried Olga, aghast, when the two girls came into the hut. 'Holy Mother of God!'

Sasha had just started to tell the tale when Gran came in with a piercing yell, swearing, Fyokla lost her temper, and all hell was let loose in the hut.

Pale and distraught, Olga tried to comfort them. 'There there. Never mind,' she said, stroking Sasha's head. 'She's your granny. You mustn't be cross with her. Never mind, child.'

Worn out by the incessant din, hunger, fumes and stink, hating and despising their poverty, Nicholas was ashamed of the impression that his parents made on his wife and daughter. He dangled his feet from the stove.

'You can't beat her,' he told his mother in an exasperated, tearful voice. 'You've no right.'

'You weakling, rotting up there on the stove!' shouted Fyokla viciously. 'What the hell brought you lot here, eating us out of house and home!'

Sasha and Motka and all the other small girls huddled on the stove in the corner behind Nicholas's back and listened, silent and terrified, their little hearts beating wildly. If someone in a family has been desperately ill for a long while, there are painful moments when, in their heart of hearts, his nearest and dearest quietly and timidly wish for his death. Only children fear the death of a loved one—the idea always horrifies them. So now the little girls held their breath, looking at Nicholas with woebegone expressions, expecting him to die soon. They wanted to cry and say something kind and loving to him.

He clung to Olga as if for protection.

'I can't stick this any more, Olga dear,' he said in a low, quavering voice. 'I can't abide it. For God's sake write to your sister Claudia and tell her for the love of Christ to sell or pawn everything she has and send us money so we can get away.

'Oh God, for one glimpse of Moscow!' he went on in anguish. 'If only I could dream of dear old Moscow town!'

When night fell and the hut grew dark, they could hardly utter a word for sheer misery. Angry Gran dipped rye crusts in a cup and spent a whole hour sucking them. Marya milked the cow, brought in a pail of milk and stood it on a bench. Then Gran poured the milk into jugs, taking her time about it, clearly glad that it was the Fast of the Assumption, so that no one would have any and it could all be kept. She just poured a tiny drop into a saucer for Fyokla's baby.

When she and Marya started taking the jugs to the cellar, Motka suddenly stirred, climbed down from the stove, went to the bench with the wooden cup of crusts on it and splashed some milk from the saucer into the cup.

Gran came back into the hut and settled down to her crusts again while Sasha and Motka sat watching on the stove, glad that she had broken her fast and would now go to hell. They cheered up and lay down to sleep. As she dozed off, Sasha imagined the Day of Judgment. There was a blazing furnace like the potter's and an evil spirit, with horns like a cow and black all over, was driving Gran into the flames with a long stick just as she had driven those geese.

V

At about half past ten on the evening of the Feast of the Assumption the young men and girls making merry down in the meadow suddenly started yelling and screaming and began running towards the village. At first people sitting up on the cliff edge could not see what was the matter.

'Fire! Fire!' came the desperate yell from below. 'The village is on fire.'

Those on top looked round, and a fantastic, grisly spectacle met their eyes. On the thatched roof of a hut at the end of the village stood a column of fire six feet high, writhing and shooting sparks all over the place like a splashing fountain. Then the whole roof went up in a bright flash of flame and there was a loud crackling.

With the whole village caught in the flickering red glare, the moonlight vanished, black shadows moved over the ground and there was a smell of burning. Out of breath, shaken, speechless, those who had run up from below jostled and fell. They could not see properly or recognize each other, being unaccustomed to the glare. It was terrifying, especially the pigeons flying about in the smoke above the fire and the singing and accordion playing that went on quite regardless in the inn, where they did not yet know about the fire.

'Old Simon's hut's on fire!' yelled someone in a rough voice.

Marya was dashing about near her hut, crying and wringing her hands, her teeth chattering, though the fire was right away at the far end of the village. Out went Nicholas in his felt boots and out rushed the children in their little smocks. Near the police constable's hut someone started banging the alarm on an iron sheet. The clang, clang, clang was borne through the air and the incessant, clamorous din caught at the heart and chilled the blood. Old women stood about holding icons. Sheep, calves and cows were driven out of the yards into the street. Trunks, sheepskins and tubs were carried out. A black stallion, usually kept apart from the other horses because he kicked and maimed them, was set free and galloped through the village and back, stamping and whinnying, then suddenly halted by a cart and lashed into it with his hind legs.

Church bells rang on the other side of the river.

Near the burning hut it was hot and so light that every blade of grass on the ground stood out clearly. Simon, a red-haired peasant with a big nose and a peaked cap pulled down to his ears, sat on one of the trunks that they had managed to drag out. He wore a jacket. His wife lay face down, swooning and groaning. An old fellow of about eighty walked about near by, hatless, carrying a white bundle. He was short, with a huge beard and looked like a gnome, and though not a local man, obviously had something to do with the fire. The flames glinted on his bald head. The village elder Antip Sedelnikov, swarthy and black-haired as a gipsy, went up to the hut with an axe and smashed the windows one after the other for no clear reason and then started chopping down the porch.

'Come on, you women! Fetch water!' he shouted. 'And let's have that fire-engine! Get a move on!'

The fire-engine was hauled along by peasants who had just been drinking in the inn. They stumbled and fell, all drunk, all looking helpless with tears in their eyes.

'Come on, you girls! Water!' yelled the elder, also drunk. 'Get a move on, girls!'

Women and girls ran down to the spring, lugged up buckets and tubs filled with water, emptied them in the engine, and ran down again. Olga, Marya, Sasha and Motka all fetched water. The women and boys worked the pump, the hose hissed and the elder directed it at the door or windows, holding back the jet with a finger, which made it hiss even more sharply.

Voices were raised in approval. 'Well done, Antip! Keep it up!'

Antip made his way into the blazing entrance-lobby. 'Pump away!' he shouted from inside. 'Do your best, mates, on this here inauspicious occasion.'

The men stood by in a huddle, idly watching the fire. No one knew what to tackle first—it was quite beyond them—and all around were stacks of wheat and hay, barns and piles of dry brushwood. Kiryak and old Osip, his father, were there as well, both the worse for drink. As if to excuse himself for doing nothing, the old man turned to the woman lying on the ground.

'Don't take on so, old girl,' he said. 'The hut's insured, so why worry?'

Simon turned to one person after another and told them how the fire started.

'It was that old fellow with the bundle—him as used to work for General Zhukov.... Used to be a cook at our old general's, God rest his soul. He comes along this evening and asks us to put him up for the night.... Well, we had a drink or two, see...? The old woman fiddles round with the samovar, getting the old fellow his tea. She puts it in the lobby, worse luck, and the flame goes straight up out of that samovar chimney and catches the thatch. That's what did it. We nearly went up too. The old man's cap was burnt—what a shame.'

They went on and on beating the iron sheet and the church bells across the river kept ringing. Lit up by the glare and out of breath, Olga kept dashing up and down the slope, staring horror-struck at red sheep and pink pigeons flying in the smoke. The ringing seemed to go right into her like a needle. It seemed that the fire would last for ever and that Sasha was lost.

When the roof of the hut crashed in, she thought the whole village was bound to burn down. Too weak to carry any more water, she sat on the cliff, putting her pails near her, while beside and below her women sat wailing as if someone had died.

Then some labourers and staff from the manor farm across the river arrived with two carts and their own fire-engine. A student rode up, a lad in a white military tunic open on the chest. Axes crashed. A ladder was placed against the blazing hulk and five men ran straight up it, the student leading the way. He was red in the face and shouted in a hoarse, biting voice and sounded as if putting out fires was all part of the day's work. They dismantled the hut beam by beam and pulled down the cow-shed, a fence and the nearest rick.

Stern voices were heard in the crowd. 'Stop them busting the place up! Stop them!'

Kiryak made for the hut looking resolute, as if he wanted to stop the newcomers breaking things up, but a labourer turned him back and hit him in the neck. That was good for a laugh and the labourer hit him again. Kiryak fell over and crawled back into the crowd on all fours.

Two pretty girls wearing hats—the student's sisters, no doubt—had also arrived from across the river. They stood watching the fire from some way off. The dismantled beams had stopped blazing, but were smoking furiously. The student worked the hose, pointing the jet at the beams, the peasants and the women bringing water.

'Georgie!' the girls shouted, reproachful and anxious. 'Georgie dear!'

The fire went out, and only when they were moving off did people notice that day was breaking and everyone was pale and rather dark-faced, as always when the last stars vanish from the sky at dawn. Going their several ways, the villagers laughed and made fun of General Zhukov's cook and his burnt cap. By now they wanted to make a joke of the fire and even seemed sorry that it had gone out so quickly.

'You managed the fire very well, sir,' Olga told the student. 'They should send you to Moscow—we have fires there most days.'

'Why, are you from Moscow?' one of the young ladies asked.

'Yes miss. My husband worked at the Slav Fair. And this is my daughter.' She pointed to Sasha who was cold and clung to her. 'She comes from Moscow too, miss.'

The two girls spoke to the student in French and he gave Sasha twenty copecks. Old Osip saw it and his face lit up.

'Thank God there was no wind, sir,' he said to the student. 'Or else the whole place would have gone up in no time. And now, Guv, and you, kind ladies,' he added sheepishly in a lower voice, 'it's a cold dawn and a man needs a bit of warmth . . . so give us the price of a noggin, Guv.'

He got nothing, cleared his throat and slouched off home. Then Olga stood on the edge of the slope and watched the two waggons fording the river and the ladies and gentleman walking across the meadow—a carriage awaited them on the other side. When she had come back to the hut she spoke to her husband.

'Aren't they nice!' she said admiringly. 'And so good-looking too! Just like little cherubs, those young ladies are.'

'Damn and blast 'em!' said sleepy Fyokla viciously.

VI

Marya thought herself unhappy and said that she longed to be dead. But Fyokla found that the life suited her—the poverty, the filth, the frantic cursing. She ate what she was given without fuss and did not care where she slept or what she slept on. She emptied slops outside the front door, splashing them out from the step, and even walked barefoot in the puddles. She took against Olga and Nicholas from the start just because they disliked the life.

'We'll see what you get to eat round here, you and your fine Moscow ways!' she said with malicious glee. 'We'll see about that.'

One morning early in September, Fyokla, pink with cold, healthy and handsome, brought up two pails of water. Marya and Olga were sitting at table drinking tea.

'Tea and sugar!' sneered Fyokla.

'Quite the ladies, aren't we?' she added, putting down the pails. 'Quite the latest fashion, I suppose, this drinking tea every day. Mind you don't burst, you and your tea!' she went on, giving Olga a look of hate. 'Fed your face all right in Moscow, didn't you, you fat bitch!'

She swung the yoke and hit Olga on the shoulder, making both her sisters-in-law throw up their hands.

'Oh, good heavens!' they said.

Then Fyokla went to the river to wash clothes, swearing so loudly all the way down that they heard her in the hut.

The day passed and the long autumn evening set in. They were winding silk in the hut—everyone except Fyokla who had gone across the river. The silk came from a near-by factory and the whole family earned a little from it, about twenty copecks a week.

'We were better off as serfs,' said the old man, winding his silk. 'You worked, you ate, you slept—everything in its proper turn. There was cabbage soup and gruel for dinner and the same again for supper. There was cucumbers and cabbage aplenty, you could eat away to your heart's content. Things were stricter too—we all knew our place.'

The only light came from a single lamp that gave a dim glow and smoked. When anyone stood in the way of it, a large shadow fell on the window and you could see bright moonlight. Old Osip told a leisurely tale about life before the serfs were freed. In these very parts where things were so drab and miserable now, there had been hunting with hounds, borzois and teams of huntsmen skilled in driving wolves towards the guns. There was vodka for the beaters, and whole waggon-trains took the game to Moscow for the young masters. Bad peasants were flogged or sent to the family estate in Tver and good ones were rewarded.

Gran also told a tale or two. She remembered every single thing. She talked about her mistress, a kind, God-fearing woman whose husband was a drunken rake. Her daughters all made unsuitable marriages—one to a drunkard and another to a tradesman, while the third eloped, helped by Gran herself, who was just a girl at the time. Like their mother they all died of broken hearts. Remembering all this, Gran even shed a tear.

Suddenly there was a knock on the door that made them all start. 'Put us up for the night, Osip old friend.'

In came a little bald old man, General Zhukov's cook, the one whose cap was burnt. He sat down and listened and then he too started recalling old times and telling stories. Nicholas sat listening on the stove with his legs dangling down and kept asking what food they cooked in the days of serfdom. They talked about rissoles, soups and sauces of various kinds. And the cook, who also had a good memory, named dishes that no longer existed. For instance there was something made from bulls' eyes and called, 'Wake me early in the morning.'

'Did you ever make cutlets à la maréchal?' asked Nicholas.

'No.'

Nicholas shook his head reproachfully. 'Call yourselves cooks!' he said.

The little girls sat or lay on the stove, looking down without blinking. There seemed to be a great many of them, like cherubs in the clouds. They liked the stories. They sighed, shuddered and grew pale with ecstasy or fear. Gran's stories were the most interesting of all and they listened breathlessly, afraid to move.

They lay down to sleep in silence. Agitated and excited by the stories, the old people thought how precious youth was, because no matter what it had been like at the time, it left only joyful, lively, stirring memories behind. And they thought of the fearful chill of death. That was not so far off—best not to think about it. The lamp went out. The darkness, the two windows sharply defined by the moonlight, the stillness and the creaking cradle somehow served only to remind them that their life was over and that there was no bringing it back.

You doze off and forget everything. But then someone suddenly touches your shoulder or breathes on your cheek and sleep is gone,

your body feels numb and thoughts of death will come into your mind.
You turn over and forget death, but the same old miserable, dreary
thoughts go round and round inside your head—about poverty, cattle
feed and the rising price of flour. Then a little later you remember once
again that life has passed you by and you can't put back the clock. . . .

'Oh Lord!' sighed the cook.

Someone tapped faintly on the window—Fyokla must be back.
Olga stood up, yawning and whispering a prayer, opened the door
and drew the bolt in the lobby. But no one came in. There was just
a breath of cold from the street and the sudden brightness of the moonlight. Through the open door Olga could see the street, quiet and
empty, and the moon riding in the sky.

'Who's there?' she called.

'It's me,' came the answer. 'Me.'

Near the door, clinging to the wall, stood Fyokla, completely naked,
shivering with cold, her teeth chattering. She looked very pale,
beautiful and strange in the bright moonlight. The shadows and glint
of moonlight on her skin stood out vividly, and her dark brows and
firm young breasts were especially sharply outlined.

'Them swine across the river stripped me and turned me loose like
this . . .' she said. 'I've come all the way home with nothing on . . .
mother naked. Bring me something to put on.'

'Well, come inside,' said Olga quietly, starting to shiver as well.

'I don't want the old folk to see me.'

Sure enough, Gran had started muttering restlessly and the old man
was asking, 'Who's there?' Olga brought her own smock and skirt
and put them on Fyokla and then both crept into the hut, trying
not to bang the doors.

'That you, my beauty?' Gran grumbled crossly, guessing who it was.
'Gadding about in the middle of the night, are you . . . ? Need your
neck wrung, you do!'

'Never mind, it's all right,' whispered Olga, wrapping Fyokla up.
'Never mind, dearie.'

It grew quiet again. They always slept badly in the hut, each with
something everlastingly nagging at him and keeping him awake. With
the old man it was backache, with Gran it was her worries and bad
temper, with Marya it was fear and with the children it was itching
and being hungry. And tonight their sleep was as troubled as ever.
They kept turning over, talking in their sleep or getting up for a drink.

Fyokla suddenly yelled out in her loud, harsh voice, but took a grip

on herself at once and went on with occasional sobs that grew quieter
and more muffled till she stopped entirely. From time to time a clock
was heard striking across the river, but there was something odd about
it, for it struck first five and then three.

'Oh Lord!' sighed the cook.

It was hard to tell by looking at the windows whether it was still
moonlight or already daybreak. Marya got up and went out and could
be heard milking the cow outside and saying, 'Stea-dy there!' Gran
went out too. It was still dark in the hut, but you could already make
things out.

Nicholas, who had not slept all night, got down from the stove.
He took his tail-coat from a small green chest, put it on and, going to
the window, smoothed the sleeves, held it by the tails and smiled.
Then he carefully took the coat off, put it back in the chest, and lay
down again.

Marya came back and started lighting the stove. She was obviously
not fully awake and was still waking up as she moved about. She had
probably had a dream or remembered last night's stories because she
said, stretching luxuriously in front of the stove, 'No, better be free
than a serf.'

VII

The 'Governor' turned up—this was what they called the local
police inspector in the village. They had known for a week when he
was coming and why. There were only forty households in Zhukovo,
but their arrears of taxes and rates had passed the two thousand rouble
mark.

The inspector put up at the inn. He 'partook of' two glasses of tea,
then walked off to the village elder's hut near which a group of defaulters awaited him.

Despite his youth—he was not much over thirty—the 'elder', Antip
Sedelnikov, was strict and always backed up the authorities, though
poor and irregular with his own tax payments. He obviously enjoyed
being elder and liked the sense of power, which he could only display
by severity. He was feared and heeded at village meetings. He was
known to pounce on a drunk in the street or near the inn, tie his arms
behind him and shove him in the lock-up. He had once even put Gran
inside for twenty-four hours for swearing when attending a meeting
in place of Osip. Never having lived in a town or read a book, he had

somehow picked up a stock of long words and liked to use them in conversation, for which he was respected, if not always understood.

When Osip went into the elder's hut with his tax-book, the inspector, a lean old man with long grey whiskers, wearing a grey tunic, was sitting at a table in the corner opposite the stove making notes. The hut was clean and pictures cut out of magazines lent variety to the walls. In the most prominent place near the icons hung a portrait of Alexander of Battenberg, one-time Prince of Bulgaria. Antip Sedelnikov stood by the table with folded arms.

'This one owes a hundred and nineteen roubles, sir,' he said when Osip's turn came. 'He paid a rouble before Easter, but not a copeck since.'

The inspector looked up at Osip. 'Why is that, my man?'

'Don't be too hard on us, sir, for God's sake,' began Osip in a great pother. 'Let me speak, sir. Last year the squire from Lyutoretsk says, "Osip," he says, "sell me your hay . . ." says he. "You sell it." Well, why not? I had a couple of tons to sell that the women had mown down on the meadow. . . . Well, we agreed on the price. . . . All nice and above board. . . .'

He complained of the elder and kept turning to the other peasants as if calling them to witness. His face was red and sweaty and his eyes were sharp and vicious.

'I don't know why you tell me all this,' said the inspector. 'I'm asking you. . . . I'm asking you why you don't pay your arrears, man. None of you pay up. Think I'm going to take the blame?'

'I can't help it.'

'These remarks haven't got no consequence, sir,' said the elder. 'Actually them Chikildeyevs are a bit impecunious like, but if you care to ask the others, you'll find it's all due to vodka and general misbehaviour. They're just ignorant.'

The inspector made a note. Quietly and evenly, as if asking for a drink of water, he told Osip to clear out.

He left soon after, coughing as he got into his cheap carriage. Even the set of his long, thin back showed that he had forgotten Osip, the elder and the Zhukovo arrears, and was thinking of his own affairs.

Before he had gone a mile Antip Sedelnikov was taking the samovar from the Chikildeyevs' hut, followed by Gran, shrieking at the top of her voice, 'You shan't have it! You shan't have it, damn you.'

He walked swiftly with long strides while she panted after him, stumbling, bent double, furious. Her kerchief had slipped onto her shoulders and her grey hair with its greenish tinge streamed in the breeze. All at once she paused.

'Christian, God-fearing people! Friends, we've been wronged,' she shouted louder than ever in a sort of sobbing chant and started beating her breast, as if taking part in a real peasants' revolt. 'They done us wrong, mates! Stick up for us, dear friends!'

'Look here, Gran,' said the elder sternly. 'Do show some sense.'

Life was very dull in the Chikildeyevs' hut without a samovar. There was something degrading and insulting about this deprivation, as if the hut had been dishonoured. Better if the elder had gone off with the table or all the benches and pots—the place would have seemed less empty. Gran shrieked, Marya wept and the little girls took their cue from her and wept too. The old man felt guilty and sat silent in the corner with a hang-dog look.

Nicholas did not say anything either. Gran was fond of him and pitied him, but now she forgot her pity and suddenly stormed at him with reproaches and abuse, thrusting her fists right under his nose. It was all his fault, she shouted. And really, why had he sent them so little money after boasting in his letters of getting fifty roubles a month at the Slav Fair? Why had he come here—with his family and all? And if he died how would they pay for his funeral?

Nicholas, Olga and Sasha looked utterly miserable.

The old man cleared his throat, took his cap and went to see the elder. It was already growing dark. Antip Sedelnikov was soldering near his stove, puffing out his cheeks. The place was full of fumes. His scraggy, unwashed children, no better than the Chikildeyevs', were messing about on the floor, and his wife—ugly, freckled, with a bulging stomach—was winding silk. It was a wretched and miserable family except for jaunty, handsome Antip. Five samovars stood in a row on a bench.

The old man said a prayer to the portrait of Prince Battenberg.

'Antip,' said he, 'don't be too hard on us, for God's sake, and give us back our samovar. Have a heart!'

'Bring three roubles and you can have it.'

'What a hope!'

Antip puffed out his cheeks and the flame droned and hissed, glinting on the samovars. The old man twisted his cap and thought for a moment.

'You give it back,' he said.

The swarthy elder looked quite black, like a sort of sorcerer. He turned to Osip.

'It all depends on the magistrate,' he said rapidly and severely. 'You can state your grounds for dissatisfaction verbally or in writing at the administrative session on the twenty-sixth of the month.'

It meant nothing to Osip, but he left it at that and went home.

About ten days later the inspector came again, stayed about an hour and left. The weather was cold and windy at the time. The river had frozen long ago, but there was still no snow and everyone was fed up because the roads were impassable.

Late one Sunday afternoon Osip's neighbours called for a chat. They sat in the dark, as it would have been sinful to work and the lamp was not lit. There were a few rather unpleasant bits of news. Two or three households had had hens seized for tax arrears. They had been taken to the local offices where they had died because no one fed them. Sheep had also been seized, carted off with their legs tied together and shifted from one cart to another at every village. One of them had died. Now they were arguing about whose fault it was.

'The council's,' said Osip. 'Who else?'

'It's the council. Stands to reason.'

The council got the blame for everything—for tax arrears, abuses generally and crop failures, though none of them knew what a council was. This went back to the time when some rich peasants, with workshops, stores and inns of their own, had done a spell on the council, which had left them with a grudge against it and a habit of cursing it in their workshops and inns.

They talked of the snow that God had not sent them. There was firewood to cart, but you could not drive or walk for the bumps in the road. Fifteen or twenty years ago and earlier the local small talk had been much more amusing. In those days every old man had looked as though he had some secret, something that he knew about and was expecting. They talked of a charter with a gold seal, land partition, new territories, buried treasure. And they were always hinting at something. But now the villagers had no secrets, their whole life was an open book for anyone to read, and all they could talk about was poverty, cattle feed and the fact that there had been no snow.

They said nothing for a while. Then they remembered about the hens and sheep, and went on arguing about whose fault it was.

'The council's,' said Osip lugubriously. 'Who else?'

VIII

The parish church was about four miles away in Kosogorovo and the peasants only went there when they had to, for christenings, weddings or funerals. For ordinary worship they just crossed the river. On fine Sundays and saints' days the girls dressed up and went to service in a body, and it was a cheering sight to see them cross the meadow in their red, yellow and green dresses. In bad weather they all stayed at home. They went to pre-communion services in the parish church. Those who had not prepared themselves for communion in Lent were charged fifteen copecks each by the parish priest when he went round the huts with the cross at Easter.

The old man did not believe in God because he hardly ever gave Him a thought. He recognized the supernatural, but thought it was women's business. When the subject of religion or miracles came up and he was asked what he thought, he would scratch himself. 'How should I know?' he would say reluctantly.

Gran believed, but somewhat vaguely. It was all jumbled up in her mind. No sooner had she started thinking about sin, death and salvation, than hardship and worries took over, whereupon she forgot what she had been thinking about. She had forgotten her prayers and usually stood in front of the icons at bedtime, whispering, 'To the Virgin of Kazan, to the Virgin of Smolensk, to the Virgin of the Three Arms. . . .'

Marya and Fyokla crossed themselves and took communion once a year, but it meant nothing to them. They did not teach their children to pray, never spoke to them of God and taught them no principles. They only told them not to eat the wrong things during fasts. It was much the same with other families—few believed, few understood. Yet they all loved the Scriptures, loved them dearly and revered them, but they had neither books nor anyone to read and explain things. They respected Olga for reading the Gospels to them sometimes and always treated her and Sasha with deference.

Olga often went to church festivals and special services in near-by villages and the local county town, which had two monasteries and twenty-seven churches. She was rather vague and forgot all about her family on these pilgrimages. Only when she came home did she suddenly discover to her great delight that she had a husband and daughter. 'God has been good to me,' she would say, smiling and radiant.

The village goings-on pained and sickened her. On Elijah's Day they drank. On the Feast of the Assumption they drank. On Holy

Cross Day they drank. The Feast of the Intercession was the parish holiday for Zhukovo and the villagers seized the chance to drink for three days. They drank their way through fifty roubles of communal funds and then the village had a whip-round for more vodka. The Chikildeyevs killed a sheep on the first day and ate vast helpings of it morning, noon and night, and even then the children got up at night for a bite. Kiryak was terribly drunk on all three days. He drank the cap off his head and the boots off his feet, and beat Marya so hard that she had to be doused with water. Later on everyone felt ashamed and sick.

But even Zhukovo or 'Lower Flunkey' had one true religious ceremony—in August when the Icon of the Blessed Life-giving Virgin was carried round the whole district from village to village. It was on a quiet, overcast day that it was expected in Zhukovo. The girls in their bright Sunday dresses had gone to meet the icon in the morning and it had been brought in with singing and a procession in the late afternoon while bells pealed across the river. A great crowd of people from the village and elsewhere blocked the street. There was noise, dust and a great crush of people.

The old man, Gran and Kiryak—all stretched out their hands to the icon, feasting their eyes on it. 'Intercessor, Holy Mother! Pray for us!' they said tearfully.

Everyone seemed to understand at once that there was no void between heaven and earth, that the rich and strong had not yet grabbed everything, that there was still someone to protect them against ill-treatment, slavery and bondage, against intolerable, grinding poverty and the demon vodka.

'Intercessor, Holy Mother!' sobbed Marya. 'Holy Mother!'

But the service ended, the icon was taken off, and everything was as before. Harsh, drunken voices once more came from the inn.

Only the rich peasants feared death. The richer they grew, the less they believed in God and salvation, and if they gave candles and had special masses said, it was only for fear of their earthly end and to be on the safe side. Poorer peasants were not afraid to die. People told Gran and the old man to their faces that their day was done and it was time they were dead. They didn't care. And people thought nothing of telling Fyokla in Nicholas's presence that when he died her husband Denis would get his discharge and be sent home from the army. Far from fearing death, Marya wished that it would come quicker and was glad when her children died.

Though not afraid of death they did have an exaggerated horror of all illnesses. The slightest thing—an upset stomach, a mild chill—was enough to make Gran lie on the stove, wrap herself up and embark on a series of hearty groans. 'I'm dy-ing!' The old man would rush off for the priest and Gran would be given the sacrament and extreme unction.

They were always talking about colds, tape-worms and tumours going round the stomach and moving up to the heart. They were more frightened of catching cold than of anything, so wrapped up well and warmed themselves on the stove even in summer. Gran liked seeing the doctor and often went to hospital, giving her age as fifty-eight instead of seventy. She thought that if the doctor knew her real age he would refuse to treat her, and say she ought to be dead—not consulting him. She usually left for hospital in the early morning, taking two or three of the little girls, and came back in the evening, hungry and cross, with drops for herself and ointment for the children. She once took Nicholas as well and for a fortnight afterwards he was taking drops and said they did him good.

Gran knew all the doctors, medical assistants and quacks for twenty miles around and disliked the lot. At the Feast of the Intercession, when the priest went round the huts with his cross, the parish clerk told her of an old fellow living near the prison in town, a former army medical orderly who was good at cures. He advised her to consult him. Gran did. She drove off to town at first snowfall and brought back a little bearded old man in a long coat, a converted Jew whose whole face was covered with blue veins. There happened to be some jobbing craftsmen working in the hut at the time. An old tailor, wearing awe-inspiring spectacles, was cutting a waistcoat out of odd bits and pieces and two young fellows were making felt boots out of wool. Having been sacked for drinking, Kiryak lived at home these days and was sitting beside the tailor mending a horse-collar. It was crowded, stuffy and smelly in the hut. The Jew examined Nicholas and said that he must be bled.

He put on the cups. The old tailor, Kiryak and the little girls stood watching and thought that they could see the illness coming out of Nicholas. Nicholas also watched the cups stuck to his chest gradually filling with dark blood. He felt that something really was leaving him and smiled with pleasure.

'Good thing, this,' said the tailor. 'Let's hope it's some use.'

The Jew put on twelve cups and then twelve more, had some tea and left. Nicholas started to shiver. His face looked peaked and seemed 'clenched like a fist', the women said. His fingers turned blue. He wrapped himself in a blanket and sheepskin, but grew colder and colder. By evening he felt very low. He wanted to be put on the floor and asked the tailor not to smoke. Then he went quiet inside his sheepskin and by morning he was dead.

IX

What a hard winter it was and what a long one!

Their own grain ran out by Christmas and they had to buy flour. Now that Kiryak lived at home he made such a din in the evenings that everyone was scared. He had such frightful headaches and felt so ashamed of himself in the mornings that it was painful to look at him. The starving cow could be heard lowing in the shed day and night, a heart-breaking sound to Gran and Marya. Needless to say, there were hard frosts all the time and deep snowdrifts. Winter dragged on. On Lady Day a real blizzard blew up and it snowed at Easter.

Anyway, winter did end. In early April the days were warm, with night frosts. Winter still held out, but one day the warmth won through at last. Streams flowed and birds sang. The whole meadow and the bushes near the river were submerged in spring floods and between Zhukovo and the far bank there was one vast sheet of water with flocks of wild duck taking wing here and there. Every evening the blazing spring sunset and gorgeous clouds presented a new, un-believable, extraordinary sight—the sort of colours and clouds that you just cannot believe if you see them in a picture.

Cranes sped past overhead, calling plaintively as if asking someone to join them. Standing on the edge of the cliff, Olga gazed for some time at the floods, the sun and the bright church which looked like new. Her tears flowed and she caught her breath, feeling a wild urge to go away somewhere into the blue, even to the ends of the earth. It had been settled that she was to go back to Moscow as a house-maid, and Kiryak was to go with her to take a hall-porter's job or some-thing. If they could only go soon!

When it was dry and warm they prepared to leave. With packs on their backs, both wearing bark shoes, Olga and Sasha left the hut at daybreak. Marya came out to see them off—Kiryak was ill and was staying at home for another week.

Olga looked at the church for the last time and said a prayer, thinking of her husband. She did not cry, but her face puckered up and looked as ugly as an old woman's. She had grown thin and plain and a little grey that winter and her bereavement had given her face a resigned, sad expression in place of her former attractive looks and pleasant smile. There was something blank and torpid about her glance, as if she was deaf. She was sorry to leave the village and the villagers. She remembered them carrying Nicholas's body and asking for a prayer to be said for him at each hut, everyone weeping in sympathy with her grief.

During the summer and winter there had been hours and days when these people seemed to live worse than beasts. They were frightful people to live with—rough, dishonest, filthy, drunken. Holding each other in mutual disrespect, fear and suspicion, they were always at loggerheads, always squabbling.

Who keeps the pot-house and makes the peasant drunk? The peasant. Who squanders his village, school and church funds on drink? The peasant. Who steals from his neighbours, sets fire to their property and perjures himself in court for a bottle of vodka? Who is the first to run down the peasant at council and other meetings? The peasant.

Yes, they were frightful people to live with. Still, they were men and women, they suffered and wept like men and women, and there was nothing in their lives for which an excuse could not be found—back-breaking work that makes you ache all over at night, cruel winters, poor harvests and overcrowding, with no help and nowhere to turn for it. The richer and stronger ones are no help, for they are rough, dishonest and drunken themselves and use the same filthy language. The pettiest official or clerk treats the peasants like tramps, even talking down to elders and churchwardens as if by right. Anyway, what help or good example can you expect from grasping, greedy, depraved, lazy persons who come to the village only to insult, rob and intimidate? Olga remembered how pitiful and crushed the old people had looked at the time when Kiryak had been taken off to be flogged that winter.

She now felt sick with pity for all these people and kept turning back to look at the huts.

Marya went with her for about two miles, then said goodbye, knelt down and began wailing, pressing her face to the ground.

'I'm on my own again. Poor me, poor lonely, unhappy me . . . !'

For a long time she moaned like this. And for a long time Olga and Sasha saw her kneeling and bowing as if to someone at her side, clutching her head while rooks flew above.

The sun rose high and it grew hot. Zhukovo was far behind. It was a nice day for walking and Olga and Sasha soon forgot both village and Marya. They felt cheerful and found everything entertaining. It might be an old burial mound or a row of telegraph poles marching who knows where over the horizon, their wires whining mysteriously. Or they would see a far-away farm-house sunk in foliage, smelling of dampness and hemp, and somehow felt that it was a happy home. Or they would see a horse's skeleton, bleached and lonely in the open country. Larks trilled furiously, quails called to each other and the corncrake's cry sounded as if someone was jerking an old iron latch.

At midday Olga and Sasha reached a large village. In the broad village street they ran across the little old man, General Zhukov's cook, all hot, with his red, sweaty bald pate shining in the sun. Olga and he did not recognize each other, but then both looked round together and saw who it was and went their ways without a word. Stopping by a hut that looked newer and more prosperous than the others, Olga bowed in front of the open windows.

'Good Christian folk,' she chanted in a loud, shrill voice, 'alms for the love of Christ, of your charity, God rest the souls of your parents, may the Kingdom of Heaven be theirs.'

'Good Christian folk,' intoned Sasha, 'alms for the love of Christ, of your charity, the Kingdom of Heaven. . . .'

ANGEL

MISS OLGA PLEMYANNIKOV, daughter of a retired minor civil servant, sat brooding on the porch in her yard. She was hot, she was plagued by flies, she was glad it would soon be evening. Dark rain clouds were moving in from the east, and there were a few puffs of damp wind from the same quarter.

In the middle of her yard stood Vanya Kukin. He was in the entertainments business—he ran the Tivoli Pleasure Gardens—and he lived in a detached cottage in the grounds of Olga's house. He gazed up at the sky.

'Oh no, not *again*!' he said desperately. 'Not *more* rain! Why does it have to rain every single blessed day? This is the absolute limit! It'll be the ruin of me—such terrible losses every day!'

He threw up his arms.

'Such is our life, Miss,' he went on, addressing Olga. 'It's pathetic! You work, you do your best, you worry, you lie awake at night, you keep thinking how to improve things. But what happens? Take the audiences, to start with—ignorant savages! I give them the best operetta and pantomime, give them first-rate burlesque. But do they want it? Do they understand any of it? They want vulgar slapstick, that's what they want. And then, just look at this weather: rain nearly every evening. It started on May the tenth, and it's been at it the whole of May and June. It's an abomination! There are no audiences, but who has to pay the rent? Who pays the performers? Not me, I suppose, oh dear me no!'

Clouds gathered again late next afternoon.

'Oh, never mind, *let* it rain,' Kukin laughed hysterically. 'Let it swamp the whole Gardens, me included. May I enjoy no happiness in this world or the next! May the performers sue me! Better still, let them send me to Siberia: to hard labour! Even better, send me to the gallows, ha, ha, ha.'

It was just the same on the third day.

Olga listened to Kukin silently and seriously, with occasional tears in her eyes, until his troubles moved her in the end, and she fell in love. He was a short, skinny, yellow-faced fellow with his hair combed back over his temples. He had a reedy, high-pitched voice, he twisted his mouth when he spoke, he always had a look of desperation. Yet he aroused deep and true emotion in her. She was always in love with someone—couldn't help it. Before this she had loved her father: an invalid, now, wheezing in his arm-chair in a darkened room. She had loved her aunt who came over from Bryansk to see her about once every two years. Earlier still, at junior school, she had loved the French master. She was a quiet, good-hearted, sentimental, very healthy young lady with a tender, melting expression. Looking at her full, rosy cheeks, at her soft white neck with its dark birth-mark, at her kind, innocent smile whenever she heard good tidings—men thought she was 'a bit of all right'. They would smile too, while her lady guests couldn't resist suddenly clasping her hand when talking to her.

'You really are an *angel*!' they would gush.

The house where she had lived since birth, and which she was due to inherit, stood on the outskirts of town: in Gipsy Lane, near Tivoli Gardens. In the evenings and at night she could hear the band in the Gardens and the crash of bursting rockets, and it all sounded to her like Kukin battling with his doom and taking his main enemy—the indifferent public—by storm. She would feel deliciously faint—not at all sleepy—and when Kukin came back in the small hours she would tap her bedroom window, showing him only her face and one shoulder through the curtains . . . and smile tenderly.

He proposed, they were married, and when he had feasted his eyes on that neck and those plump, healthy shoulders, he clapped his hands.

'You *angel*!' he said.

He was happy, but it rained on his wedding day—*and* his wedding night—so that look of desperation remained.

They lived happily after the marriage. She would sit in the box-office, look after the Gardens, record expenses, hand out wages. Her rosy cheeks, her charming, innocent, radiant smile could be glimpsed, now through the box-office window, now in the wings, now in the bar. Already she was telling all her friends that there was nothing in this world so remarkable, so important, so vital as the stage. True pleasure, culture, civilization . . . only in the theatre were these things to be had.

'But does the public understand?' she would ask. 'They want slap-stick. We put on *Faust Inside Out* yesterday, and almost all the boxes were empty. But if we'd staged some vulgar rubbish, me and Vanya, we'd have had a full house, you take my word. We're presenting *Orpheus in the Underworld* tomorrow, me and Vanya. You must come.'

Whatever Kukin said about the theatre and actors, she echoed. Like him she scorned the public for its ignorance and indifference to art. She interfered in rehearsals, she corrected the actors, she kept an eye on the bandsmen. Whenever there was an unfavourable theatrical notice in the local newspaper she would weep—and then go and demand an explanation from the editor's office.

The actors liked her, they called her 'Me and Vanya' and 'Angel'. She was kind to them, she lent them small sums, and if any of them let her down she would go and cry secretly without complaining to her husband.

They did quite well in winter too. They had taken the town theatre for the whole season, and rented it out for short engagements to a Ukrainian troupe, a conjurer, some local amateurs. Olga grew buxom and radiated happiness, while Kukin became thinner and yellower, and complained of his appalling losses though business was pretty good all winter. He coughed at night, and she would give him raspberry or lime-flower tisane, rub him with eau-de-Cologne and wrap him up in her soft shawls.

'Oh, you are such a splendid little chap,' she would say, stroking his hair and meaning every word. 'You're such a handsome little fellow.'

When he was away in Moscow in Lent recruiting a new company she couldn't sleep, but just sat by the window looking at the stars. She compared herself to a hen—they too are restless and sleepless at night without a cock in the fowl-house. Kukin was held up in Moscow. But he'd be back by Easter, he wrote, and he was already making certain plans for the Tivoli in his letters. Then, late on Palm Sunday evening, there was a sudden ominous knocking at the gate as someone pummelled it till it boomed like a barrel. Shuffling barefoot through the puddles, the sleepy cook ran to answer.

'Open up, please,' said a deep, hollow voice outside. 'A telegram for you.'

Olga had had telegrams from her husband before, but this time she nearly fainted for some reason. She opened it with trembling fingers, and read as follows:

MR KUKIN PASSED AWAY SUDDENLY TODAY
NUBSCUTCH AWAIT INSTRUCTIONS FUFERAL
TUESDAY

That's what was printed in the telegram: FUFERAL. And there

was this meaningless NUBSCUTCH too. It was signed by the operetta producer.

'My darling!' Olga sobbed. 'My lovely, darling little Vanya, oh why did I ever meet you? Why did I have to know you, love you? For whom have you forsaken your poor, miserable little Olga?'

Kukin was buried in the Vagankov Cemetery in Moscow on the Tuesday. Olga returned home on Wednesday, flopped down on her bed as soon as she reached her room, and sobbed so loudly that she could be heard out in the street and in the next-door yards.

'Poor angel!' said the ladies of the neighbourhood, crossing themselves. 'Darling Olga—she is taking it hard, poor dear.'

One day three months later Olga was coming dolefully back from church, in full mourning. A neighbour, Vasya Pustovalov, manager of the Babakayev timber-yard—also on his way back from church—chanced to be walking by her side. He wore a boater and a white waistcoat with a gold chain across it. He looked more like a country squire than a tradesman.

'There's always a pattern in things, Mrs. Kukin,' said he in a grave, sympathetic voice. 'The death of a dear one must be God's will, in which case we must be sensible and endure it patiently.'

He saw Olga to her gate, he said good-bye, he went his way. Afterwards she seemed to hear that grave voice all day, and she need only close her eyes to see his dark beard in her imagination. She thought him very attractive. And she must have made an impression on him, too, because not long afterwards a certain elderly lady, whom she barely knew, came to take coffee with her . . . and had hardly sat down at table before she was on about Pustovalov. What a good steady man he was, said she—any young lady would be glad to marry him. Three days later Pustovalov called in person. He only stayed about ten minutes, he hadn't much to say for himself, but Olga fell so much in love with him that she lay awake all night in a hot, feverish state. In the morning she sent for the elderly lady, the match was soon made, a wedding followed.

After their marriage the Pustovalovs lived happily. He was usually at the timber-yard till lunch. Then he would do his business errands while Olga took his place—sitting in the office till evening, keeping accounts, dispatching orders.

'Timber prices rise twenty per cent a year these days,' she would tell customers and friends. 'We used to deal in local stuff, but now—just fancy!—Vasya has to go and fetch it from out Mogilyov way every year. And what a price!' she would say, putting both hands over her cheeks in horror. 'What a price!'

She felt as if she had been a timber dealer from time immemorial. The most vital and essential thing in life was wood, she felt. And she found something deeply moving in the words joist, logging, laths, slats, scantlings, purlins, frames, slabs. When she was asleep at nights, she would dream of mountains of boards and laths, and of long, never-ending wagon trains taking timber somewhere far out of town. She dreamt of a whole battalion of posts, thirty foot by one foot, marching upright as they moved to take the timber-yard by storm. Beams, baulks, slabs clashed with the resounding thud of seasoned wood, falling down and getting up again, jamming against each other, and Olga would cry out in her sleep.

'What's the matter, Olga dear?' Pustovalov would ask tenderly, and tell her to cross herself.

She shared all her husband's thoughts. If he thought the room too hot, if he thought business slack—then she thought so as well. Her husband disliked all forms of entertainment, and stayed at home on his days off. So she did too.

'You spend all your time at home or in the office,' her friends would say. 'You should go to the theatre or the circus, angel.'

'We haven't time for theatre-going, me and Vasya,' she would answer gravely. 'We're working people, we can't be bothered with trifles. What's so wonderful about your theatres, anyway?'

The Pustovalovs attended vespers on Saturday nights. On Sundays and saints'-days they went to early service, and walked back from church side by side—with rapt expressions, both smelling sweet, her silk dress rustling agreeably. At home they drank tea with fine white bread and various jams, and then ate pasties. At noon each day their yard, and the street outside their gate, were deliciously redolent of beetroot soup, roast lamb and duck—and of fish in Lent. You couldn't pass their gate without feeling hungry. They always kept the samovar boiling in the office, and they treated their customers to tea and buns. Once a week they both went to the public baths, and they would walk back side by side, red-faced.

'We're doing all right,' Olga told her friends. 'It's a good life, praise be. God grant everyone to live like me and Vasya.'

When Pustovalov went to fetch timber from the Mogilyov district she missed him terribly, she couldn't sleep at night, and she cried. She had an occasional evening visitor in young Smirnin, an army vet who was renting her cottage. He would tell her stories or play cards with her, and this cheered her up. She was fascinated by his accounts of his own family life—he was married and had a son, but he and his wife had separated because she had been unfaithful. Now he hated her and sent her forty roubles a month for the son's keep—hearing which, Olga would sigh, shake her head and pity Smirnin.

'God bless you,' she would say as she bade him good night and lighted his way to the stairs with a candle. 'Thank you for sharing your sorrows with me. May God and the Holy Mother keep you.' She always spoke in this grave, deliberate way, imitating her husband.

Just as the vet was vanishing through the door downstairs she would call him back. 'Mr. Smirnin, you should make it up with your wife, you know. Do forgive her, if only for your son's sake—that little lad understands everything, I'll be bound.'

On Pustovalov's return she would talk in low tones about the vet and his unhappy family history. Both would sigh, shake their heads—and discuss the little boy, who probably missed his father. Then, strange as it might seem, by association of ideas both would kneel before the icons, bow to the ground and pray to God to give them children.

Thus quietly and peacefully, in love and utter harmony, the Pustovalovs spent six years. But then, one winter's day, Vasya drank some hot tea in the office, went out to dispatch some timber without his cap on, caught cold and fell ill. He was attended by all the best doctors, but the illness took its course and he died after four months' suffering. Olga had been widowed again.

'Why did you forsake me, dearest?' she sobbed after burying her husband. 'How ever can I live without you? Oh, I'm so wretched and unhappy! Pity me, good people, I'm all alone now——'

She wore a black dress with weepers, she had renounced her hat and gloves for all time, she seldom went out of the house—and then only to church or her husband's grave—she lived at home like a nun. Not until six months had passed did she remove those weepers and open the shutters. She could sometimes be seen of a morning shopping for food in the market with her cook, but how did she live now, what went on in her house? It was a matter of guesswork . . . of guesswork based—shall we say?—on her being seen having tea in her garden with the vet while he read the newspaper to her, and also on what she said when she met a lady of her acquaintance at the post-office.

'There are no proper veterinary inspections in town, which is why we have so many diseases. You keep hearing of people infected by milk and catching things from horses and cows. We should really take as much care of domestic animals' health as of people's.'

She echoed the vet's thoughts, now holding the same views on all subjects as he. That she could not live a single year without an attachment, that she had found a new happiness in her own cottage . . . so much was clear. Any other woman would have incurred censure, but no one could think ill of Olga—everything about her was so aboveboard. She and the vet told no one of the change in their relations. They tried to hide it, but failed because Olga couldn't keep a secret. When his service colleagues came to visit she would pour their tea or give them their supper, while talking about cattle plague, pearl disease and municipal slaughter-houses . . . which embarrassed him terribly. He would seize her arm as the guests left.

'Haven't I asked you not to talk about things you don't understand?' he would hiss angrily. 'Kindly don't interfere when us vets are talking shop, it really is most tiresome.'

She looked at him in consternation and alarm. 'What can I talk about then, Volodya?'

She would embrace him with tears in her eyes, she would beg him not to be angry—and they would both be happy.

Their happiness proved short-lived, though. The vet left with his regiment. And since that regiment had been posted to far-away parts —Siberia practically—he left for good. Olga was alone.

She really was alone this time. Her father had died long ago, and his old arm-chair was lying around the attic minus one leg and covered with dust. She became thin, she lost her looks. People no longer noticed her, no longer smiled at her in the street. Her best years were over and done with, obviously. A new life was beginning, an unknown life—better not think about it. Sitting on the porch of an evening, Olga could hear the band playing and the rockets bursting in the Tivoli, but that did not stimulate her thoughts. She gazed blankly at her empty yard, she thought of nothing, she wanted nothing. When night came she went to bed and dreamt about that empty yard. She did not seem to want food and drink.

The main trouble was, though, that she no longer had views on anything. She saw objects around her, yes, she did grasp what was going on. But she could not form opinions. What was she to talk about? She did not know. It's a terrible thing, that, not having opinions. You see an upright bottle, say—or rain, or a peasant in a cart. But what are they for: that bottle, that rain, that peasant? What sense do they make? That you couldn't say . . . not even if someone gave you a thousand roubles, you couldn't. In the Kukin and Pustovalov eras—and then in the vet's day—Olga could give reasons for everything, she would have offered a view on any subject you liked. But now her mind and heart were as empty as her empty yard. It was an unnerving, bitter sensation: like eating a lot of wormwood.

The town has been gradually expanding on all sides. Gipsy Lane is a 'road' now. Houses have mushroomed and a set of side-streets has sprung up where once Tivoli and timber-yard stood. How time does fly! Olga's house looks dingy, her roof has rusted, her shed is lop-sided, her entire premises are deep in weeds and stinging nettles. Olga herself looks older, uglier. In summer she sits on her porch with the same old heartache and emptiness, there is the same old taste of wormwood. In winter she sits by her window looking at the snow. If she scents the spring air, or hears the peal of cathedral bells borne on the breeze, memories suddenly overwhelm her, she feels a delicious swooning sensation, tears well from her eyes. It lasts only a minute, though. Then the old emptiness returns, and life loses all meaning. Her black cat Bryska rubs up against his mistress, purring gently, but these feline caresses leave Olga cold. She needs a bit more than that! She needs a love to possess her whole being, all her mind and soul: a love to equip her with ideas, with a sense of purpose, a love to warm her ageing blood. She irritably shakes black Bryska off her lap. 'Away with you, you're not wanted here.'

So day follows day, year follows year: a life without joy, without opinions. Whatever her cook Mavra says goes.

Late one warm July afternoon, as the town cows are being driven down the street, filling the whole yard with dust clouds, there is a sudden knock at the gate. Olga opens it herself, looks out—and is dumbfounded. At the gate stands veterinary surgeon Smirnin—now grey-haired and wearing civilian clothes. It all comes back to her at once and she breaks down and cries, laying her head on his chest without a word. She is so shaken that they have both gone into the house and sat down to tea before she has realized what is happening.

'Dearest Volodya,' she mutters, trembling with joy. 'What brings you here?'

'I want to settle down here for good,' he tells her. 'I've resigned and I want to try my luck as a civilian—want to put down some roots.

Besides, it's time my son went to school, he's a big boy now. I've made it up with my wife, you know.'

Olga asked where she was.

'She's at a hotel with the boy while I look for somewhere to live.'

'Goodness me, then why not take *my* house, dear? It would be ideal for you! Oh, for heaven's sake, I wouldn't *charge* you anything.'

Overcome by emotion, Olga burst out crying again. 'You can live here and I'll manage in the cottage. Goodness, how marvellous!'

Next day they were already painting the roof and whitewashing the walls, while Olga strode up and down the yard, arms akimbo, seeing to everything. Her old smile shone on her face, but she was like a new woman—she seemed as fresh as if she had woken up after a long sleep. The vet's wife arrived—a thin, plain woman with short hair and a petulant expression—bringing little Sasha. He was small for his age (nine), he was chubby, he had bright blue eyes and dimpled cheeks. And no sooner had that boy set foot in the yard than he was off chasing the cat. His cheerful, merry laughter rang out.

'Is that your cat, Aunty?' he asked Olga. 'When it has babies, may we have one, please? Mummy's so scared of mice.'

Olga talked to him and gave him tea. She suddenly felt warm inside, and a delicious faintness came over her, just as if he was her own son. When he sat in the dining-room of an evening doing his homework she would gaze at him with loving pity.

'My darling, my little beauty, my child,' she would whisper. 'What a clever little, pale little fellow you are.'

'An island,' he read out, 'is a piece of land entirely surrounded by water.'

'An island is a piece of land—' she repeated. This, after so many years' silence and empty-headedness, was her first confidently expressed opinion.

Yes, she now had opinions of her own. At supper she would tell Sasha's parents how hard schoolchildren had to work these days. Better, even so, to have a classical than a modern education because the classical curriculum opens all doors. Doctor, engineer . . . you can take your pick.

After Sasha had started going to school his mother went to her sister's in Kharkov and did not return. His father was off every day inspecting cattle, and there were times when he was away from home for three days on end. They were completely neglecting Sasha, Olga felt—he wasn't wanted in the house, he was dying of starvation. So she moved him to her cottage and fixed him up with his own little room.

Now Sasha has been living in the cottage for six months. Every morning Olga goes to his room and finds him sound asleep with his hand beneath his cheek—not breathing, apparently. It seems a pity to wake him up.

'Get up, Sasha darling,' she says sadly. 'Time for school.'

He gets up, dresses, says his prayers, sits down to breakfast. He drinks three glasses of tea, he eats two large rolls, half a French loaf and butter. He is still not quite awake, and so is in rather a bad mood.

'That fable, Sasha—' says Olga. 'You didn't learn it properly.' She looks at him as though she is seeing him off on a long journey. 'Oh, you *are* such a handful! You *must* try and learn, dear, you must do what teacher says.'

'Oh, don't bother me, please!' replies Sasha.

Then he starts off down the street to school: a small boy in a large cap, satchel on back. Olga follows him silently.

'Sasha, dear,' she calls.

He looks round and she puts a date or caramel in his hand. When they turn off into the school road he feels ashamed of being followed by a tall, stout woman. He looks round.

'Go home, Aunty,' says he. 'I'll make my own way now.'

She stands and watches without taking her eyes off him until he disappears up the school drive. How she loves him! None of her earlier attachments has been so profound, never before has her innermost being surrendered as wholeheartedly, as unselfishly, as joyfully as it does now that her maternal feelings are increasingly welling up inside her. For this boy—no relative at all—for his dimpled cheeks, for his cap she would give her whole life, give it gladly, with tears of ecstasy. Why? Who knows?

After taking Sasha to school she goes home quietly—contented, at peace, overflowing with love. Her face glows—she has been looking younger these last six months—and she smiles. It is a pleasure to see her.

'Hallo, Olga, angel,' people say when they meet her. 'How are you, angel?'

'They do work schoolchildren so hard these days,' she says in the market. 'No, seriously—the First Form had to learn a whole fable by heart yesterday. *And* do a Latin translation. Sums too. It's too much for a little lad.'

What she says about teachers, lessons and textbooks . . . it's all pure
Sasha!

At about half past two they lunch together, and in the evening
they do Sasha's homework together, weeping. Putting him to bed, she
makes the sign of the cross over him at great length, whispering a
prayer. Then she goes to bed herself, and she dreams of that future—
vague, far distant—when Sasha will take his degree and become a
doctor or engineer . . . when he will own his own big house, his
horses and carriage, when he will marry and have children.

Still thinking these same thoughts, she falls asleep. From her closed
eyes tears course down her cheeks, and the black cat lies purring by
her side.

Then, suddenly, there is a loud knock on the garden gate and Olga
wakes up, too scared to breathe, her heart pounding. Half a minute
passes, there is a second knock.

'A telegram from Kharkov,' thinks she, trembling all over. 'Sasha's
mother wants him in Kharkov. Oh, goodness me!'

She is in despair. Her head, hands and feet are cold, and she feels as
if she's the most unhappy person in the world. But another minute
passes, voices are heard. It's the vet coming back from his club.

'Oh, thank God,' she thinks.

Her anxiety gradually subsides and she can relax again. She lies down
and thinks of Sasha: deep in slumber in the next room, and occasionally
talking in his sleep.

'You watch out!' he says. 'You go away! Don't you pick quarrels
with me!'

THE RUSSIAN MASTER

I

WITH a clatter of hooves on the wooden floor three fine, expensive horses were brought out of the stable: Count Nulin, the black, and then the grey, Giant, with his sister Mayka. While saddling Giant old Shelestov spoke to his daughter Masha.

'Come on, Marie Godefroi, up you get and off with you!'

Masha Shelestov was the youngest in the family. She was eighteen, but they still thought of her as a child, calling her by the pet names Manya and Manyusya. And when the circus had come to town she had enjoyed it so much that they had nicknamed her Marie Godefroi after the famous equestrienne.

'Off we go!' she shouted, mounting Giant.

Her sister Varya got on Mayka, Nikitin on Count Nulin, the officers mounted their own horses, and the long, picturesque cavalcade ambled out of the yard in single file with a gleam of officers' white tunics and ladies' black riding habits.

As they mounted and rode into the street Nikitin noticed that Masha had eyes for him alone, looking anxiously at him and Count Nulin.

'Hold him tight, Mr. Nikitin. Don't let him shy, he's only playing up.'

Whether by accident or because her Giant was a great friend of his Count Nulin, she rode beside Nikitin all the time, as she had the day before and the day before that, while he looked at her small, graceful form as she sat the proud grey, at her fine profile and the wholly unbecoming chimney-pot hat which seemed to age her. Enchanted, enthralled, enraptured, he looked and listened without taking much in.

'I swear I'll pluck up my courage,' he told himself. 'I'll speak to her this very day, by God I will.'

It was after six in the evening, the hour when white acacias and lilacs smell so strongly that the air and the very trees seem to congeal in their own perfume. The band played in the town park. Horses' hooves rang on the road. Laughter, voices, banging gates were heard on all sides. Soldiers they met saluted the officers, schoolboys bowed to Nikitin. Strollers, and those hurrying to the park for the music, all obviously enjoyed looking at the riders. How warm it was and how soft the clouds looked, scattered at random about the sky, how gently soothing were the shadows of the poplars and acacias—shadows reaching right across the wide street to grasp the houses on the other side as high as their first floors and balconies.

They rode on out of town, trotting down the highway. Here was no more scent of acacia and lilac, nor band music—just the smell of fields and the bright green of young rye and wheat. Gophers whistled, rooks cawed. Wherever one looked all was green apart from a few black melon-plots here and there, and a white streak of late apple-blossom in the graveyard far to their left.

They passed the slaughterhouses and brewery, they overtook a military band hurrying to the country park.

'Polyansky has a fine horse, I admit,' Masha told Nikitin with a glance at the officer riding beside Varya. 'But it does have its blemishes. The white patch on its left leg is wrong, and you'll notice it jibs. There's no way of training it now, so it'll go on jibbing till its dying day.'

Like her father, Masha was keen on horses. To see anyone else with a fine horse was agony to her, and she liked faulting other people's mounts. Nikitin knew nothing about horses, though. Reining or curbing, trotting or galloping—it was all one to him. He just felt he looked out of place, which was why he thought the officers must attract Masha more than he, being so much at home in the saddle. And so he was jealous of them.

As they rode past the country park someone suggested calling in for a glass of soda water. They did. The only trees in this park were oaks just coming into leaf, and through the young foliage the whole park could be seen—bandstand, tables, swings and crows' nests like huge fur caps. Dismounting near a table, the riders and their ladies ordered soda water. Friends strolling in the park came up, including an army medical officer in riding boots and the bandmaster awaiting his bandsmen. The doctor must have taken Nikitin for a student because he asked whether he had come over for the summer holidays.

'No, I live here,' Nikitin answered. 'I teach at the high school.'

'Really?' The doctor was surprised. 'So young and teaching already?'

'Young indeed! Good grief, I'm twenty-six!'

'You do have a beard and moustache, yet you don't seem more than twenty-two or three. You certainly do look young.'

'Oh, not again—what bloody cheek!' thought Nikitin. 'The fellow takes me for a whipper-snapper.'

It riled him when people said how young he looked, especially in women's or schoolboys' company. Ever since coming to town and taking this job he had found himself disliking his own youthful appearance. The boys were not afraid of him, old men called him 'young chap', and women would rather dance with him than listen to his long speeches. He would have given a lot to be ten years older.

From the park they rode on to the Shelestovs' farm, stopped at the gate and called for the bailiff's wife Praskovya to bring them fresh milk. But no one drank it—they just looked at each other, laughed and started cantering back. As they rode back the band was playing in the country park, the sun had sunk behind the graveyard, and half the sky was sunset-crimson.

Again Masha rode with Nikitin. He wanted to tell her he was madly in love with her—but said nothing, afraid of the officers and Varya hearing. Masha was silent too. Sensing why this was and why she rode beside him, he felt so happy that everything—earth, sky, town lights, the brewery's black silhouette—blended before his eyes into something delightfully soothing while Count Nulin seemed to float on air, wanting to climb the crimson sky.

They arrived home. A samovar hissed on the garden table at one edge of which old Shelestov sat with some friends, officers of the local assizes. As usual he was criticizing someone.

'It's the act of a bounder, an utter bounder—yes, of a bounder, sir.'

Since falling in love with Masha, Nikitin had found everything about the Shelestovs to his liking—their house, its garden, afternoon tea, wicker chairs, their old nanny and even the old man's favourite word, 'bounder'. He only disliked the horde of cats and dogs and the Egyptian pigeons moaning lugubriously in their big cage on the terrace. There were so many dogs about house and yard that he had learnt to distinguish only two since meeting the family—Bluebottle and Fishface.

Bluebottle was a small, mangy, shaggy-muzzled, spiteful, spoilt little tyke. She hated Nikitin, and at sight of him would put her head on one side, bare her teeth and embark on a long, liquid, nasal-guttural snarl. Then she would sit under his chair, and give a great piercing peal of yelps when he tried to chase her away. 'Don't be afraid,' his hosts would say. 'She's a good little dog.'

Fishface was a huge, black, long-legged hound with a tail like a ramrod. During tea and dinner it usually stalked silently beneath the table, banging that tail on boots and table-legs. This was a good-natured, stupid hound, but Nikitin couldn't stand it because it would put its muzzle on your lap at mealtimes and slobber on your trousers. He had often tried hitting its large head with his knife handle, had flicked its nose, cursed it, complained. But nothing saved his trousers from spots.

Tea, jam, rusks and butter tasted good after the ride. Everyone drank his first glass with silent relish, but by the second they were already arguing. It was always Varya who began these mealtime disputes. She was twenty-three. A good-looking girl, prettier than Masha, she was considered the cleverest and most cultured person in the household and she wore the responsible, severe air befitting an older daughter who has taken the place of her dead mother. As mistress of the house she felt entitled to wear a smock when she had guests, she called the officers by their surnames, and she treated Masha as a child, addressing her in schoolmistressy style. She called herself an old maid—she was quite sure she was going to get married, in other words.

Every conversation, even on the weather, she needs must convert into an argument. She was a great one for quibbling, detecting inconsistencies, splitting hairs. Start talking to her and she would be glaring into your face, suddenly interrupting with a 'now, just you look here, Petrov, you were saying the exact opposite only the day before yesterday'. Or she would smile sardonically with an 'ah, so now we're advocating the principles of the secret police, are we? Hearty congratulations!' If you made a joke or pun she'd pitch in at once with her 'feeble' or 'dead as a door nail'. Or, should an officer jest, she would give a scornful grimace and call it 'barrack-room wit', rolling her Rs so impressively that Bluebottle would growl back from under a chair.

Today's teatime quarrel began with Nikitin talking about school examinations and Varya interrupting.

'Now, you look here, Nikitin. You say the boys have a hard time. And whose fault is that, pray? For instance you set the eighth form an essay on Pushkin as a psychologist. Now, in the first place you shouldn't set such difficult subjects. And secondly how can you call Pushkin a psychologist? Shchedrin, now, or Dostoyevsky, say—that's a different story. But Pushkin is a great poet and nothing more.'

'Shchedrin is one thing, Pushkin is something else,' Nikitin sulkily rejoined.

'I know Shchedrin isn't on your syllabus, but that's beside the point. Just you explain what makes Pushkin a psychologist.'

'But it's plain as a pikestaff. Very well, then, I'll give examples.'

He recited some passages of *Eugene Onegin* and then of *Boris Godunov*.

'I see no psychology there,' sighed Varya. 'A psychologist delves into the crannies of the human soul. Those are fine verses, nothing more.'

Nikitin was offended. 'I know your sort of psychology. You want somebody to saw my finger with a blunt saw while I yell my head off, that's your idea of psychology.'

'Feeble! And you still haven't proved that Pushkin's a psychologist.'

When Nikitin found himself arguing against views which he thought hackneyed, conventional and the like, he usually jumped out of his seat, clutched his head in both hands and ran up and down the room groaning—which is what he did now. He jumped up, he clutched his head, he walked round the table groaning, and then sat away from it.

The officers took his part. Captain Polyansky assured Varya that Pushkin really was a psychologist, citing two lines of Lermontov to prove it, and Lieutenant Gernet said that Pushkin wouldn't have had a statue erected to him in Moscow had he not been a psychologist.

'It's the act of a bounder,' was heard from the other end of the table. 'I said as much to the Governor. "It's the act of a bounder, sir", I told him.'

'I shan't argue any more!' shouted Nikitin. 'This could go on till doomsday, I've had enough. Oh, clear off, you bloody dog!' he shouted at Fishface who had put his head and paw on his lap.

A guttural snarl came from under his chair.

'Admit you're in the wrong!' Varya shouted. 'Own up!'

But some young ladies came in, and the dispute died a natural death. They all went into the drawing-room, where Varya sat at the grand piano and played dances. They danced a waltz, a polka and a quadrille with a grand chain led through the whole house by Captain Polyansky, after which they waltzed again.

Watching the youngsters in the drawing-room, the older folk sat out the dances and smoked, among them the municipal bank manager Shebaldin, renowned for his love of literature and dramatic art. He had founded the local music and drama group, taking part in performances himself, but for some reason only playing comic footmen or intoning Alexis Tolstoy's poem 'The Sinful Woman'. He had been nicknamed 'the Mummy' in town because he was tall, emaciated and sinewy with a fixed, solemn expression and dull, glazed eyes. So sincere was his love of the theatre that he even shaved his moustache and beard, which made him look still more like a mummy.

After the grand chain he shuffled up sideways to Nikitin.

'I had the pleasure of being present at the argument during tea,' he remarked, coughing. 'And I fully share your opinion. We're fellow-spirits, you and I, and I'd much welcome a chat. Now, have you read Lessing's *Hamburgische Dramaturgie?*'

'No.'

Shebaldin looked horrified, waved his hands as if he had burnt his fingers, and backed away from Nikitin without a word. The man's figure, his question, his surprise—all seemed absurd to Nikitin, who yet wondered whether it wasn't 'really rather embarrassing. Here I am teaching literature, and I still haven't read Lessing. I shall have to.'

Before supper everyone, young and old, sat down to play forfeits. They took two packs of cards. One was dealt round, the other laid on the table face downwards.

'Whoever holds this card,' said old Shelestov solemnly, lifting the top card of the second pack, 'his forfeit is to go straight to the nursery and kiss Nanny.'

The good fortune of kissing Nanny devolved upon Shebaldin. They all flocked round him, they took him to the nursery and they made him kiss the nanny in an uproar of laughing, clapping and shouting.

'Less passion, I insist!' shouted Shelestov, tears rolling down his cheeks.

Nikitin's forfeit was to take confession. He sat on a chair in the middle of the drawing-room, a shawl was brought and put over his head. Varya came to confess first.

'I know your sins, madam.' Nikitin gazed at her stern profile in the gloom. 'How, pray, do you account for going out with Polyansky every day? Oho, there's more to this than meets the eye!'

'Feeble,' said Varya. And went.

Then Nikitin saw big, lustrous, unwavering eyes under his shawl, a lovely profile emerged from the gloom, and he caught a familiar, precious fragrance redolent of Masha's room.

'Marie Godefroi, what are your sins?' he said, and did not know his own voice—so tender, so soft was it.

Masha screwed up her eyes, put out the tip of her tongue, laughed and went away. A minute later she was standing in the middle of the room clapping her hands.

'Supper, supper, supper,' she shouted, and all trooped into the dining-room.

At supper Varya had another argument, with her father this time. Polyansky stolidly ate his food, drank his claret, and told Nikitin about a winter's night which he had once spent knee-deep in a bog when on active service. The enemy had been so near that they were forbidden to speak or smoke, it had been cold and dark, there had been a piercing wind. Nikitin listened, watching Masha out of the corner of his eye while she gazed at him without wavering or blinking, as if deep in thought and oblivious of her surroundings. This pleased and tormented him.

'Why does she look at me like that?' he agonizingly wondered. 'It's embarrassing, someone may notice. Oh, how young, how innocent she is.'

The party broke up at midnight. When Nikitin had gone through the gate a first-floor window banged open, Masha showed herself, and called his name.

'What is it?'

'It's just that—.' Masha was obviously wondering what to say. 'Er, Polyansky's promised to bring his camera in a day or two and photograph us all. We must have a get-together.'

'Fine.'

Masha disappeared, the window slammed, and someone in the house at once started playing the piano.

'Oh, what a house,' thought Nikitin, crossing the street. 'A house where the only moaning comes from the Egyptian pigeons, and that simply because they have no other way to express their joy.'

Fun was not confined to the Shelestovs', though, for Nikitin had not taken two hundred steps before piano music was heard from another house. He walked on a bit and saw a peasant playing a balalaika near a gate. The band in the park struck up a pot-pourri of Russian folksongs.

Nikitin lived a quarter of a mile from the Shelestovs in an eight-roomed flat, rented at three hundred roubles a year, which he shared with his colleague Hippolytus, the geography and history master. This Hippolytus—a snub-nosed, reddish-bearded, middle-aged man with a rather coarse but good-natured expression more like a workman's than an intellectual's—was sitting at his desk correcting pupils' maps when Nikitin returned. According to Hippolytus, drawing your maps was the most crucial and essential aspect of geography, while with history it was knowing your dates—he would sit up night after night with his blue pencil correcting the maps of boys and girls he taught, or compiling lists of dates.

'Wonderful weather today,' said Nikitin, going into Hippolytus's room. 'I don't know how you can stay indoors.'

No great talker, Hippolytus would either say nothing at all or utter the merest platitudes. He now vouchsafed the following reply.

'It is indeed excellent weather. It is May now, and it will soon be full summer. Summer differs from winter. Stoves must be lit in winter, whereas in summer you can keep warm without them. Open your windows on a summer night and you'll still be warm, whereas in winter you are cold even with the double frames.'

After sitting near the desk for less than a minute, Nikitin felt bored and stood up, yawning.

'Good night,' he said. 'I wanted to tell you something romantic affecting myself, but you have geography on the brain. One talks to you of love, and you ask for the date of the Battle of Kalka. To hell with your battles and your Siberian capes.'

'But why are you so cross?'

'I'm just fed up.'

Annoyed at not having proposed to Masha and having no one to tell about his love, he went and lay on his study sofa. The room was dark and quiet. Lying and gazing into the darkness, Nikitin imagined that some errand would take him to St. Petersburg in a couple of years, and that the weeping Masha would see him off at the station. In St. Petersburg he would receive a long letter from her in which she would entreat him to hurry back home. He would write her a reply beginning 'Darling little rat——'

'Just so, "darling little rat",' he laughed.

He was lying uncomfortably, so he put his hands behind his head and canted his left leg on to the sofa back. That was better. Meanwhile dawn was breaking beyond the window, sleepy cocks crowed outside. Nikitin went on thinking—how he would come back from St. Petersburg, how Masha would meet him at the station and throw her arms round his neck shrieking with joy. Better still, he would play a trick. He would come back secretly late at night, the cook would let him in, and he would tip-toe to the bedroom, undress noiselessly and dive into bed. She would wake up—ah, bliss!

It was quite light now, but instead of his study and its window he saw Masha, who sat talking on the steps of the brewery they had ridden past that afternoon. She took Nikitin's arm and they went to the country park where he saw those oaks and crows' nests like fur caps. One nest swayed and óut peeped Shebaldin with a vociferous 'Who hasn't read his Lessing?'

Shuddering all over, Nikitin opened his eyes. There by the sofa stood Hippolytus, head thrown back as he tied his cravat.

'Get up, it's time for school,' he said. 'Now, you shouldn't sleep in your clothes, it spoils them. One sleeps in óne's bed after first removing one's attire.'

And he embarked on his usual long, emphatic string of platitudes.

Nikitin's first period was Russian grammar with the second form. Going into the classroom at nine o'clock precisely, he saw two capital letters chalked on the blackboard: **M. S.** They stood for Masha Shelestov no doubt.

'So the little devils have found out,' thought Nikitin. 'How do they always know everything?'

His second period was Russian literature with the fifth form. Here too he saw an M. S. on the board, and as he left the classroom at the end of the lesson a cry rang out behind him like a catcall from a theatre gallery. 'Good old Masha!'

He felt muzzy after sleeping in his clothes, his body drooped from fatigue. His pupils, daily looking forward to the break before their examinations, were idle and depressed, and they misbehaved out of boredom. Also depressed, Nikitin ignored their little tricks and kept going to the window. He saw the street bathed in sunlight, the limpid blue sky above the houses, the birds—while far, far away beyond green gardens and houses stretched an infinitely remote expanse with dark blue coppices and a puff of steam from a moving train.

Two white-tunicked officers flicked their whips as they walked down the street in the shade of the acacias. A party of grey-bearded Jews in peaked caps drove past in a brake, the governess was taking the headmistress's grand-daughter for a walk, Fishface dashed past with two mongrels. And there went Varya in her plain grey dress and red stockings, carrying a *European Herald*—she must have been to the municipal library.

It was a long time before school would end at three o'clock. Nor could Nikitin go home or visit the Shelestovs after school, for he had to give a lesson at Wolf's. This Wolf was a rich Jewish protestant convert who did not send his children to school, but got schoolmasters to coach them privately at five roubles a lesson.

Nikitin was bored, bored, bored.

At three o'clock he went to Wolf's and spent what seemed like all eternity there. He left at five o'clock, and was due back at school by seven for a teachers' meeting to fix the oral examination timetable for the fourth and sixth forms.

That night, on his way from school to the Shelestovs', he felt his heart pounding and his face burning. A week ago, a month ago—every time he had been about to propose he had had an entire harangue ready complete with introduction and peroration, but now he didn't have one word prepared, his head was awhirl. All he knew was that he was going to declare himself this evening for sure and that there was no more putting it off.

He would ask her into the garden, he reflected. 'I'll stroll about a bit and I'll propose.'

There was no one in the hall. He went into the drawing-room and parlour, but there was no one there either. He heard Varya arguing with someone upstairs and the dressmaker clicking her scissors in the nursery.

There was a lobby with three names: the 'small', the 'corridor', the 'dark' room. It contained a big old cupboard full of medicines, gunpowder and hunting gear, and a narrow wooden staircase, with cats always asleep on it, leading to the first floor. The lobby had two doors—one to the nursery, one to the drawing-room. When Nikitin went in on his way upstairs the nursery door suddenly opened and slammed so hard that staircase and cupboard rattled. Out rushed Masha in a dark dress, carrying a piece of blue material, and darted to the stairs without seeing him.

'Hey', Nikitin said to stop her. 'Hallo, Godefroi. May I, er——'

He gasped, he didn't know what to say, clutching her hand with one hand and the blue material with the other. Half frightened, half surprised, she gazed at him wide-eyed.

'Look here—,' Nikitin went on, afraid she would go away. 'I have something to say, only it's, er, awkward here. I can't do it, it's beyond me, Godefroi, it's more than I can manage and that's all there, er, is to it.'

The blue material slipped to the floor and Nikitin took Masha's other hand. She turned pale, moved her lips and backed away from him, ending up in the corner between wall and cupboard.

'I swear, I assure you,' he said softly. 'I take my oath, Masha, er——'

She threw her head back and he kissed her lips, holding her cheek with his fingers to make the kiss last longer. Then he somehow found himself in the corner between cupboard and wall, while she had twined her arms round his neck and was pressing her head against his chin.

Then they both ran into the garden.

The Shelestovs had a large, ten-acre garden with a score of old maples and limes. There was a fir, a sweet chestnut, a silvery olive, and all the rest were fruit-trees—cherries, apples, pears. There were masses of flowers too.

Nikitin and Masha ran down the paths, now silent, now laughing, now asking disconnected questions which went unanswered, while a half moon shone over the garden. On the ground—dark grass, dimly lit by the moon's crescent—drowsy tulips and irises stretched up as if they too longed to hear words of love.

When Nikitin and Masha came back to the house the officers and young ladies were already assembled, dancing a mazurka. Again Polyansky led a grand chain through the house, again they played forfeits after dancing. But when the guests went into the dining-room before supper, Masha was left alone with Nikitin.

She pressed close to him. 'You must talk to papa and Varya, I'm too embarrassed.'

After supper he spoke to the old man, who heard him out. 'I'm most grateful,' said he, after some thought, 'for the honour which you are conferring on myself and my daughter, but permit me to speak as a friend—not as a father, but as between gentlemen. Now, why oh why the great rush to marry so early? Only farm labourers marry so young, but then we all know they're a lot of bounders, sir. But you—what's got into you? A ball and chain at your tender age—where's the fun in that?'

Nikitin took umbrage. 'I'm *not* young, I'm nearly twenty-seven.'

'Father, the farrier's here,' shouted Varya from another room. And that ended the conversation.

Varya, Masha and Polyansky saw Nikitin home.

'Why does your mysterious Mr. Hippolytus never emerge?' Varya asked when they reached his gate. 'He might come and see us.'

The mysterious Mr. Hippolytus was sitting on his bed taking off his trousers when Nikitin went into his room.

'Don't go to bed yet, old man,' Nikitin gasped. 'Just give me a moment, please.'

Hippolytus quickly put his trousers on again and asked anxiously what the matter was.

'I'm getting married.'

Nikitin sat down beside his colleague with the amazed look of one who has succeeded in surprising himself. 'Just fancy, I'm getting married. To Masha Shelestov, I proposed this evening.'

'Well, she seems a nice girl. She is very young, though,'

'Yes, young she is,' sighed Nikitin with a worried shrug. 'Very young indeed.'

'She was a pupil of mine once. I remember her, she wasn't bad at geography but she was no good at history. And she was inattentive in class.'

Nikitin suddenly felt rather sorry for his colleague and wanted to say something kind and consoling. 'Why don't *you* get married, old man?' he asked. 'My dear Hippolytus, why don't you marry Varya, say? She's a splendid girl, quite first-rate. Oh, she is very argumentative, I know, but she's so very, very good-hearted. She was asking about you just now. So you marry her, old chap, how about it?'

That Varya wouldn't have this boring, snub-nosed character Nikitin knew perfectly well, yet he still tried to persuade him to marry her. Why?

Hippolytus pondered. 'Marriage is a serious step,' he said. 'One must look at all the angles, weigh every issue, one mustn't be too casual. Caution never comes amiss—especially in wedlock when a man, ceasing to be a bachelor, begins a new life.'

He began uttering his platitudes, but Nikitin stopped listening to him, said goodnight and went to his room. Hastily undressing, he quickly lay down in a great hurry to brood on his happiness, his Masha, his future. Then he smiled, suddenly remembering that he still hadn't read Lessing.

'I must read him,' he thought. 'But then again, why should I? To hell with him.'

Exhausted by bliss, he fell asleep at once and smiled through till morning. He dreamt of the clatter of horses' hooves on the wooden floor. He dreamt of black Count Nulin and the grey, Giant, with his sister Mayka, being brought out of the stable.

II

It was very crowded and noisy in church. At one point someone in the congregation actually shouted aloud, and the priest who was marrying me and Masha peered over his spectacles.

'Don't wander about the church,' he said sternly. 'Just keep still and worship. This is God's house, remember.'

I had two of my colleagues in attendance, while Masha was attended by Captain Polyansky and Lieutenant Gernet. The bishop's choir sang superbly. The sputtering candles, the glitter, the fine clothes, the officers, the mass of joyful, contented faces, Masha's special ethereal look, the entire ambience, the words of the nuptial prayers—they moved me to tears, they filled me with exultation. How my life has blossomed out, I thought. How romantically, how poetically it has been shaping of late. Two years ago I was just a student living in cheap lodgings in Moscow's Neglinny Drive, with no money, no relatives and—I then fancied—no future. But now I teach at the high school in one of the best county towns, I'm secure, I'm loved, I'm spoilt. For me this congregation is assembled, thought I. For me three chandeliers burn, for me the archdeacon booms, for me the choir puts forth its efforts. For me too this young creature, soon to be called my wife, is so youthful, so elegant, so happy. I remembered our first meetings, our country rides, my proposal and the weather which seemed to have gone out of its way to be wonderfully fine all summer. That happiness which, in my old Neglinny Drive days, only seemed possible in novels and stories—I was actually experiencing it now, apparently, I was taking it in my hands.

After the ceremony everyone crowded round Masha and me, they expressed their sincere pleasure, they congratulated us, they wished us happiness. A retired major-general in his late sixties congratulated Masha alone.

'I trust, my dear, that now you're married you'll still be the same dear little rosebud,' he told her in a squeaky, senile voice audible throughout the church.

The officers, the headmaster, the teachers—all gave the socially incumbent grin, and I could feel that ingratiating, artificial smile on my face too. Dear old Mr. Hippolytus—history master, geography master, mouther of platitudes—shook my hand firmly and spoke with feeling. 'Hitherto you've been a bachelor and have lived on your own. But now you're married and single no longer.'

From church we went to the two-storeyed house with unrendered walls which comes to me with the dowry. Besides the house Masha is bringing about twenty thousand roubles in cash and a place called Meliton's Heath complete with a shack where I'm told there are lots of hens and ducks running wild because no one looks after them.

When I got home from church I stretched and lounged on the ottoman in my new study, smoking. I felt more snug, more comfortable, more cosy than ever in my life. Meanwhile wedding guests cheered, a wretched band played flourishes and sundry trash in the hall. Masha's sister Varya ran into the study carrying a wineglass, her face oddly strained as if her mouth was full of water. Apparently she had meant to run on, but she suddenly burst out laughing and sobbing, while the glass rolled, ringing, across the floor. We took her by the arms and led her off.

'No one understands,' she muttered later as she lay on the old nurse's bed at the back of the house. 'No one, no one—God, no one understands.'

Everyone understood perfectly well, though, that she was four years older than her sister Masha, that she still wasn't married, and that she wasn't crying through envy but because she was sadly aware that her time was passing—or had perhaps already passed. By the time the quadrille began she was back in the drawing-room with a tearful, heavily powdered face, and I saw her spooning up a dish of ice-cream held for her by Captain Polyansky.

It is now past five in the morning. I have taken up my diary to describe my complete, my manifold happiness, intending to write half a dozen pages and read them to Masha later in the day, but oddly enough my mind is just a vague, dreamy jumble, and all I remember distinctly is this business of Varya. 'Poor Varya', I want to write. Yes, I could go on sitting here and writing 'poor Varya'. And now the trees have started rustling, which means rain. Crows are cawing and my dear Masha, who has just fallen asleep, has a rather sad expression.

Nikitin did not touch his diary for a long time afterwards. He had various entrance and other school examinations at the beginning of August, and after the fifteenth of the month term started again. He usually left for school before nine, and an hour later was already missing Masha and his new home, and kept looking at his watch. In the lower forms he would get one of the boys to dictate and would sit in the window day-dreaming, eyes shut, while his pupils wrote. Picturing the future, recalling the past—he found everything equally splendid, like a fairy-tale. In the senior forms they read Gogol or Pushkin's prose aloud, which made him drowsy, conjuring up in his imagination people, trees, fields, horses.

'Superb,' he would sigh, as if bewitched by the author.

At the lunch break Masha would send him his meal in a snow-white napkin, and he would eat it slowly, with pauses to prolong his enjoyment, while Hippolytus—who usually lunched on a single roll—looked at him with respectful envy, uttering some such platitude as that 'man cannot live without food'.

From school Nikitin would go to his coaching, and when he at last reached home about half past five he would feel as happy and excited as if he had been away a whole year. He would run panting upstairs, find Masha, take her in his arms, kiss her, swear he loved her and couldn't live without her, claiming to have missed her terribly, asking in panic whether she was well and why she looked so solemn. Then they would dine together. After dinner he would lie smoking on his study ottoman while she sat beside him, talking in a low voice.

His happiest days were Sundays and holidays, when he stayed at home from morning till evening. On these days he shared an unsophisticated but most agreeable life reminiscent of pastoral idylls. Constantly watching the sensible, practical Masha as she wove her nest, he too wanted to show that he was some use about the house, and would do something pointless like pushing the chaise out of the shed and inspecting it from all sides. Masha had set up a regular dairy and kept three cows. Her cellar and larder contained many jugs of milk and pots of sour cream, all of which she kept for butter. Nikitin would sometimes ask her for a glass of milk as a joke, and she would take fright at this breach of discipline, while he laughed and put his arms round her.

'There, there, it was only a joke, my treasure—just a little joke.'

Or he would laugh at how strict she was when she found an old stone-hard piece of salami, say, or cheese in the cupboard and solemnly said that 'they can eat that out in the kitchen'.

He would tell her that such a scrap was fit only for a mousetrap, while she hotly contended that men know nothing of housekeeping, and that you could send food out to those servants by the hundred-weight and you still wouldn't get any reaction from them. He would agree and embrace her ecstatically. When she said something sensible he found it unique and astounding, and whatever contradicted his own sentiments was deliciously unsophisticated.

Sometimes, in philosophical vein, he would discourse on an abstract theme, while she listened and looked inquiringly into his face. 'I'm infinitely happy with you, darling,' he would say, playing with her fingers, or plaiting and unplaiting her hair. 'But I don't regard my happiness as a windfall or manna from heaven. My felicity is a wholly natural, consistent and impeccably logical phenomenon. I believe that man makes his own happiness, so I'm now enjoying something I myself created. Yes, I can say so without false modesty: I created this bliss, and I have every right to it. You know my past. Having no mother and father, being poor, an unhappy childhood, a miserable adolescence— all that was a struggle, a road to happiness built by myself.'

In October the school suffered a grievous loss when Hippolytus succumbed to erysipelas of the head and died. He was unconscious and delirious for two days before dying, but even when rambling he rambled only platitudes.

'The Volga flows into the Caspian Sea, horses eat oats and hay——'

There was no school on the day of his funeral. Colleagues and pupils carried coffin-lid and coffin, and the school choir sang the anthem 'Holy, holy, holy' all the way to the cemetery. The procession included three priests, two deacons, all the boys' high school and the bishop's choir in their best cassocks. Seeing so solemn a cortège, passers-by crossed themselves and prayed to God to 'grant us all such a death'.

Nikitin went home from the cemetery very moved, and took his diary from the desk.

Today Mr. Hippolytus Ryzhitsky was consigned to his grave (he wrote). Rest in peace, thou humble toiler. Masha, Varya and the other ladies at the funeral all wept sincerely, perhaps because they knew that no woman ever loved so unattractive, so downtrodden a man. I wanted to say a word of appreciation at my colleague's grave, but was warned that the Head might take exception since he disliked the deceased. I think this has been the first day since the wedding that I've felt depressed.

There was no other event of note during the school year.

Winter was a half-hearted affair—sleety, without hard frosts. All Twelfth Night, for instance, the wind howled piteously as in autumn, the roofs dripped, and during the Consecration of the Waters in the morning the police stopped people walking on the frozen river because they said the ice had swollen up and looked dark. Despite the dismal weather Nikitin was just as happy as in summer, though, and had even acquired a new hobby—he had learnt to play bridge. There only seemed to be one fly in the ointment, only one thing that got on his

nerves and riled him—the cats and dogs which he had acquired as part
of the dowry. The house smelt like a zoo, especially in the mornings,
and there was no getting rid of the stench. The cats often fought the
dogs. That spiteful Bluebottle was fed a dozen times a day, but still
wouldn't accept Nikitin, still treated him to her liquid, nasal-guttural
growls.

One midnight in Lent Nikitin was on his way home from the club
after cards. It was raining, dark and muddy. Things felt unsavoury,
somehow. Was it the twelve roubles he had lost at the club? Or was it
that when they were settling up one of the players had remarked that
Nikitin had pots of money—a clear hint at that dowry? The twelve
roubles didn't matter to him, and there had been nothing offensive in
the man's words. Still, it was distasteful, and he didn't even feel like
going home.

'Oh, how awful,' he said, halting by a street lamp.

The reason he didn't care about the twelve roubles was that he had
got them for nothing, it struck him. Now, if he had been a labourer he
would have valued every copeck, he would not have been so casual
about winning or losing. But then, all his good fortune had come to
him free and gratis, he reasoned—it was a luxury, really, like medicine
to a healthy man. Had he been harassed like the great majority by
worrying about his livelihood, had he been struggling for existence,
had his back and chest ached from hard work, then his supper, his
warm, snug quarters and his domestic bliss would be a necessity, a
reward, an adornment of his life. As it was the significance of all that
was oddly blurred, somehow.

'Oh, how awful,' he repeated, knowing full well that these very
broodings were a bad sign.

Masha was in bed when he arrived home. Her breathing was even,
and she smiled, obviously relishing her sleep. Next to her curled the
white cat, purring. While Nikitin was lighting his candle and cigarette
Masha woke up and thirstily drank a glass of water.

'I ate too much jam,' she laughed, and asked after a pause whether he
had been visiting her family.

'No.'

Nikitin knew that Captain Polyansky, on whom Varya had been
counting heavily of late, was being posted to the west country, and
was now making his farewell visits in town for which reason there was
an air of gloom at his father-in-law's.

Masha sat up. 'Varya called this evening. She didn't say anything, but you can see from her face how depressed she is, poor thing. I can't stand Polyansky. He's so fat, so frowsty, and his cheeks wobble when he walks or dances. He's not my type. Still, I did think he was a decent person.'

'Well, I still do think he is a decent person.'

'What, after he's treated Varya so badly?'

'Badly in what sense?' Nikitin was irked by the white cat stretching and arching its back. 'To the best of my knowledge he never proposed or made any promises.'

'Then why did he visit our house so often? He shouldn't have come if he didn't mean business.'

Nikitin put out the candle and lay down. But he did not feel like sleeping or lying there. His head seemed like some vast, empty barn with new, rather weird thoughts drifting about it like tall shadows. Away from the soft icon-lamp beaming on their quiet family happiness, away from this cosy little world in which he and that cat both lived in such delectable serenity, there was a very different world, he reflected. And for that other world he felt a sudden pang of anguished longing. He wanted to toil in some factory or big workshop, to lecture to audiences, to write, to publish, to make a splash, to exhaust himself, to suffer. He craved some obsession to make him oblivious of self and indifferent to personal happiness with its monotonous sensations. And then suddenly, in his mind's eye, the living image of clean-shaven Shebaldin arose and spoke in horror.

'Who hasn't even read Lessing? How backward you are—God, how you have gone to seed.'

Masha drank more water. He looked at her neck, plump shoulders and breasts, remembering what the retired major-general had called her in church that day—'a dear little rosebud'.

'Dear little rosebud,' he muttered. And laughed. Under the bed sleepy Bluebottle growled her guttural response.

Inside Nikitin a cold, heavy, spiteful urge seemed to hammer and twist. He wanted to be rude to Masha, or even jump up and hit her. His heart throbbed.

'So that's the way of it,' he stated, trying to restrain himself. 'By visiting your house I thereby undertook to marry you, I suppose?'

'Of course you did, you know that as well as I do.'

'Charming, I must say.'

A minute later he said it again. 'Charming.'

To stop himself adding something which he would regret, and to calm his emotions, Nikitin went to his study and lay on the ottoman without a pillow. Then he lay on the carpet on the floor.

He tried to reassure himself. 'This is all nonsense. You, a teacher, have a most admirable calling. What other world can you need? What utter rubbish!'

But then he at once answered himself with certainty that, far from being a teacher, he was a mediocre, featureless hack like the Greek master, a Czech. He had never had a vocation for teaching, he knew nothing of pedagogic theory, he had never been interested in it, he had no idea how to treat children. The significance of his teaching was lost on him, perhaps he was even teaching all the wrong things. The late Hippolytus had been frankly stupid, but all his colleagues and pupils had known who he was and what to expect of him—whereas he, Nikitin, was like the Czech who could conceal his dullness and adroitly deceive people by pretending that everything was, thank God, just as it should be. These new ideas alarmed Nikitin, he spurned them, he called them stupid, he put them down to nerves, he thought he would soon be laughing at himself.

Towards morning, indeed, he already was laughing at his nerves and calling himself an old woman. And yet he also realized that his peace of mind was lost, probably for ever, and that there was no happiness for him in this two-storeyed house with its unrendered walls. The illusion was gone, he sensed, and a new, uneasy, conscious life had begun—a life incompatible with peace of mind and personal happiness.

On the next day, a Sunday, he went to the school chapel where he met the headmaster and his colleagues. Their sole business in life seemed to consist of sedulously concealing their own ignorance and dissatisfaction, and he too smiled affably and indulged in small talk to avoid betraying his unease. Then he walked to the station. He watched the mail train come and go, pleased to be alone and not to have to talk to anyone.

At home he found his father-in-law and Varya who had come over for dinner. Varya's eyes were red from crying, and she complained of a headache, while Shelestov ate a lot and went on about young people being so unreliable and ungentlemanly nowadays.

'It's the act of a bounder,' he said. 'And so I shall tell him to his face— the act of a bounder, sir.'

Nikitin smiled amiably and helped Masha entertain their guests, but after dinner he went and locked himself in his study.

The March sun shone brightly, and warm rays fell on the desk through the double frames. It was only the twentieth of the month, but sledges had now given way to wheeled traffic and starlings were singing in the garden. He had the feeling that Masha was about to come in, put one arm around his neck, say that the horses or chaise had been brought round to the porch, and ask what she was to wear to keep warm. Spring had begun—a spring just as exquisite as the previous year's, promising just the same joys. But Nikitin thought he would like to take a holiday, go to Moscow and stay in his old lodgings in Neglinny Drive. In the next room they were drinking coffee and talking about Captain Polyansky while he tried not to listen.

Ye gods, where am I (he wrote in his diary)? I'm surrounded by smug, complacent mediocrities, dreary nonentities, pots of sour cream, jugs of milk, cockroaches, stupid women.

There is nothing more terrible, insulting and mortifying than the smug complacency of the second-rate. I must run away, I must escape this very day or I shall go out of my mind.

TERROR

MY FRIEND'S STORY

HAVING taken a university degree and been a civil servant in St. Petersburg, Dmitry Silin had given up his job at the age of thirty to take up farming. Though he had made a fair success of it I felt he was out of his element and would have done better to return to St. Petersburg. Sunburnt, grey with dust and toil-worn, he would meet me near his gate or entrance, then battle with drowsiness over supper until his wife took him off to bed like a baby. Or else he would conquer his fatigue and begin expounding edifying sentiments in his gentle, sincere and apparently pleading voice—at which times I never saw him as a farmer or agriculturalist, but only as a tormented human being. He needed no farm, I realized, he just wanted some way of getting through the day without mishap.

I liked going over there and sometimes stayed at his farm for two or three days at a stretch. I liked his house, his park, his big orchard, his little river, and I liked his general outlook: rather passive and over-elaborate, yet lucid. I must have liked him personally too, though I cannot say for certain as I am still unable to analyse my feelings of the time. He was an intelligent, good-natured, genuine, quite interesting person, but I well remember how upset and embarrassed I was when he told me his most intimate secrets and said what great friends the two of us were. There was something uncomfortable and tiresome about this great affection for me, and I would far rather have had us just ordinary friendly acquaintances.

The fact is, I was greatly attracted by his wife Mary. Not that I was in love with her, but I liked her face, her eyes, her voice, her walk. I used to miss this good-looking, elegant young woman when I hadn't seen her for some time and I liked to dwell on her image in fancy: more so than on anyone else's. I had no specific designs on her, no romantic aspirations, but whenever we were alone together I somehow remembered that her husband took me for his great friend, which was so embarrassing. I enjoyed listening when she played my favourite piano pieces or told me anything of interest, yet I was also rather irked by the thought of her loving her husband, of him being my great friend, of her thinking me *his* great friend, and all this spoilt my mood, making me listless, uncomfortable and bored. She would notice these changes in me.

'You're bored without your friend,' she usually said. 'I must get him back from the fields.'

'See, your friend's here,' she would say when Silin arrived. 'You can cheer up now.'

This situation continued for about eighteen months.

One Sunday in July Silin and I happened to have nothing to do, so we drove over to the large village of Klushino to buy some food for supper. The sun set while we were shopping and evening came on: an evening which I shall probably never forget as long as I live. After buying soap-like cheese and petrified salami smelling of tar, we went to the inn in quest of beer. Our coachman drove off to the smithy to have our horses shod and we told him we would wait for him by the church. While we walked, spoke and laughed at our purchases, our steps were dogged, with an air of silent mystery befitting a detective, by one known in the county under the rather odd nickname of Forty Martyrs. This Forty Martyrs was none other than a Gabriel ('Gavryushka') Severov whom I had once briefly employed as footman before dismissing him for drunkenness. He had worked for Dmitry Silin too and had also been dismissed by him: again for the same shortcoming. He was a raging drunkard—his whole way of life, indeed, was as tipsy and debauched as the man himself. His father had been a priest and his mother a gentlewoman, so he had been born into the privileged classes. But carefully though I might scrutinize his haggard, respectful, always sweaty face, his ginger beard now turning grey, his wretched, tattered little jacket and his red shirt worn outside his trousers—of what are commonly called privileges I found not the faintest trace. He called himself educated—said he had studied at a church school, but hadn't stayed the course since he was expelled for smoking. Then he had sung in the bishop's choir and spent a couple of years in a monastery from which he was also dismissed: not for smoking this time, but for 'my weakness'. He had tramped all over two provinces, had put in certain applications to the provincial church authorities and various government offices, and had been had up in court four times. In the end he had become stranded in our county, working as footman, forester, kennelman and church caretaker. He had married a widowed cook of loose character and had eventually been swallowed up in this menial swamp, growing so inured to its dirt and brawls that even he now referred to his genteel origin somewhat sceptically, as to a myth. At the time of

which I write he was running around jobless, pretending to be a farrier
and huntsman. His wife had vanished without trace.

From the inn we went to the church and sat in the porch waiting for
our coachman. Forty Martyrs stood a little way off, holding his hand
to his mouth so that he could cough respectfully into it should need
arise. It was dark. There was a strong smell of evening dampness and
the moon was about to come up. There were only two clouds in the
clear, starry sky: exactly overhead, one big, the other smaller, like
mother and child. Alone up there, they were chasing each other
towards the dying sunset's embers.

'What a marvellous evening,' said Silin.

'Exceptionally so,' Forty Martyrs agreed with a respectful cough
into his hand.

'Whatever possessed you to come here, Mr. Silin?' he asked in an
ingratiating voice, evidently wanting to chat.

Silin made no answer and Forty Martyrs heaved a deep sigh.

'My sufferings are all on account of a cause for which I must answer
to Almighty God,' he said quietly, not looking at us. 'Now, I'm a lost
man, no doubt about it, and I ain't no good at anything, and I ain't
got nothing to eat, honest, I'm worse off than a dog, I'm sorry to
say.'

Silin propped his head on his fists, unheeding, and meditated. The
church stood on a high bank at the end of the street and through the
churchyard railing could be seen a river, water-meadows on the far
side and the crimson glare of a camp fire round which black figures
were moving: men and horses. Beyond the fire, further away, were
more lights: those of a hamlet whence came the sound of singing.

Mist rose above the river and there were patches of it above the
meadow. High, narrow coils of thick, milky haze drifted over the river,
masking the stars' reflections and clinging to the willows. They were
constantly changing shape, some seemingly locked in embrace, others
bowing low, while yet others lifted broad-sleeved arms aloft like priests
at prayer. They probably suggested ghosts and departed spirits to
Silin, for he turned his face to me with a sad smile and asked me why
it was, 'that when we want to tell some frightening, mysterious,
grotesque tale, we never cull our material from life, my dear chap, but
always from the world of phantoms and shades of the hereafter?'

'We fear what we don't understand.'

'But we don't understand life, do we? Do we understand life any
better than the world hereafter, you tell me that?'

Silin sat down so close to me that I could feel his breath on my cheek. His pale, lean face seemed yet paler in the gloaming and his dark beard was black as soot. His eyes were sad, earnest and rather frightened, as if he was about to tell me something terrifying.

'Our life and the world hereafter . . . they're both equally mysterious and terrifying,' he went on in his habitual pleading voice, gazing into my eyes. 'Anyone who's scared of ghosts should also be afraid of me, those lights and of the sky—for when you really come to think of it these things are all just as mysterious and grotesque as any manifestations from another world. The reason why Hamlet didn't kill himself was dread of "in that sleep of death what dreams may come". I like that famous soliloquy, but it never really got home to me, quite frankly. I tell you, my friend, there have been anguished moments when I have pictured my last hour in my mind's eye, when my fancy has conjured up thousands of utterly lugubrious vistas, when I have managed to work myself up into a lather of agonized, nightmarish exaltation. Yet none of that has ever scared me anything like as much as everyday life, you take my word for it. Ghosts *are* frightening, it goes without saying, but so is life too. I can't make any sense of life, old boy, and I fear it. I don't know—perhaps I'm being morbid, perhaps I've gone off the rails. A sane, healthy man believes he understands everything he sees and hears, but I have lost any such impression and I'm poisoning myself with terror day in day out. There is a complaint called fear of open spaces, but it's fear of life that ails me. When I lie on the grass watching a little beetle—born only yesterday, understanding nothing—its life seems one long chain of horror. And that is just how I see myself.'

'But what exactly are you scared of?' I asked.

'Everything. I am not naturally profound, I'm not much interested in such questions as the hereafter or the fate of humanity and I'm not much of a one for flights into the sublime either. What terrifies me most is just ordinary everyday routine, the thing none of us can escape. The things I do . . . I can't tell the true from the false, and they trouble me. My living conditions and upbringing have imprisoned me in a closed circle of lies, I know. Worrying how to deceive myself and others every day without noticing that I'm doing so . . . that's my entire existence, I know that too, and I dread not being rid of this fraud until I'm in my grave. I do something one day and next day I have no idea why I did it. I entered government service in St. Petersburg and took fright. Then I came here to farm and took fright again. We know so little, which is why we make mistakes every day, I see that—we're

unfair, we slander people or pester the life out of them, we lavish all
our efforts on futilities which only make things more difficult, and that
scares me because I can't see what use it is to anyone. I don't understand
people, old man, I'm so scared of them. The peasants are a terrifying
spectacle—what lofty purposes their sufferings serve, what they live
for, I have no idea. If life exists for pleasure they are superfluous and
redundant. But if life's purpose and meaning is hardship and crass,
hopeless barbarism, then what use is this ordeal to anyone? That's
what I don't see. I don't understand anyone or anything.

'Just you try and make sense of this specimen,' said Silin, pointing
to Forty Martyrs. 'You just puzzle him out!'

Seeing us both looking at him, Forty Martyrs coughed deferentially
into his fist.

'I have always been a faithful servant when I've had good masters,
but it was drinking spirits, mainly, what done for me. Now, if you
was to take pity on a poor man and give me a job I'd take the pledge,
like. My word is my bond.'

The verger walked by, gave us a baffled look and began tugging his
rope. Slowly, lengthily, rudely shattering the calm of evening, the bell
tolled ten.

'What—ten o'clock already!' said Silin. 'It's time we were going.

'Yes, old man,' he sighed, 'if you did but know how I dread my
ordinary, everyday thoughts which one wouldn't expect to contain
anything terrible. To stop myself thinking I seek distraction in my work
and I try to tire myself out so that I may sleep soundly at night.
Children, a wife . . . to other men these are perfectly normal things,
but they're such a burden to me, old man.'

He rubbed his face with his hands, cleared his throat and gave a
laugh.

'If only I could tell you what an idiotic role I've played,' he said.
'I have a lovely wife, I have delightful children, everyone tells me, and
I'm a good husband and father. They think I'm so happy, they envy
me. Well, since we've gone so far I'll let you into a secret: my happy
family life's just a deplorable blunder, and I fear that too.'

A wry smile disfigured his pale face and he put an arm around my
waist.

'You're a true friend,' he continued in hushed tones. 'I trust you,
I profoundly respect you. Heaven sends us friendship so that we can
open our hearts and find relief from the mysteries which oppress us.
Let me exploit your affection, then, and tell you the full truth. My

family life, which you think so enchanting . . . it's my chief misfortune,
it's what scares me most. I made a strange and foolish marriage. I was
madly in love with Mary before we married, I may say, and I courted
her for two years. Five times I proposed, but she refused me because
she didn't care for me at all. On the sixth occasion I went down on my
knees, aflame with passion, and besought her hand like one begging for
mercy. She said yes.

'"I don't love you," she told me, "but I will be faithful to you."

'I was delighted to accept this condition. It made sense to me at the
time, but now, by God, it makes sense no more. "I don't love you, but
I'll be faithful to you" . . . what *does* it mean? It's all so muzzy and
obscure. I love her every bit as much now as I did on our wedding day,
while she seems to care as little for me as ever and she must be glad
when I'm away from home. Whether she likes me or not I don't know
for sure, I just don't know, but we live under the same roof, don't we?
We speak intimately to each other, we sleep together, we have children,
we hold our property in common. But what on earth does it signify?
What's it all in aid of? Do *you* understand anything, old man? Oh, it's
sheer torture, this! Understanding nothing about our relationship, I
hate her or myself by turns, or the two of us together, and my head's
in a complete whirl. I torment myself, I grow duller and duller, while
she . . . she looks prettier every day, as if to spite me, quite fantastic
she's becoming. She has such marvellous hair, I think, and her smile's
unlike any other woman's. I love her, yet I know my love is hopeless.
A hopeless love for a woman who has already borne you two children
. . . not easy to make sense of, that, is it? Pretty frightening, eh? More
frightening than your ghosts, wouldn't you say?'

He was in a mood to go on talking for some time, but luckily the
coachman's voice rang out: our carriage had arrived. As we got in
Forty Martyrs doffed his hat and helped us both into our seats, his
expression suggesting that he had long been awaiting the opportunity
to touch our precious bodies.

'May I come and see you, Mr. Silin?' he asked, blinking furiously, his
head cocked to one side. 'Have pity on me, for God's sake, seeing as
how I'm dying of hunger.'

'Oh, all right then,' said Silin. 'Come along for three days and we'll
see how it goes.'

Forty Martyrs was delighted. 'Very good, sir, I'll be along tonight, sir.'

We were about four miles from the house. Content to have un-
burdened himself to his great friend at last, Silin kept his arm round my

waist all the way. He had put his griefs and fears behind him, and cheerfully explained that he would have gone back to St. Petersburg and taken up academic work had his family situation been favourable. The mood which had banished so many gifted young people to the countryside . . . it was a deplorable trend, said he. Russia had rye and wheat in plenty, but no civilized people whatever. Talented and healthy young folk should take up science, the arts, politics. Any other course was irrational. He enjoyed such theorizing and said how sorry he was that we must part early next morning as he had to go to a timber sale.

Now, I felt uncomfortable and depressed. I had the impression of deceiving the man, yet that feeling was also agreeable. Looking at the huge, crimson moon, I pictured that tall, shapely blonde with her pale face, always so well-dressed and smelling of some special musky scent, and I was somehow happy to think that she didn't love her husband.

We reached home and sat down to supper. Mary laughingly regaled us with our purchases. She really did have marvellous hair, I found, and a smile unlike any other woman's. Watching her, I sought signs in her every movement and glance of her not loving her husband, and seemed to find them.

Silin was soon struggling with sleep.

'You two can do what you like,' he said, having sat with us for ten minutes after supper. 'But I have to be up at three o'clock in the morning, you must excuse me.'

He kissed his wife tenderly, and he pressed my hand firmly and gratefully, making me promise to come next week without fail. To avoid oversleeping on the morrow he went to spend the night in a hut in the grounds.

Mary always sat up late, in St. Petersburg style, and now I was rather glad of this.

'Well, now,' I began, when we were alone together. 'Well now, do please play me something.'

I didn't want music, but I didn't know what to start talking about. She sat down at the piano and played—what, I don't remember—while I sat near by, looking at her plump white arms and trying to read her cold, impassive expression. Then she smiled at some thought and looked at me.

'You miss your friend,' she said.

I laughed.

'For purposes of friendship one visit a month would be adequate, but I come here more than once a week.'

This said, I stood up and paced the room excitedly. She stood up too and moved away to the fireplace.

'What do you mean by that?' she asked, raising her large, clear eyes to me.

I made no answer.

'What you say is untrue,' she went on, after some thought. 'You only come here for Dmitry's sake. All right, I'm very glad you do, one doesn't often see such friendship these days.'

'Well, well,' thought I, and not knowing what to say I asked whether she would like a stroll in the garden.

'No.'

I went out on to the terrace. My scalp was tingling and I felt a chill of excitement. I was certain now that our conversation would be utterly trivial and that we shouldn't manage to say anything special to each other. And yet the thing I did not even dare to dream of . . . it was definitely bound to come about this night: this night, most definitely, or never.

'What marvellous weather,' I said in a loud voice.

'I just don't care about it either way,' I heard in answer.

I went into the drawing-room. Mary was still standing by the fireplace with her hands behind her back, thinking and looking away.

'And why don't you care about it either way?' I asked.

'Because I'm so bored. You are only bored when your friend isn't here, but I'm bored all the time. Anyway, that's of no interest to you.'

I sat down at the piano and struck a few chords, waiting to hear what she would say next.

'Pray don't stand on ceremony,' she said, looking at me angrily, as if ready to weep with vexation. 'If you're tired go to bed. Don't think that being Dmitry's friend means having to be bored by his wife. I don't require any sacrifices, so please go.'

I didn't go of course. She went out on to the terrace while I stayed in the drawing-room and spent five minutes leafing through the music. Then I went out too. We stood side by side in the curtains' shadow above steps flooded with moonlight. Black tree shadows lay across flower-beds and on the paths' yellow sand.

'I shall have to go away tomorrow too,' I said.

'But of course, you can't stay here if my husband's away,' she said mockingly. 'I can just think how miserable you would be if you fell in love with me. Just wait, one day I'll suddenly throw myself at you just to see your look of outrage as you run away from me. It should be an interesting sight.'

Her words and her pale face were angry, but her eyes were full of the tenderest, the most passionate love. I was now looking at this lovely creature as my own property and I noticed for the first time that she had golden eyebrows: exquisite eyebrows the like of which I had never seen before. The thought that I might take her in my arms, fondle her, touch that wonderful hair . . . it suddenly seemed so fantastic that I laughed and shut my eyes.

'It's bed-time, though,' she said. 'I wish you a restful night.'

'I don't want a restful night,' I said, laughing and following her into the drawing-room. 'I'll see this night in hell if it proves restful!'

Pressing her arm, escorting her to the door, I saw from her face that she understood me and was pleased that I had understood her.

I went to my room. Near the books on the table lay Dmitry's cap, reminding me of our great friendship. I took my stick and went into the garden. Mist was rising and tall, narrow phantoms were trailing near trees and bushes, embracing them: the same phantoms seen not long ago on the river. What a pity I couldn't talk to them.

In air unusually clear each leaf, each dew-drop, was sharply outlined and all these things seemed to smile at me in the drowsy silence. As I passed the green benches I recalled words from some play of Shakespeare's: 'How sweet the moonlight sleeps upon this bank!'

There was a little hillock in the garden. I climbed it, I sat down and a swoon of enchantment came over me. I knew for certain that I was soon going to hold her in my arms, that I would press against that voluptuous body, kiss those golden eyebrows. Yet I wanted not to believe that this was so, I wanted to tantalize myself and I was sorry that she had tormented me so little by yielding so quickly.

Then, suddenly, heavy footsteps were heard. A man of medium height appeared on the path and I at once recognized Forty Martyrs. He sat on the bench, heaved a deep sigh, crossed himself three times and lay down. A minute later he stood up and lay on his other side. The gnats and the dampness of the night prevented him from sleeping.

'What a life!' he said. 'What a wretched, miserable existence.'

Looking at his gaunt, stooped body and hearing his heavy, hoarse sighs, I remembered another wretched, miserable existence as confessed to me that day and I felt aghast—terrified of my own ecstatic mood. I climbed down the knoll and went to the house.

'Silin finds life terrifying,' I thought. 'So don't stand on ceremony with it, break it, snatch everything you can from it before it crushes you.'

Mary was standing on the terrace. I put my arms round her without a word and began greedily kissing her eyebrows, her temples, her neck. . . .

In my room she told me that she had loved me for a long time, for more than a year. She swore she loved me, she wept, she begged me to take her away. I kept leading her over to the window to see her face in the moonlight. She seemed like a lovely dream and I quickly gripped her tight in my arms to convince myself that she was really there. Not for a long time had I known such raptures. And yet I felt a certain disquiet. In some remote cranny of my heart I was ill at ease. There was something as incongruous and oppressive about her love for me as in Dmitry's friendship. It was a grand passion, this, all very serious with tears and vows thrown in, whereas I didn't want it to be serious, I wanted no tears, no vows, no talk about the future—this moonlit night should just flash through our lives like a bright meteor and let that be the end of it.

She left me at exactly three o'clock and I was standing in the doorway watching her go when Dmitry Silin suddenly appeared at the end of the corridor. Seeing him, she shuddered and made way for him to pass, her whole figure expressing revulsion. He gave a rather strange smile, coughed and came into my room.

'I left my cap here last night,' he said, not looking at me.

He found the cap, put it on his head with both hands, and then looked at my embarrassed face and slippers.

'I must be doomed never to understand anything,' he said in a rather strange, husky voice quite unlike his own. 'If you can make sense of anything I can only congratulate you. I see nothing.'

He went out, coughing. Then I saw him through the window harnessing his horses near the stable. His hands trembled, he was hurrying and he kept looking back at the house. He probably felt scared. Then he climbed into his carriage and struck the horses. There was a strange, hunted expression on his face.

A little later I set off too. The sun was already rising, and yesterday's mist clung timidly to bushes and hillocks. Forty Martyrs sat on my carriage box. He had already got himself a drink somewhere and was talking drunken gibberish.

'I'm a free man,' he shouted to the horses. 'Hey there, my darlings! I was born a gentleman, just in case you're interested.'

Dmitry Silin's terror . . . I had been unable to get it out of my mind and it infected me too. Thinking of what had happened, I could make nothing of it. I looked at the rooks and their flight puzzled me, terrified me.

'Why did I do it?' I wondered, baffled and frantic. 'Why did it have to happen just like that? Why not in some different way? Why did she have to fall in love with me so seriously? Why must he come into the room to fetch his cap? What use was it all? And to whom? And why should his cap be involved?'

I left for St. Petersburg that day and I have never set eyes on Dmitry Silin or his wife again. They are said to be still living together.

THE ORDER OF ST. ANNE

I

No food was served after the wedding, not even light refreshments.
Bride and groom just drank their glass of champagne, changed and
drove to the station. There was no gay wedding breakfast, no party,
no band and no dancing—they were going to stay at a monastery
instead, a hundred and fifty miles away.

A good idea too, many people thought. Modeste Alekseyevich was
pretty high up in the service now and not so young as all that either,
so a hearty wedding reception might well have seemed not quite the
thing—or so people said. Who feels like music, anyway, when a civil
servant of fifty-two marries a girl barely turned eighteen? Besides,
being a man of principle, Modeste Alekseyevich was said to have
arranged this monastery trip on purpose, to let his bride know that
even as a married man he still put religion and morality first.

A crowd went to see them off at the station, colleagues and relatives
who stood glass in hand waiting to cheer when the train pulled out.
Peter Leontyevich, the bride's father, wore a top hat and the tail-coat
belonging to his schoolmaster's regulation dress. Already drunk and
white as a sheet, he kept reaching up to the train window, holding
his glass and pleading with his daughter.

'Anne, dear. A word in your ear, Anne.'

Anne leant out of the window towards him and he whispered to her,
breathing alcohol all over her, blowing in her ear—not one word
could she understand—and making the sign of the cross over her face,
breast and hands. His breathing was unsteady and tears shone in his
eyes. Anne's schoolboy brothers Peter and Andrew were tugging at
his coat.

'Oh really, Father,' they whispered, somewhat put out. 'Do stop it.'

When the train started, Anne saw her father run a few steps after
the coach, staggering and spilling his wine. He had such a pathetic,
good-natured, hang-dog air.

He gave a long cheer.

Now bride and bridegroom were alone. Modeste looked round the
compartment, put their things on the racks and sat down, beaming,
opposite his young wife. He was a civil servant of average height,

rather round and plump and extremely sleek. He had long whiskers, but no moustache, and his round, clean-shaven, sharply defined chin looked like the heel of a foot. That missing moustache—the freshly shaved bare patch that gradually merged into fat cheeks quivering like jellies—was the most typical thing about his face. He bore himself with dignity, his movements slow and his manner mild.

'At this juncture I cannot but recall a certain incident,' he said with a smile. 'Five years ago Kosorotov received the Order of St. Anne, second class, and called on the Governor of the Province to thank him. "So you have three Annes now," declared His Excellency. "One in your buttonhole and two round your neck." I must explain that Kosorotov's wife had just come back, a bad-tempered, giddy creature called Anne. When I receive the Order of St. Anne, second class, His Excellency will, I trust, have no cause to pass the same remark.'

A smile lit up his small eyes and Anne smiled back. Any moment the man might kiss her with his full, wet lips and there was absolutely nothing she could do about it—a disturbing thought. The sleek motions of his plump body scared her. She felt frightened and disgusted.

He stood up, slowly took the medal from his neck, removed his coat and waistcoat, and put on his dressing-gown.

'That's better,' he said, sitting down beside her.

She remembered the ordeal of the marriage service, with the priest, the guests and everyone else in church looking at her sadly as if wondering why on earth such a lovely girl should be marrying this unattractive elderly gentleman. Only that morning she had been terribly pleased that everything had worked out so well, but during the ceremony and here in the train she had a guilty feeling—felt she had been let down and made to look silly. Yes, she had her rich husband. But she still had no money. Her wedding dress had still not been paid for, and her father and brothers had not had a copeck between them when they had seen her off that morning—she could tell by the look on their faces. Would they have any supper tonight? Or tomorrow night? Somehow she thought that Father and the boys must be starving now that she had left home, and would be sitting there in the depths of despair as on the night after Mother's funeral.

'Oh, I'm so unhappy,' she thought. 'Why am I so unhappy?'

As clumsy as any other pillar of society unused to women's company, Modeste kept touching her waist and patting her shoulder, while she thought about money, about her mother, and her mother's death.

After Mother's death, her father—art master at the local high school

—had taken to drink and then they really had been in a bad way, what with the boys having no boots or galoshes, Father being continually had up in court, and bailiffs coming and making an inventory of the furniture.

What a shameful business! Anne had had to look after her drunken father, darn her brothers' socks and do the shopping. And any compliment to her beauty, youth and elegant manners made her feel as if the whole world could see her cheap hat and the worn patches on her shoes that she had smeared with ink. At nights she cried and could not shake off the nagging worry that Father might lose his job any day because he drank. That might well be the last straw, and then he would follow Mother to the grave.

But then some ladies who knew the family bestirred themselves and started looking out a husband for her. And before long this Modeste Alekseyevich had emerged. He was not young or handsome, but he did have money. He had something like a hundred thousand in the bank and a family estate which he let to a tenant. He was a man of principle, in His Excellency's good books, and could easily—or so Anne was told—obtain a note from His Excellency to the headmaster, or even to the local education officer, and then Father would not lose his job. . . .

She was musing on these points when a snatch of music and a buzz of voices suddenly burst through the window. The train had stopped at a wayside halt. Someone in the crowd on the other side of the platform had struck up a rousing tune on an accordion accompanied by a cheap, squeaky fiddle. There were tall birches, poplars, moonlit cottages, and beyond them a military band was playing. The summer visitors must be holding a dance. People were strolling along the platform—holiday-makers and visitors from town who had made the trip for a breath of fresh air on a fine day. And Artynov was there. He owned the whole holiday area. A rich man, tall and stout with dark hair, a face like an Armenian's and bulging eyes, he wore peculiar clothes—an open-necked shirt, riding boots and spurs, and a black cloak hanging from his shoulders and trailing on the ground like the train of a dress. At his heels, their pointed muzzles lowered, were two borzoi hounds.

Anne's eyes were still bright with tears, but now Mother, money problems, wedding—all were forgotten. She shook hands with schoolboys and officers that she knew, laughed merrily and showered greetings on them.

She went out onto the small platform at the end of her carriage and stood there in the moonlight to show off her marvellous new dress and hat. She asked why the train had stopped.

'This is a loop-line,' she was told. 'They're waiting for the mail train.'

Seeing that Artynov was watching her, she coyly fluttered her eye-lids and began to speak loudly in French. The splendid ring of her own voice, the strains of the band and a glimpse of the moon reflected in the pond, together with the general high spirits and the fact that Arty-nov, notorious gay spark and ladies' man, had his eye on her—all these things suddenly combined to make her happy. When the train started off again and her officer friends gave her a goodbye salute, she was already humming a polka—the tune blown after her by the brass band blaring away somewhere behind the trees. Back in her compartment, she felt that the halt at that country station had proved that she was bound to be happy in spite of everything.

Bride and groom stayed two days at the monastery, then returned to town and lived in the flat which went with Modeste's job. Anne used to play the piano when he was at the office, or felt bored to tears, or lay on the sofa reading novels and looking at fashion magazines. At dinner her husband ate a lot and talked about politics, appointments, staff transfers and honours lists.

'Hard work never harmed anyone,' he would say, or, 'Family life is not pleasure, but duty,' or, 'Take care of the copecks and the roubles will take care of themselves.' He thought religion and morality the most important things in life. 'We all have our responsibilities,' he would say, holding a knife in his fist like a sword.

Listening to him scared Anne so much that she could not eat and usually left the table hungry.

After dinner her husband would take a nap, snoring noisily, while she went off to see the family. Father and the boys always gave her a special look as if they had just been saying as she came in how wrong she was to have married an abysmal bore for his money when she didn't even like the man. The rustle of her dress, her bracelets, her ladylike air—they found it vaguely inhibiting and offensive. It was a little em-barrassing having her there and they did not know what to say to her, though they were as fond of her as ever and still could not get used to her not being around at supper time. She would sit down with them and eat cabbage soup, porridge or potatoes fried in mutton dripping that smelt of tallow. Her father's hand would shake as he poured out a glass of vodka from the decanter and drank it down rapidly and greedily, with disgust, followed by a second glass and a third.

Peter and Andrew, thin, pale boys with large eyes, would take the decanter from him, quite at their wits' end.

'Oh really, Father . . .' they would say. 'Do stop it. . . .'

When Anne grew worried as well and begged him to stop drinking, he would suddenly flare up, thumping his fist on the table. 'No one orders me about,' he would shout. 'Young puppies! Wretched girl! I'ye a good mind to chuck you out!'

But his voice sounded so feeble and good-natured that no one was afraid. After dinner he usually dressed up. Pale, with his chin cut from shaving, he would spend half an hour craning his thin neck in front of the mirror and trying to make himself look smart, brushing his hair or twirling his black moustache. He would sprinkle himself with scent, put on a bow tie, gloves and top hat and go out to give private lessons. On holidays he stayed at home, painting or playing the wheezy, groaning harmonium. He tried to squeeze out delicious harmonies, humming an accompaniment, or else lost his temper with the boys.

'Monsters! Scoundrels! They've ruined the instrument.'

In the evening Anne's husband played cards with colleagues from the office who lived in the same block of government flats. During these sessions the wives forgathered as well. Hideous women, dressed in appallingly bad taste and as vulgar as could be, they would start gossiping and telling tales as ugly and tasteless as they were themselves.

Sometimes Anne's husband took her to the theatre. He kept her by his side in the intervals, holding her arm and strolling in the corridors and foyer. He would bow to someone.

'Fairly high up in the service,' he would tell Anne in a rapid whisper. 'Received by His Excellency,' or, 'Rather well off. Has a house of his own.'

They were going past the bar once when Anne felt that she would like something sweet. She was fond of chocolate and apple tart, but had no money and did not like to ask her husband. He picked up a pear, squeezed it and asked doubtfully how much it cost.

'Twenty-five copecks.'

'Well, I must say!'

He put the pear back. But it was awkward to leave the bar without buying anything, so he asked for soda water and drank the whole bottle himself, which brought tears to his eyes. Anne hated him at times like these.

Or else, suddenly blushing scarlet, he would hurriedly say, 'Bow to that old lady.'

'But I don't know her.'

'Never mind. She's the wife of our provincial treasurer. Oh, go on!' he nagged. 'Bow, I tell you. Your head won't fall off.'

So Anne would bow, and in fact her head never did fall off. But it was a painful experience.

She always did what her husband wanted, furious with herself for letting him make such a complete fool of her. She had only married him for his money, but she had less money now than before her marriage. In those days her father at least gave her the occasional twenty copecks, but now she never had any money at all. She could not just take it behind his back or ask for it, being so afraid of her husband, scared stiff in fact.

She felt as if her fear of the man had long been part of her. As a little girl she had always thought of the high-school headmaster as a terrifying, overwhelming force bearing down on her like a storm cloud or a railway engine that was going to run over her. Another menace of the same kind, continually invoked in the family—feared too for some reason—was His Excellency. And there were a dozen lesser horrors, among whom were clean-shaven schoolmasters, stern and unbending. Now they included this Modeste as well, the man of principle, who even looked like the headmaster. In Anne's imagination all these menaces seemed to be rolled into one and she saw them as a colossal polar bear, terrifying as it advanced on weak, erring creatures like her father. Afraid to protest, she forced herself to smile and pretend to be pleased when defiled by clumsy caresses and embraces that sickened her.

Only once did Peter Leontyevich pluck up courage to ask his son-in-law for a loan of fifty roubles so that he could meet some particularly irksome debt. And that was quite an ordeal.

'All right, you can have it,' Anne's husband had said after some thought. 'But I warn you, you get no more help from me till you stop drinking. Such self-indulgence is disgraceful in a government employee. I feel obliged to point out what is generally recognized, that this craving has been the ruin of many an able man who, given a little self-control, might in time have become a person of consequence.'

One rolling period succeeded another—'in so far as', 'basing ourselves on the assumption that', 'in view of what has just been stated'. And Anne's poor father suffered agonies of humiliation. He was dying for a drink.

When the boys visited Anne—usually with holes in their boots and in threadbare trousers—they came in for these lectures too.

'We all have our responsibilities,' Modeste Alekseyevich told them. But they got no money out of him. He gave Anne presents instead —rings, bracelets and brooches, 'just the thing to put by for a rainy day' —and often opened her chest of drawers to make sure that none of the stuff was missing.

II

Meanwhile winter had set in. Long before Christmas the local news-paper announced that the usual winter ball would 'duly take place' in the Assembly Rooms on the twenty-ninth of December. Much excited, Anne's husband held whispered consultations with his colleagues' wives every evening after cards, shooting an anxious glance or two at Anne. Then he would walk up and down the room for a while, thinking. At last, late one evening, he stopped in front of Anne.

'You must get yourself a ball dress,' he said. 'Is that clear? But mind you consult Marya Grigoryevna and Natalya Kuzminishna.'

He gave her a hundred roubles, which she took. But she ordered the dress without consulting anyone, though she did have a word with her father and tried to imagine how her mother would have dressed for the ball. Her mother had always followed the latest fashions and had always taken great pains with Anne, dressing her up like an ex-quisite little doll, teaching her to speak French and dance an excellent mazurka—she had been a governess for five years before her marriage. Like her mother, Anne could make a new dress out of an old one or clean her gloves with benzine and she knew about hiring jewellery. And she could flutter her eyelids like her mother, talk Russian with a Parisian r, adopt elegant poses, go into raptures when necessary or look melancholy and mysterious. She had her dark hair and eyes from her father. Like him she was highly strung and was used to making the most of her looks.

Half an hour before they were to leave for the ball Modeste Alek-seyevich came into her room without his coat on to tie his medal ribbon round his neck in front of her wardrobe mirror. Dazzled by her beauty and the glitter of her new dress that seemed light as thistle-down, he combed his whiskers, looking rather smug.

'I must say, Anne . . .' he said, 'you really are, er, quite a girl. My dear,' he went on, suddenly solemn, 'I've made you happy and tonight it's your turn to make me happy. Will you please present yourself to His Excellency's good lady? Do, for heaven's sake. She can get me a more senior post.'

They left for the ball and reached the Assembly Rooms. There was a door-keeper at the entrance. The vestibule was full of coat-racks and fur coats, with servants scurrying about and ladies in low-necked dresses trying to keep off the draught with their fans. The place smelt of gas lights and soldiers. Anne went upstairs on her husband's arm. She heard music and saw a full-length reflection of herself in an enormous mirror brightly lit by innumerable lights. Her heart seemed to leap for joy and she felt that she was going to be happy—the same feeling that had come over her on that moonlit night at the wayside station. She walked proudly, sure of herself. Feeling for the first time that she was no longer a girl, but a grown woman, she unconsciously modelled her walk and manner on her mother. For the first time in her life she felt rich and free. Even her husband's presence did not hamper her because the moment she stepped inside the Assembly Rooms her instinct told her that she lost nothing by having an elderly husband at her side—far from it, for it lent her the very air of piquancy and mystery that men so relish.

In the large ballroom the orchestra was blaring away and dancing had begun. Plunged straight from her very ordinary official flat into this whirl of light, colour, noise and music, Anne surveyed the room and thought how marvellous it all was. She at once picked out everyone she knew in the crowd, everyone she had met at parties or on outings, officers, schoolmasters, lawyers, civil servants, landowners, His Excellency, Artynov, society ladies in their finery and low-necked dresses—some beautiful, others ugly as they took their places at the kiosks and stalls of the charity bazaar, ready to open shop in aid of the poor.

An enormous officer with epaulettes—Anne had met him in the Old Kiev Road when she was still at school, but could not remember his name—seemed to pop up from nowhere and asked her to waltz. She bounced away from her husband, feeling as if she was sailing a boat in a raging storm and had left him far behind on the shore. She danced like one possessed—a waltz, a polka and a quadrille—passing from one partner to another, dizzy with music and noise, mixing up French and Russian, pronouncing the Russian r as if she came from Paris, laughing, not thinking of her husband or of anything or anyone else. She had made a hit with the men, that was obvious. And no wonder. Breathless and excited, she gripped her fan convulsively and felt thirsty. Her father came up, his tail-coat creased and smelling of benzine. He held out a plate of pink ice-cream.

'You're enchanting this evening,' he said, looking at her with great enthusiasm. 'Oh, why did you have to rush into that marriage? I've never regretted it more. I know you did it for us, but. . . .' His hands shook as he pulled out a bundle of notes.

'I was paid for some coaching today,' he said. 'So I can pay your husband back.'

She thrust the plate into his hands and someone pounced on her and whisked her off. Over her partner's shoulder she caught a glimpse of her father gliding over the parquet floor, his arms round a lady as he whirled her through the ballroom.

'Isn't he nice when he's sober!' she thought.

The big officer partnered her again in the mazurka. He moved along, solemn, ponderous, like a uniformed dummy, twitching his chest and shoulders and just faintly tapping his feet. It seemed as if he did not want to dance at all, but she fluttered round him and provoked him with her beauty and bare neck, her movements impetuous and her blazing eyes a challenge. He looked more and more bored and stretched his arms towards her like royalty conferring a favour.

Everyone cheered.

Gradually the big officer caught on too. He seemed to wake up and come to life. He yielded to the spell and really let himself go, his movements lithe and youthful, while she just twitched her shoulders with a sly look as if to say that she was queen now and he the slave. She felt everyone's eyes on them and everybody in the ballroom seemed to be swooning with envy. The big officer had hardly had time to thank her when everyone suddenly formed a gangway and the men drew themselves up in a curiously stiff way with their arms at their sides.

The reason was—His Excellency. He was advancing towards her and he wore a tail-coat with two stars on the chest. She was his target sure enough, for he was staring straight at her with a sickly smile, his lips working as always happened when he saw a pretty woman.

'Delighted, delighted . . .' he began. 'I'll have to put your husband under arrest for sitting tight on such a treasure all this time. I've a message from my wife,' he went on, holding out his hand. 'You must help us. . . . M'm, yes. . . . We ought to give you a prize for beauty . . . as they do in America. . . . M'm, yes. . . . Those Americans—er, my wife is longing to meet you.'

He took her to a stall, to an elderly woman with a vast chin so out of proportion to the rest of her face that she might have had a big stone in her mouth.

'Do come and help,' she said in a nasal drawl. 'All the pretty women are helping with the charity bazaar and for some reason you're the only one idle. Why don't you join us?'

She left. Anne took her place by a silver samovar and tea cups and did a roaring trade from the start. She charged at least a rouble for a cup of tea and made the big officer drink three cups. Artynov, the rich man with the protruding eyes and the wheeze, came up. Tonight he was not wearing the strange clothes that Anne had seen him in that summer, but sported a tail-coat like everyone else. Without taking his eyes off Anne, he drank a glass of champagne and paid a hundred roubles. Then he drank some tea and put down another hundred. He was suffering from asthma and said not a word.

Anne cried her wares and took the customers' money, quite sure by this time that these people found nothing but sheer delight in her smiles and glances. She knew now that this was what she was born for, this hectic, brilliant life of laughter, music, dancing and admirers. Now she could laugh at her old fear of the force that bore down and threatened to crush her. She was afraid of no one now and was only sad that her mother was not there so that they could both enjoy her success.

Pale, but still steady on his feet, her father came up to her stall and asked for a glass of brandy. Anne thought that he was going to say something out of turn and blushed—she already felt ashamed of such a poor, such a very ordinary father. But he just drank his brandy, tossed her ten roubles from his bundle of notes and moved away with dignity. Not a word had he said. A little later she saw him dancing the *grand rond*, staggering now and shouting, at which his partner seemed greatly put out. He had staggered and shouted just like this at a ball about three years ago, Anne remembered. That had ended with a police inspector taking him home to bed, and next day the headmaster had threatened to dismiss him. Not quite the sort of thing Anne wanted to remember just now!

When the samovars had gone cold in the booths and the exhausted helpers had handed their takings to the elderly woman with the stone in her mouth, Artynov took Anne's arm and they went into the hall where supper was served for the charity workers. There were not more than a score of people at table, but things were pretty lively. His Excellency gave a toast. 'In this magnificent dining-room it is fitting that we should drink to the cheap canteens which are the occasion of tonight's bazaar.' An artillery brigadier proposed 'the power that can bring even a gunner to his knees', and the men all clinked glasses with the ladies.

It was all great fun.

Day was breaking when Anne was taken home, and cooks were on their way to market. Happy, drunk and absolutely dead beat, her head awhirl with new impressions, she undressed, flopped on the bed and fell straight asleep. . . .

At about half past one in the afternoon her maid woke her to say that Mr. Artynov had called. She dressed quickly and went into the drawing-room.

Not long after Artynov, His Excellency came to thank her for helping with the bazaar. Giving her his sickly look, his lips working, he kissed her hand, asked permission to call again, and left. She stood in the middle of the drawing-room, absolutely dumbfounded, almost in a trance, unable to believe that a change, and such a staggering change, had taken place in her life so quickly.

Then her husband came in.

He stood before her with the look that she knew so well. It was the crawling, sugary, slavish, deferential look that he kept for powerful and distinguished people. Triumphant, indignant, scornful—quite certain that she could get away with anything and articulating each word clearly—she spoke.

'Get out! Idiot!'

After that Anne never had a day to herself as she was always off on some picnic or outing or taking part in theatricals. She always came home in the small hours and would lie down on the drawing-room floor, after which she would tell everyone the pathetic story of how she had slept beneath the flowers. She needed a lot of money, but she no longer feared Modeste Alekseyevich and spent his money as if it was her own. She made no requests or demands—just sent him bills or notes saying, 'Give bearer 200 roubles', '100 roubles—pay at once.'

At Easter her husband received the Order of St. Anne, second class, and called to thank His Excellency. His Excellency laid aside his newspaper and settled back in his arm-chair.

'So you now have three Annes,' he said, studying his white hands and pink finger-nails. 'One in your button-hole and two round your neck.'

Modeste laid two fingers to his lips for fear of laughing out loud.

'Now we must await the appearance of a tiny Vladimir,' he said. 'Dare I ask your Excellency to be godfather?'

He was hinting at the Order of St. Vladimir, fourth class, and could already see himself dining out on a quip so brilliantly apt and audacious. He was about to make some other equally happy remark when His Excellency plunged back into his newspaper and nodded. . . .

As for Anne, she took troika rides, went hunting with Artynov, acted in one-act plays, went out to supper, and saw less and less of her family. They always had supper on their own these days. Her father was drinking more than ever, his money had run out, and the harmonium had been sold to pay his debts.

Nowadays the boys never let him out in the street on his own and were always watching in case he fell down. When he met Anne driving along the Old Kiev Road in her coach with a pair of horses and a side-horse while Artynov sat on the box and acted as coachman, her father would take off his top hat and start to shout something. Then Peter and Andrew would hold his arms and plead with him.

'Oh really, Father. Please don't.'

NOTES

1 'Kazan.' Town on the Volga, about 500 miles east of Moscow.

1 'at Cubat's Restaurant.' Probably the Bellevue Restaurant (pro-prietor Cubat), on one of the islands (Kamenny ostrov) in the north of St. Petersburg. Most large restaurants in St. Petersburg were run by Frenchmen or Germans.

2 'a passport.' A Russian citizen was required to possess a passport for purposes of internal as well as external travel. Wives, who were legally obliged to reside with their husbands, had to have the husband's permission in order to apply for a passport.

A LADY WITH A DOG

7 'Yalta.' Town and seaside resort on the Crimean coast, where Chekhov built a villa in 1899, and which was his main residence from then until his death in 1904; Vernet's café is mentioned in Baedeker's *Russia* (1914), p. 417.

8 'Belyov.' Small town about 150 miles south of Moscow.

8 'Zhizdra.' Small town about 200 miles south-west of Moscow.

8 'sunny Spain.' The text has 'Grenada' (an island in the West Indies), but it seems more likely that Chekhov had the Spanish 'Granada' in mind.

12 'Oreanda.' On the coast about five miles south-west of Yalta, Oreanda contained a park which extended down to the sea.

12 'Feodosiya.' Resort on the Crimean coast, about 70 miles north-east of Yalta.

13 'the waterfall.' The waterfall of Uchan-Su, about six miles from Yalta, was a favourite target for excursions.

16 '*The Geisha.*' The operetta by Sidney Jones, first produced in London (1896).

18 'The Slav Fair.' A large hotel in central Moscow, at which Chekhov himself sometimes stayed.

THE DUEL

23 'Superfluous Men.' Reference is to a well-known Russian literary type—the man at odds with society, as found particularly in certain works by Griboyedov, Pushkin, Lermontov, Turgenev and Goncharov. See *The Oxford Chekhov*, ii, 5–6.

24 'Tolstoy.' The novelist and thinker L. N. Tolstoy (1828–1910).

24 'Herbert Spencer.' The English philosopher (1820–1903).

26 'Tula.' Provincial capital, about 120 miles south of Moscow.

26 'Vereshchagin.' The Russian painter V. V. Vereshchagin (1824–1904).

28 'Order of St. Vladimir.' The imperial Russian 'orders', or decorations for distinction in peace or war, were instituted by Peter the Great and added to as the years went by.

28 'Circassians.' Inhabitants of an area in the northern Caucasus.

29 'Anna Karenin.' The reference is to Tolstoy's novel *Anna Karenin* (1875–7).

29 'Abkhazians.' Inhabitants of Abkhazia, an area north-west of Georgia.

30 'Sevastopol.' The Crimean port.

30 'Kursk.' City in central Russia, about 300 miles south of Moscow.

33 'Prince Vorontsov.' Field Marshal M. S. Vorontsov (1782–1856), Viceroy of the Caucasus (1844–53).

36 'Onegin.' Reference is to Yevgeny Onegin, a Superfluous Man and hero of the verse novel *Yevgeny Onegin* (1823–31) by A. S. Pushkin (1799–1837).

36 'Pechorin.' Reference is to Pechorin, a Superfluous Man and hero of the novel *A Hero of Our Time* (1840) by the poet M. Yu. Lermontov (1814–41).

36 'Byron's Cain.' Reference is to *Cain* (1821) by the English poet Byron (1788–1824).

36 'Bazarov.' Reference is to Yevgeny Bazarov, hero of the novel *Fathers and Children* (1862) by I. S. Turgenev (1818–83).

36 'serf system.' That is, they are descended from owners of the serfs, who were emancipated in 1861.

41 'Dorpat.' Reference is to the Estonian town of Tartu, which lay within the Russian Empire, seat of a university reopened in 1802, at which the language of instruction was German until 1895.

48 'Vladivostok.' Russian port in the far east of Siberia on the Sea of Japan.

48 'Bering Straits.' Between far north-eastern Siberia and Alaska.

48 'Yenisey.' Large river in central Siberia.

50 'Pushkin's "Ukrainian Night".' Reference is to a celebrated descriptive passage beginning 'Quiet is the Ukrainian night' from the Second Canto of Pushkin's narrative poem *Poltava* (1829).

55 'His beaver collar...' The lines are from Verse xvi of Chapter One of Pushkin's *Yevgeny Onegin*, being part of a description of a winter scene in St. Petersburg.

60 'Stanley.' Sir Henry Morton Stanley (1841–1904), the explorer.

64 'Whosoever shall offend...'. Mark 9:42.

71 'Turgenev's Rudin.' Reference is to the hero of Turgenev's novel *Rudin* (1856), a Superfluous Man.

74 'Anna Karenin.' Reference is to the tragic climax of Tolstoy's novel *Anna Karenin*, where the heroine commits suicide by throwing herself under a train as the result of an unhappy adulterous love affair.

83 'New Athos.' New Athos (or Akhali Afoni), a settlement on the Abkhazian shore of the Black Sea, now a spa in the Gudauta District of the Abkhazian A.S.S.R.

83 'Novorossisk.' Black Sea port in the Krasnodar (formerly Yekaterinodar) Region of the northern Caucasus.

92 'Leskov.' N. S. Leskov (1831–95), the Russian novelist and short-story writer.

94 'Peter and Paul dungeons.' The Peter and Paul Fortress in St. Petersburg, founded in 1703, where many political prisoners were held.

94 'In my oppressed and anguished mind...' The last lines of Pushkin's famous lyric *Memory* (1828).

99 'Chechen.' A people of the northern Caucasus still not entirely subjected to Russian rule at the end of the nineteenth century.

105 'Lermontov.' Reference is to the duel between Pechorin and Grushnitsky in *A Hero of Our Time* (see note to p. 36 above).

105 'Turgenev's Bazarov.' Reference is to Bazarov's duel with Paul Kirsanov in *Fathers and Children* (see note to p. 36 above).

A HARD CASE

114 'the village elder's barn.' It was the practice for the heads of households in a village to elect an elder who became the head of the *mir* or village commune. He presided over and summoned its meetings, and was in charge of village administration.

116 'their Turgenev and their Shchedrin.' The novelist Turgenev (see note to p. 36) was a well-known liberal; M. Ye. Saltykov (1826–89) was a satirist and a well-known radical (who wrote under the pseudonym 'Shchedrin', and is often known as Saltykov-Shchedrin).

116 'Henry Buckles.' Reference is to Henry Thomas Buckle (1821–62), the English social historian and author of *History of Civilization* (1857–61), which enjoyed a great vogue in Russia.

117 '"Where Southern Breezes Blow".' A popular Ukrainian folk-song.

118 'Gadyach.' A small town in the Ukraine about 150 miles east of Kiev.

GOOSEBERRIES

129 'six foot of earth.' Reference is to Tolstoy's short story *Does a Man Need much Earth?* (1886).

132 'To hosts of petty truths....' From the poem *A Hero* (1830) by Pushkin.

CONCERNING LOVE

136 '"this is a great mystery".' Ephesians 5:32.

137 '*European Herald*.' *Vestnik Yevropy*—a historico-political and literary monthly of liberal complexion published in St. Petersburg/Petrograd, 1866–1918.

PEASANTS

147 'Whosoever shall smite thee....' Matthew 5:39.

148 'Come unto me all ye that labour....' Matthew 11:28.

148 'Vladimir.' Provincial capital about 120 miles east of Moscow.

149 'since the days of serfdom.' Since 1861, the year of emancipation.

149–50 'at the Hermitage Garden Theatre.' The Hermitage Variety Theatre in Karetny ryad in Moscow (not to be confused with the Hermitage Restaurant in Trubny Place in Moscow or the Hermitage Museum in St. Petersburg).

150 'And when they were departed. . . .' Matthew 2:13.

155 'the Assumption.' 15 August, the end of the harvest.

159 'huntsmen skilled in driving wolves towards the guns.' Translation of Russian *pskovichi*. These are not 'retrievers', as in some earlier translations, but specialists in wolf- or fox-hunting—their function being to drive the beasts from cover while the guns wait at a pre-arranged spot. The *pskovichi* originally came from Pskov Province, whence their name, and usually worked in teams of three.

160 'Tver.' Town about 140 miles north-west of Moscow, named Kalinin in 1931.

163 'Alexander of Battenberg' (1857–93). Prince of Bulgaria 1879–86. He was forced to abdicate by Alexander III of Russia. 'This detail . . . indicates perhaps the elder's ignorance, for one so loyal would not otherwise have given the place of honour to an enemy of his Tsar.' (W. H. Bruford, *Chekhov and his Russia*, p. 55.)

166 'Elijah's Day.' 20 July, the beginning of the harvest.

166–7 'Holy Cross Day.' 14 September.

167 'The Feast of the Intercession' [of the Virgin]. 1 October.

ANGEL

173 'Bryansk.' Town about 250 miles south-west of Moscow.

173 '*Faust Inside Out.*' Perhaps a burlesque of the opera *Faust* (1859) by Charles Gounod (1818–93).

173 '*Orpheus in the Underworld.*' The operetta *Orfée aux enfers* (1858, revised 1874) by Jacques Offenbach (1819–80).

175 'Mogilyov.' Town about 350 miles west-south-west of Moscow.

180 'Kharkov.' Large city in the Ukraine.

THE RUSSIAN MASTER

183 'Count Nulin.' The horse is named after the hero of Pushkin's comic poem *Count Nulin* (1825).

183 'Marie Godefroi.' A well-known equestrienne of the period, of whom A. A. Suvorin had written to Chekhov from Feodosiya in the Crimea, on 6 September 1888, as 'that *prima donna* of the ring, a rather handsome, well-built brunette—a truly fabulous horsewoman and a devastating trick rider' (*Works*, 1944–51, xiv, 512).

186 'Shchedrin.' See note to p. 116 above.

186 'Dostoyevsky.' F. M. Dostoyevsky (1821–81), the novelist.

187 '*Eugene Onegin*.' See note to p. 36 above.

187 '*Boris Godunov*.' Pushkin's historical play (1824–5).

187 'Lermontov.' See note to p. 36 above.

187 'Alexis Tolstoy's poem "*The Sinful Woman*".' This work by A. K. Tolstoy (1817–75) also figures in Act Three of Chekhov's *Cherry Orchard*—see *The Oxford Chekhov*, iii, 181.

188 'Lessing's *Hamburgische Dramaturgie*.' The treatise on drama (1769) by the German critic and dramatist G. E. Lessing (1729–81).

190 'Battle of Kalka.' At the battle by the River Kalka in south Russia, on 31 May 1223, the Russians were routed by a Mongol–Tatar army.

190 'Siberian capes.' Literally, 'Cape Chukotskys'—reference being to the Chukotsky Peninsula in the far north-east of Siberia, opposite the Bering Straits.

191 '*European Herald*.' See note to p. 137 above.

195 'Neglinny Drive.' Street leading north from the Maly Theatre in central Moscow.

196 'Gogol.' N. V. Gogol (1809–52), the novelist and short-story writer.

198 'the Consecration of the Waters.' Annual ceremony of the Orthodox Church held on 5 January, the Eve of Epiphany.

204 'Klushino.' Name of a locality about a hundred miles west of Moscow.

206 'in that sleep of death...' From the soliloquy 'To be, or not to be' in Shakespeare's *Hamlet*, Act III, Scene i.

209 'The mood which had banished so many gifted young people to the countryside.' The reference is to a recurrent tendency for young Russian intellectuals to attempt to help (or 'repay their debt to') the peasantry by working as village teachers, doctors, political agitators, etc.

211 'How sweet the moonlight...' Shakespeare, *Merchant of Venice*, Act V, Scene i.

212 'I was born a gentleman.' A deliberately loose translation for literal 'I am a hereditary honorary citizen' (*potomstvenny pochotny grazhdanin*). This was one of the many categories to which Imperial Russian citizens were assigned. In the present instance 'Forty Martyrs' was neither a gentleman (since his father had been a priest) nor a cleric (since he himself had not entered the church). As an 'honorary citizen' he retained certain privileges denied to peasants and other members of the lower classes.

214 'The Order of St. Anne' and 'the Order of St. Anne, second class.' See note to p. 28. The Order of St. Anne, third class, was worn in the button-hole, while the Order of St. Anne, second class, was worn on a ribbon round the neck.

225 'the Order of St. Vladimir, fourth class.' This rated just above the Order of St. Anne, second class.

The Oxford World's Classics Website

www.worldsclassics.co.uk

- Browse the full range of Oxford World's Classics online

- Sign up for our monthly e-alert to receive information on new titles

- Read extracts from the Introductions

- Listen to our editors and translators talk about the world's greatest literature with our Oxford World's Classics audio guides

- Join the conversation, follow us on Twitter at OWC_Oxford

- Teachers and lecturers can order inspection copies quickly and simply via our website

www.worldsclassics.co.uk

American Literature

British and Irish Literature

Children's Literature

Classics and Ancient Literature

Colonial Literature

Eastern Literature

European Literature

Gothic Literature

History

Medieval Literature

Oxford English Drama

Poetry

Philosophy

Politics

Religion

The Oxford Shakespeare

A complete list of Oxford World's Classics, including Authors in Context, Oxford English Drama, and the Oxford Shakespeare, is available in the UK from the Marketing Services Department, Oxford University Press, Great Clarendon Street, Oxford OX2 6DP, or visit the website at www.oup.com/uk/worldsclassics.

In the USA, visit www.oup.com/us/owc for a complete title list.

Oxford World's Classics are available from all good bookshops. In case of difficulty, customers in the UK should contact Oxford University Press Bookshop, 116 High Street, Oxford OX1 4BR.